Killing Time

Imagine your worst nightmare.
Arrested and interrogated for a murder you know
nothing about.
Sentenced to years behind bars for a crime you did
not commit.
But there's a final, chilling detail to this nightmare.
You are an ex-policeman, hated by everyone in the
600-strong prison.
This nightmare is the true story of Noel Fellowes.

'It would be an understatement to say that this is an
extremely disturbing case.'
The Lord Chief Justice, Lord Lane

'It is clear that police officers handling the case either
ignored or deliberately withheld vital evidence.'
Sunday Express

KILLING TIME

Noel Fellowes

A LION PAPERBACK

Oxford · Batavia · Sydney

I dedicate this book to
more than a woman,
more than a wife,
more than a mother –
to a truly remarkable lady,
Coral,
with my deepest love.

Copyright © 1986 Noel Fellowes

Published by
Lion Publishing plc
Sandy Lane West, Littlemore, Oxford, England
ISBN 0 7459 1051 3
Albatross Books Pty Ltd
PO Box 320, Sutherland, NSW 2232, Australia
ISBN 0 86760 830 7

First edition 1986
Reprinted 1987, 1988, 1989

**The author can be contacted c/o Bracknell Baptist Church,
Church Road, Bracknell RG12 1EH**

Printed and bound in Great Britain by
Cox & Wyman Ltd, Reading

Contents

Foreword

During the thirty years or so I have been studying miscarriages of justice, I have found the most common cause to be 'over-zealousness' on the part of the police.

What sometimes happens is this. The police light on some tiny, circumstantial piece of evidence to connect some person with the crime. Unable to find any further evidence, yet desperate to get results, they allow their suspicions to harden into certainty. Believing they are serving the best interests of justice, they then:

a) Try to browbeat the suspect into a confession.
b) Pressurize witnesses to say what they want them to say.
c) Suppress or ignore the evidence of other witnesses whose evidence is favourable to the accused.
d) 'Lose' documents such as timesheets that support the accused's alibi.

The case of Noel Fellowes, a taxi-driver and former policeman, is a classic example of this sort of malpractice. Arrested in 1970 for the murder of a 67-year-old debt-collector called Harold Parkinson, the only evidence against him was that his mother-in-law's name had been found in Parkinson's debt collection book, and that someone had seen Parkinson get into a taxi on the day of the murder!

On this flimsy scenario the Lancashire CID, under the leadership of Detective Chief Superintendent Mounsey, went to work. Having grilled Noel Fellowes all night to extract a confession and failed, they then 'persuaded' various witnesses to say that he had a grudge against Parkinson (whom he had never met) and that the cravat found on Parkinson's body belonged to Fellowes (who didn't own a cravat). They suppressed evidence that pointed to others and failed to ascertain that the cravat belonged to Parkinson. In addition, the taxi firm's records that would have established Noel Fellowes' alibi mysteriously went missing.

Faced with this mass of false evidence, it is not surprising that the jury found Mr Fellowes guilty of manslaughter. Sentenced to seven years, he served four before being released on parole. One of the most heartening sections of this book is Noel Fellowes' refusal to be crushed by the prison system and how, despite recurrent nightmares and two beatings-up (for no other reason than he had been a copper) he succeeded in blossoming physically and educationally.

It wasn't for another nine years however that, thanks to a supergrass, Parkinson's real assailant was discovered. Upholding Noel Fellowes' appeal against conviction, the Lord Chief Justice had some mildly critical things to say about the conduct of the Lancashire police ('A combination of misfortunes, one must also say misbehaviour or errors, and of mistaken conclusions, which conspired to produce this result').

In my view that was not enough. What was needed was not just the clearing of his name, but a searching inquiry into just how an innocent man had come to be convicted. In his new-found Christian faith the author has forgiven his transgressors. But we need to ensure that this does not make it easier for those who come after to become transgressors themselves.

What in the long run can be done to prevent further miscarriages of justice? In my view there is only one solution, which is to abandon the accusatorial system of justice which has been responsible for so many miscarriages in the past, and in its place to adopt a modified form of the inquisitorial or European system, in which initial investigations into serious cases are not conducted by policemen hungry for results, but by a supervisory, neutral legal official.

Had such officials been operating in Britain these last thirty years, a score of prisoners or ex-prisoners I could name (and some of whom I have named) would never have come to trial, let alone have been convicted. Noel Fellowes is the latest; but not, I fear, the last.

Ludovic Kennedy
March 1986

1

The Wrong Man

It was the afternoon of 26 February 1970. I woke up feeling tired after my all-night stint at the taxi office. Nightwork seemed to suit some people but I saw it as a gross inconvenience to my social life. Still, a cold washdown, a cup of tea and I would be ready to face another day. The flat I shared with a friend was in disarray, but that could wait for a cleaning blitz at the weekend. It seemed such a waste of time cleaning and clearing up every day. Who wanted to be domesticated anyway? My brain started to function at last, recovering from the shock of waking up after insufficient sleep. My stomach was telling me I was very hungry. I managed to find a few slices of stale bread and a small tin of baked beans. Cooking wasn't one of my greater gifts so I decided to buy fish and chips on the way to work.

It was a typical cold, grey, damp February day. I walked down Thornton Road towards the chip-shop. Better get some cigarettes as my packet showed signs of urgent crisis. 'Twenty Embassy and a *Lancashire Evening Post* please,' I muttered to the shop assistant. I came out of the shop with my newspaper and emergency supply of cigarettes. I remember glancing at the headlines of the paper: 'KILLING IN OVERTON', it said.

I thought, *That doesn't happen in places like this*. It was places like London, Liverpool or Manchester. How could such a thing happen in a village like Overton? Or in a place like Morecambe? It was the end of the winter. No one moved in the town; all the people hibernated. Still, if nothing else, it would certainly liven up conversation. There's nothing like gossip and speculation to wake people up.

I strolled down Euston Road thinking of what I had read and wondered what could have happened. The reporting detail was sparse. No specific detail—only that a large team of detectives had been drafted into the area. When I got to the taxi office, I was greeted with, 'Have you seen the paper? There's been a murder in Overton.' The place was buzzing with excitement.

Who needs all this? I thought to myself. I had only surfaced a couple of hours ago and I hadn't even had anything to eat. Betty told me Lynn had phoned and wanted picking up from work at the hairdressers to be taken home. I took my driver's log-sheets, jumped in the car and went to pick her up. As we drove back to her parents' home we discussed the mystery killing in Overton and other more mundane things. Lynn was disappointed I was working nights for a couple of weeks as it meant we could only see each other coming to or going from work.

I had met Lynn after my recent separation from my wife. In retrospect, the marriage breakdown was a combination of incompatibility and a reluctance on my part to accept the responsibility and dedication which marriage demanded. The emotional strain of unhappiness and incompatibility, coupled with a general disenchantment, had led to my recent resignation from the Lancashire Constabulary as a police constable. I had taken a job as a taxi driver to give myself time to recover and to take stock of my life, a breathing space before deciding what course and career to take. Besides, Morecambe was a seaside resort which offered very little other than seasonal work.

The opportunity of a carefree romance was refreshing. It boosted my ego and allowed me to share my innermost thoughts with an independent person on the rights or wrongs of my decision to separate. I had never tried to hide or disguise the fact that I was going out with Lynn. I had no reason to try to deceive anyone, as I had met Lynn after I had left my wife. It was a good, wholesome relationship and we seemed to complement each other's personalities. Lynn came from a good family background and was stable and secure. Her parents were friendly and welcomed me into their house at any time. I had, of course, already told them of my circumstances and assured them that my involvement with their daughter wasn't just a quick fling—as indeed it wasn't. I was very fond of her and the feeling was mutual.

After taking Lynn home, I was busy carrying passengers until about midnight. Then I headed for the office to take over the manning of the phone and to do general office duties until the day staff started at 6 a.m. The conversation in the small hours was taken up with the Overton killing and the intense activity of the police. There seemed to be more police cars and policemen than residents and we joked about needing to watch our speed around town until they had left the area.

Days passed slowly by as they always did in the winter months of a heavily-shuttered seaside town. The only topic of conversation was the recent mystery of the killing in Overton. By now the place was littered with policemen. There seemed to be one or two at the end of every street, clipboards and pencils at the ready. Posters of the dead man were all over the town and police vans using tannoys were appealing for anyone who had known Harold Parkinson to come forward. The whole town was gripped in the intensity of the murder enquiry.

There was a breakthrough when the police revealed that they had received an anonymous phone call from a man saying that he had seen Mr Parkinson board a taxi on the night before he died. Following up this lead, the police decided to interview all taxi drivers in the area. They arrived at the taxi office on 5 March and were given the names of all the drivers. As a result, I was asked to go to the Murder HQ at the Memorial Hall, Overton to answer some questions. Naturally, I agreed. I had nothing to hide.

At the Murder HQ the two detectives sat me down and began routine questioning. Did I know the man or not? I told them I didn't. They showed me a photograph of the dead man and asked if I had ever carried him as a passenger. Again I told them I had not—to the best of my recollection. I told them

11

that Mr Parkinson's face looked familiar, but in a town like Morecambe with a very high intake of retired people I couldn't be certain. Besides, our taxi business was in Morecambe, seven or eight miles from Overton. If Mr Parkinson had wanted a taxi he would have taken one locally.

Then the detectives told me that Mr Parkinson fancied himself as a private investigator. They knew that I was separated from my wife and suggested there might be some connection. I replied that I had nothing to hide—all my friends and family knew my situation. Next they told me that my mother-in-law's name was found in a book belonging to Harold Parkinson and they thought he might have been employed by her to follow me. My mother-in-law was always interfering and was always trying to make trouble for me, I told them. I had no knowledge of her hiring anyone, but then I wouldn't, as I had no contact with her at all. Perhaps my wife and/or mother-in-law had employed him. But how would I know? 'Why don't you ask them?' I replied.

Again they asked if I knew Harold Parkinson. They reminded me that he used to frequent Morecambe Police Station with information about all sorts of happenings in the town. I said that I *may* have seen him or heard some talk of him in the station whilst I was still a policeman. And I conceded that if he *were* a private detective, my wife might have put him on to me to tail my movements. It was all speculation and I certainly had never met him. Indeed, I felt rather shocked to learn that my wife or mother-in-law had possibly hired him.

The interview lasted about half an hour and they asked me to make a statement to confirm what I had said. I was quite willing to do so, as the enquiry had nothing to do with me—or so I thought.

That afternoon I returned to the taxi office feeling a little disturbed that my mother-in-law's name was in one of Harold Parkinson's books. When I picked Lynn up from work I told her of the interview with the detectives, including their revelation about my mother-in-law. To take the intensity out of the situation I jokingly said, 'Next stop Walton

12

Jail'. She said I shouldn't joke about things like that. It was a part of my make-up—I never took anything seriously.

As I ate with Lynn and her family we discussed the murder. I threw in a few remarks like, 'I told them I didn't tie him that tight'. In retrospect they were in bad taste but I was trying to make light of the matter. Little did I know that those remarks, although made in jest, were to cost me a number of years of terrible suffering.

The afternoon of 6 March I was awoken by a loud banging on the door of the flat. Trying to get my head together I stumbled into my trousers and answered the door. Two hefty six-foot men stood at the door.

'Noel Fellowes?' asked one.

'That's me. Who on earth are you?'

They flashed their warrant cards and walked into the flat. I was still half asleep but tried to understand what was happening and, more importantly, what they wanted. They informed me that with my consent they wanted to take some of my clothing for forensic analysis, for the purpose of elimination. I inferred that they were joking. To my utter dismay they were not.

This can't be real, I thought to myself. *I must be dreaming.* I asked them again why they wanted my clothes and again they said it was for elimination. At that point I told them that the joke was going too far and I was going to consult a solicitor. The whole incident didn't make sense and in my short experience in the police force I had never encountered this sort of procedure. But after quick consideration I told them to take what they wanted as I had nothing to hide. They did.

After they left a deep feeling of bewilderment and insecurity seemed to well up in my stomach. I made myself a drink and sat for a while, trying to comprehend what had taken place a few minutes earlier. What on earth did they want my clothing for? Did they suspect I was somehow involved in the crime? I sat there in complete disbelief. After thinking for some time I asked myself, 'What am I worrying about? It's nothing to do

13

with me at all.' It was strange to feel so frightened by the police. Off I went to work again. When I told my colleagues about the trauma of the afternoon, they were just as bewildered as I was.

In the early evening of 8 March I was in the taxi office when two men entered. They identified themselves as detectives and said that Chief Superintendent Mounsey, in charge of the murder investigation, wanted to interview me at the Murder HQ in Overton. They gave no reason for this request, but added that it would look better if I went. I agreed to go with them and they drove me to the Memorial Hall in Overton to meet Mounsey.

It was a strange journey. No one spoke. I tried to collect my thoughts, reasoning out why they wanted to interview me again. As we arrived at the Memorial Hall I felt apprehensive about what they wanted from me. I had already told them everything I knew. We walked through the main entrance and were met by the noise of telephones ringing, typewriters clicking and an atmosphere of intense human activity. There were small mountains of paper stacked on every desk and teams of detectives sifting through them. There were large street maps on the wall with colour coding and comments written on them.

The two detectives led me down the avenue of desks to a single glazed door at the rear of the main hall. A small doorplate greeted us with the inscription 'Det. Chief Sup. Mounsey'. We had arrived. I was ushered in by the detectives and ordered to sit down on a wooden chair. Little did I know that this was to be my last night of freedom for a number of years.

A tall, overweight, middle-aged man walked in. I knew immediately it was Mounsey as the other detectives jumped to their feet in nervous respect. With a gruff introduction of himself and the opening words 'I am not very happy about the statement you have given my officers,' the interview began. My first response was to tell him that I wasn't happy at being brought back to the Murder HQ. This remark seemed to incense him and he retorted that his men had been working round the clock on this investigation and he wasn't going to be messed about by an upstart who had a little knowledge about the law. *Not the best start to the interview*, I thought. *Perhaps I had better keep my thoughts to myself.*

Mounsey was an awesome character. He studied the statement I had made earlier, casting a casual glance at me now and then. Then he asked me about my previous knowledge and involvement with Harold Parkinson. I reiterated that I had never met him and didn't know him. The line of questioning continued, involving my separation and the name of my mother-in-law in Parkinson's diary. I made the same statement I had made earlier. But Mounsey was having none of it. He told me that he had further information from two people—that I had told them Mr Parkinson was following me and I had seen him in Morecambe and duffed him up. At this I stayed calm, saying that it was impossible because I had never met the man. Indeed, the first thing I had heard about the possibility of Mr Parkinson following me was from his own two detectives, who told me my mother-in-law's address was found in his book.

By this time, the adrenalin was flowing and I could feel the sensation of fear creeping upon me. *What on earth is happening?* I thought to myself. *They wouldn't invent things like this*.

The fear grew as Mounsey started to say things like, 'We know you've done it, lad. Why don't you get it off your chest? We know you didn't really mean to kill him.' As I continued to plead my innocence, he became more determined. He started shouting and banging his fist upon the table. By this time fear had totally engulfed me and I just broke down. I could not control my emotions. As hard as I tried to fight the tears back, they just kept on flowing. Deep shock set in and I was inwardly fighting to get words out of my mouth: 'I've told you over and over again. I have never met the man. I know nothing about this crime,' I said.

'Right, lads,' Mounsey said to the other detectives. 'Wrap it up here. Let's go to Lancaster Police Station. We've got him.' I broke into a cold sweat in total disbelief at what I had just heard. Surely this was a dream? It wasn't happening. Before I could utter another word, I found myself standing between the two detectives and a pair of handcuffs were snapped tightly over my wrists. How ironic. I thought of the number of times as a policeman I had snapped handcuffs on other people so routinely, never ever having considered what it was like or how the person had felt. Now I had first-hand experience of both the feeling and result—complete and utter horror.

They led me out of the room and into the main hall, Mounsey in front proclaiming to his army of busy administrators, 'We've got him. Have an early night.' Two stone-faced detectives grabbed my arms and continued to walk me through the narrow corridor of chairs and desks. What a contrast! An hour ago when I had entered the hall it was a mass of activity. Now as I was being led out there was a deathly stillness. The typewriters had stopped, telephones were silent. There was not even the sound of rustling paper. Only a few minutes before all these people had been feverishly sifting, collating, double-checking, looking for any vital clue they had missed and now they had been told it was over. I was conscious of people staring and assessing me as I passed by each of them. Most faces were expressionless but I could hear their thoughts in unison saying, 'You're for it, you are.'

We travelled to Lancaster at high speed, in silence. I was still trying to comprehend what had happened in the last hour or so. I was now so gripped with fear that my whole body was shaking and a feeling of nausea began to creep steadily over me. 'If this is the way one feels when innocent, how on earth do people feel when they are guilty?' I asked myself. Surely there had to be a mistake of wrong identity, gross incompetence or absolute lies on someone's part. It was difficult even attempting to think straight. So many questions buzzed through my head at such a speed I didn't seem able to catch up with them. The silence in the car was strange after the brow-beating exchanges in the Memorial Hall. Perhaps it was a psychological tactic employed by top-line detectives—a lull before the storm.

The journey to Lancaster seemed shorter than usual. On arrival I was hurriedly escorted into an interview room. By this time my nervous state had subsided a little and a small protective shield of inner assurance raised itself. Mounsey came into the room armed with a bundle of papers and wearing a menacing expression on his face. Then the interrogation started.

We started where we left off at the Memorial Hall, going over the same questions and the same ground we had covered before. I repeatedly told him that I didn't know Parkinson, had never ever met him and had no interest in coin collecting.

'What about the fight you had with him?' he asked.

'I never met the man,' I said.

The same questions were fired at me over and over again by Mounsey and the other three detectives in the room. They seemed to be trying to outdo each other by approaching the same questions from different angles. I remember thinking how strange it was that I had been telling them the truth all the time, but they refused to accept it. Still, it would only be a matter of time before they would come to the conclusion that I was telling the truth. After all, I knew I had never met the man and had no involvement in the murder they were investigating, so there couldn't be any evidence whatsoever to support their ridiculous accusations.

By this time I was tired of all the repetitive questioning and told Mounsey that I had answered all his questions in total truth and now I wanted to go home. He told me I wasn't going anywhere until he had finished with me.

The tactics changed and so did the detectives. They all left, including Mounsey, and a fresh team took over. When I got up to go they pushed me back down in my seat. I asked them if they were the heavy mob. One of them replied, 'You should know we don't do things like that.'

They took a new approach, showing me large photographs of the dead man. He had obviously been badly beaten, tied up in a most intricate fashion and gagged. They were, to say the very least, horrific.

'How did he get the cuts and bruises?' they asked.

'I haven't got a clue. I wasn't there and have never met him,' I replied.

'You're separated from your wife; your mother-in-law employed him to follow you; we had a phone message that he got in a taxi and furthermore, we have two witnesses who confirm that you told them he was following you and you beat him up a few days before. Now come on, make it easy on yourself. Tell us what really happened.'

Again I could only deny the accusations. I knew nothing. Questions and counter-questions were fired at me over and over again. The strain was starting to tell on me and my mind drifted into confusion. By this time I had been *interrogated* (that is the only appropriate word for what was happening) for about six hours. It was now one o'clock in the morning.

Six hours of intense questioning and still they didn't believe a word I said. All I repeated throughout that time was that I had never met the man and that I had absolutely nothing to do with the offence. By now signs of tiredness and frustration appeared in both their faces and voices. The tension mounted and they became more irate. We had done the full circle and were back to the more aggressive style of injecting fear by shouting accusations and desk-banging with clenched fists. This approach certainly worked to raise the level of fear within me, but if you are innocent, how can you confess to something you haven't done?

Later on, Mounsey returned with another team and told the other detectives to have a break. They were obviously disappointed. He turned to me.

'You have done very well keeping us all up. Now let's get it over with. Tell us about the person or persons you are covering up for. We know there must have been more than one person who committed this crime.'

'I'm not covering up for anyone. I've repeatedly told you that I know absolutely nothing,' I said wearily.

'You're an ex-policeman and probably quite a clever one to have covered your tracks after killing this man. Now the game is over. We know you've done it. Everything points to you. At the very worst it will only be manslaughter. Come on—tell us the truth,' insisted Mounsey.

Again I denied any knowledge of the crime. By this time I was totally fatigued, mentally and physically. There seemed no escape from the barrage of questions and their eagerness to trap me into confessing something I hadn't done. They seemed hell-bent on stitching me up, but why? Here I was, a free man, living in a democratic society, being interrogated by not one, but several teams of Lancashire's top detectives. I had been refused permission to leave, denied access to a telephone, denied access to contact both friends and family and—worst of all—denied legal representation. So much for democratic rights and entitlements. 1984 had obviously arrived fourteen years early.

I told Mounsey my head was spinning and I felt totally washed up. I wanted to go.

'Not until you've given us what we want,' he said.

'I've told you all I know. Stop this merry-go-round. You cannot hold me against my will. Either charge me or let me go,' I said.

'You're going nowhere, mister,' he shouted.

The questioning continued. We covered the same ground yet again and my denials continued. I was down to single word answers. No. No. No. At around 2.30 a.m. another detective came in and sheepishly whispered something into Mounsey's ear, then left again.

Mounsey looked at me and said, 'Your wife is downstairs. You can see her if you want.'

What on earth was my wife here for? I hadn't seen her for a couple of months. Still, anything to get out of this room, I thought. They handcuffed me again and led me down to another interview room, pushed me into the room and there was my wife, looking pale and nervous.

Our only greeting was to stare at each other. My opening comment was 'What's going on? They think I have some-thing to do with the murder in Overton.'

19

My wife sat impassively and said, 'You must tell them the truth, Noel, and everything will be all right.'

'I've told them the truth all along,' I said.

She kept on saying, 'Tell them the truth and they will help you.'

I just couldn't believe my own ears. Now they had my wife in on the act. It was at that point that I knew I was a scapegoat for someone. It was my first realization that a conspiracy was being built—and I was the victim. It was amazing. Now they were trying to use my wife as an emotional buffer to break down my defences in order to extract the confession that eluded them. I pleaded with my wife to phone my parents or a solicitor. She said the police had told her to tell no one. They would look after it. How naive people are. They presume that just because someone has a uniform, is called a policeman and is employed to uphold the law, they are beyond reproach and must be telling the truth in any given circumstance.

I pleaded with her to contact someone as the situation was desperate and I knew I needed outside help. But she gave no indication whether she would or wouldn't. With that the visit ended and the detectives led me back to the original interview room.

'Now we have let you see your wife, how about clearing up this whole mess?' asked Mounsey.

Without prompting, my voice echoed the same reply: 'I know nothing and can tell you nothing.'

Again they were obviously determined that time and expertise were on their side and it would only be a matter of time before they broke through. They started from the beginning again—same questions, different approach. This time it was a case of asking leading and subtle questions like, 'When you hit him you didn't mean to hurt him, did you?' I had to call upon my deepest resolve and concentration to understand what they were trying to orchestrate. They had obviously decided that as a confession wasn't going to be forthcoming, their best tactic was to adopt leading questions and to break down my defences in a more subtle approach.

I had nothing left—no strength of mind or physical energy. I felt dizzy, sick and totally insecure. What had started as another ordinary day had turned into a terrible nightmare beyond my control. From that point on I remained totally silent and at about 5.30 a.m. Mounsey decided I had clammed up, so he directed his men to lock me up and let me rest for a while.

I had been questioned non-stop by teams of detectives for a period of some ten-and-a-half hours and they had achieved nothing more than what had been achieved in the first fifteen minutes on the previous evening. Surely by now they *must* know I was telling the truth. They had produced no evidence to support their theory or their accusations. What they said was nothing more than speculation and at the very best circumstantial, but even the latter was ridiculous. They took me down to the basement which turned out to be the cell block and handed me over to the constable in charge. He demanded I took off my jacket, emptied my pockets and proceeded to lock me up. By this time I was so exhausted I couldn't even be bothered to protest. All I wanted to do was lie down and sleep. They could have thrown me in a rat-infested dungeon for all I cared—just let me sleep.

I emerged from the depths of sleep feeling a hand shaking me vigorously. I reluctantly opened my eyes to the strange surroundings of a cell and a uniformed policeman telling me to get up. The full horror of my predicament flooded back into my mind. I was really here. It wasn't a figment of some devilish nightmare. It was for real. The constable said the lads in the station reckoned I had done extremely well standing up to all the questioning I encountered. Big deal, I thought to myself. They had all but destroyed me mentally and physically and now this jerk was giving me a back-handed compliment. He supplied me with a towel and soap to wash with, then brought me something to eat and drink. Shortly afterwards two detectives came down and told me they were taking me upstairs again. Strange, really—after all I had endured the previous night my mind was alert, but my body was functioning with nervous disorder.

I remained silent and decided that whatever happened I was not going to say anything until I had legal representation. The detectives tried to engage me in conversation but I kept my mouth shut. I was escorted to a room to meet the 'police surgeon'. He was not a policeman but was employed at times in his own professional capacity as a doctor. He gave me a short examination, then explained that the police wanted to take samples of my hair, nails, scrapings from beneath my nails, a sample of blood and numerous other samples. At this I broke my silence and told him I had no objection as I had nothing to hide.

Then the detectives took me for fingerprinting. I told them it was unnecessary—they already had my fingerprints on record. All policemen are fingerprinted, and mine would still be on file. But they insisted, so I obliged. They said they had some more questions to ask me. At each question, I just stared at them and remained silent. I had decided that I was not going to carry on with this ridiculous game. I also knew that time was on my side and that by now people were bound to be asking questions about my whereabouts. The police would have to allow me either legal representation or charge me within a short space of time. Before long they came to the conclusion I wasn't going to assist them, so they locked me up in the cell again.

Now followed a time of immense mental activity, trying to relive the previous day and night, searching my memory for clues as to why they thought it was me. The worst thing was to try and remember all my movements from 6 p.m. on Tuesday 24 February 1970 until mid-morning on Thursday 26 February 1970. How does one account for every minute of forty odd hours a couple of weeks previously? I remembered being on nights and knew that my work-sheets could account for that time. The rest was pretty sketchy. It would have been much easier if I could have spoken to people but I was isolated, cut off from any outside contact. There was only me and I was trapped in a situation in which I didn't even understand the rules. I spent the afternoon thinking over my dilemma and trying to analyze the past twenty-four hours. The most horrifying aspect of it all was the uncertainty of my immediate freedom and liberty.

In the evening two detectives took me upstairs again and showed me into a room. Chief Inspector Howson stood there, in company with Mounsey, with a piece of paper in his hand and started reading out its contents.

'Keith Noel Fellowes, you are charged that between the 24th and 26th February you murdered Harold Parkinson . . .' And so on. I heard him say, 'You are not obliged to say anything; anything you say will be taken down and . . .' I couldn't believe what I was hearing. My heart pounded faster and faster. My legs began to crumple beneath the weight of the shockwaves jerking through my body. I looked coldly at Mounsey eyeball to eyeball—a pregnant silence—then I spoke.

'Not guilty.'

He looked at me with a fixed expression on his face.

The exercise over, Howson told me that they would inform my solicitor for me. I told them I didn't have one.

'Never mind,' he said. 'We'll pick one off the legal aid list for you.'

And that was it.

2

The Scene of the Crime

Harold Parkinson was an old man who saw life through the eyes of a comic-strip hero. A man of sixty-seven, he was a private investigator, a police informer and a martial arts warrior—in his own mind. He was a man who dreamed of doing great things but achieved little; an old man who lived in the world of his own imagination. There weren't many like him in the tiny village of Overton. The population was 831—a sedate mixture of retired, farming or professional people not given to eccentricity and play-acting. The isolation of their small community—cut off daily at one end by the tide—was a comforting barrier both to the hustle and bustle of the crowds of tourists who flocked to the seaside at Morecambe and to the everyday business of the rest of Lancashire.

Harold John Driscoll Parkinson had only lived in the terraced cottage in Overton's Main Street for seven years. But he was a local man and many had seen him become progressively more wayward at different addresses over several decades. He had been born into a well-off family. His father, a noted alderman, ran a successful jewellery store in Morecambe and Harold Parkinson had inherited his wealth without ever having to work hard for a living. His parents had never felt he was the 'right sort' to serve behind their counter, and over the years he had tried his hand at several things, but he had never really settled on anything. It is difficult to piece together exactly what he had done because of the embellishments he laid in later life. He said that he had made his a fortune buying and selling coins and antiques. But the truth was that the money left him by his parents set him up in a comfortable existence which he did not need to improve upon.

Mr Parkinson was a colourful local figure, and he was always the subject of interest and speculation. When he introduced the first Volkswagen ever to grace the streets of the village, many peered through their curtains in wonder. Later, they couldn't conceal their curiosity when he bought a diesel-powered Mercedes. Unfortunately one of his other habits—drinking—interrupted his freewheeling days. He was banned from driving after being stopped by the police.

Even in his old age, Mr Parkinson liked to be active. He was out and about most days, even if it was just to go down to the library. Occasionally, local firms would contact him to do some minor debt-collecting work—picking up small sums of money from families who hadn't found the time or the means to pay up for their coal, their furniture or other goods. His success in this role was largely a result of his impressive frame—over six feet tall and well-built, with a swaggering gait which any sergeant-major would have been proud of.

Mr Parkinson was a frequent visitor to the Queen's Hotel in Morecambe at lunchtime and Overton's two pubs, the Ship and the Globe, in the evening. It was here that his harmless ramblings became a source of irritation to people, for Mr Parkinson enjoyed heated debate. Occasionally he became too disruptive and the landlord or landlady would be forced to take the rare step of barring a pensioner from the premises—the ban would soon be lifted, though. In a small town like Overton there was no room for malice.

Retired fisherman Jimmy Braid had known Harold Parkinson since his teens. He remembers him marry, separate, and eventually move to just a few doors down from his own Main Street home.

'During the war, he told me that he worked on security at Vickers shipyards where he lost the little finger off one hand. He was always vague about his activities, associates and relatives. He could very easily upset people with his off-handed attitude.'

Not everyone shared this view, however, and indeed there was little standing room when he threw a New Year's Eve party a few weeks before his death.

The cottage in Main Street was attractive and had a distinctive charm, with its stone fireplace, low timber-beamed ceiling and an interesting collection of antiques and curios. Family photographs decorated a grand Welsh dresser and display cabinet. Harold Parkinson was not a tidy man and had persuaded local villager Mrs Josephine Hockenhull to come in and clean for him. She has mixed memories of her four years as 'home help'.

'He sometimes showed off, saying he could chop a man down with one blow. He would grip my hand. I'm no weakling but I couldn't get loose. He fancied himself in Kung Fu and would act the fool waving his hands in front of his face. But I never took any notice of him. He wouldn't do anybody any harm. He was full of stories. Told me surgeons had put a plate in his head after a serious road accident.'

Mr Parkinson was famous for his magnificent coin collection. It was started by his father, Alderman J. W. Parkinson, who gave him a set of Edward VII coins, including Maundy money. Over the years Harold collected coins from many parts of the world, some dating back centuries. He helped found the Morecambe, Lancaster and District Numismatic Society and joined the respected International Coin Group. Mr Parkinson's hobby was featured in local newspapers, who photographed and interviewed him. Word of his expertise spread throughout the country—ultimately into the wrong hands. The collection of gold, silver and copper coins was kept in a cabinet in a back room which could apparently be seen from an outside window. But he was very security-conscious—typical of a man who for years had wanted to be a policeman—and visitors would hear the clicking of locks and bolts the instant they left either the front or back door.

The desire to be a policeman was very strong. Mr Parkinson often sought out police company and yet had little of real importance to tell them. Gradually he began to see himself in the role of 'Dick Barton' super-sleuth, the private eye who would fearlessly tackle any case. In truth, he probably never did any private investigation work in his life. But this whim was later to have a significant bearing on how others were to regard him. And it had a direct effect on my life.

On Tuesday 24 February 1970, Harold Parkinson woke up with nagging stomach pains. It ruined his plans for the day. When a friend, Bernard Darby, a shop proprietor, arrived to take him to the library at 9.30 a.m., he found him not well enough to travel the few miles. Mr Darby and Mrs Hockenhull both made sure he was feeling better before leaving. It was the last time they were to see him alive.

Both later recalled that Mr Parkinson was expecting a telephone call that day, probably something to do with his coins, and sharp-eyed Mrs Hockenhull was even able to give police a detailed description of the clothes he had been wearing.

Three of Harold Parkinson's acquaintances saw him the following day at different times, evidence that he had recovered from his tummy pains. But a terrible shock lay in store for Mr Darby on Thursday 26 February when he returned to the cottage to pick up the old man.

'I first noticed that the curtains downstairs were drawn and there was no sign of him outside his home. It was usual on a sunny morning for him to be outside in the garden. I went to the front door and saw that there was a newspaper stuck through the letter-box and a bottle of milk nearby. The door was ajar about one-and-a-half inches, just caught on the frame. I pushed it open and shouted "Harold". There was no reply and I went into the living-room which was generally disturbed, with papers strewn over the floor and the settee. A copper kettle that was usually on the hearth was lying on its side and there was a pile of silver coins and an eye-glass strewn about. I shouted "Harold" again, by this time thinking he was ill or had gone to bed drunk. I then saw the door to the understairs cupboard was open wide. I saw a bundle lying on the floor. I went to it and realized it was a body. It had a gag round the face. I looked at the hands and saw that there was a finger missing and realized it was Harold Parkinson. There was blood coming from his mouth.'

Mr Darby could tell by the colour of his friend's hands that he was dead. He quickly rang the police, who arrived two minutes later. Amid all the tragic confusion, the telephone rang. It was Elizabeth Barrett, a fellow coin enthusiast, who had planned to invite Harold for a meal. Mr Darby had the unenviable task of telling her he was dead.

What was even worse, the old man was tied and bound from head to foot, in a manner later to be described by a barrister as 'trussed like a turkey'. Starting at the bottom, the victim's ankles were pinned together with an 18-inch red tie, fastened in a tight granny knot. The calves were held firm by a bandage fastened in the same way. A few inches above the knees, a cable was tied in figure-of-eight fashion, completely immobilizing movement of the thighs. Just for good measure, a metal-buckled webbing strap was wrapped round the upper legs. One loose end was looped round the left arm. The wrists were clasped together at the front of the body, right hand on top of left. Here, there was a silk neckerchief, again in a figure-of-eight, the first loop tied in a granny knot, the second with a reef knot. There was more calico bandage or white cloth round the hands, some of it crossing in a big X over his chest and, fatally, round his neck. Electrical cable still connected to a small Hoover dustette vacuum cleaner was circled round his bulky frame. The lower half of Mr Parkinson's head was obscured by a purple piece of material, which was to assume vital importance in days to come.

It later took mortuary staff hours to untie the ligatures from the stiffening corpse of Harold Parkinson. Whoever had bound him had gone to inordinate lengths to stop him raising the alarm. But their caution had proved too successful. The old man, found lying on his back with his knees raised slightly, had probably struggled so much that he had tightened his bonds, and eventually strangled himself. It was clear, too, that Mr Parkinson had suffered a thorough beating before being trussed up. A quarter of his face was covered in dried blood and there was bruising and discoloration in other parts.

Uniformed and CID officers quickly started to try to piece together his last moments and identify the many various possibilities surrounding his death. Was it a robbery or a burglary which went wrong? Had Mr Parkinson many enemies? Could he have tied himself up in a masochistic search for kicks? The first officers to arrive faced many unanswered questions. For one officer, the death was a double shock. Det. Constable Jack Ellison had known Mr Parkinson for six years and had enjoyed passing the time of day with him.

Within an hour of the discovery of the body, word had leaked to the local press. Three *Lancashire Evening Post* reporters were assigned to the story. A local shopkeeper told one journalist: 'He used to bring his coins to show us and we thought they were pretty valuable. He didn't come in for his bread yesterday and we wondered what was wrong.' The killing had a big impact on local newspaper front pages but was dismissed in only a few lines in the national press. Their editors were more concerned with the sudden wave of aeroplane bombings and hijackings, the cruelty of South African troops who fired on crowds and the long-running dispute over whether Britain should join the Common Market.

On 26 February 1970, when the body of Harold Parkinson was found, *The Times* had one story of great interest to many of the 'official' callers to his house. An eight-and-a-half per cent interim pay rise for almost 100,000 policemen and women had been agreed at a meeting in London. The starting salary for a 19-year-old PC would be £900 a year; Chief Inspectors could expect £2,100. The paper also reported the discovery of a hole in a wall at Walton prison—sealed before any of the inmates of the Liverpool jail could take advantage of it. Mia Farrow had twins. Twenty policemen were continuing the search for the body of Muriel McKay, a newspaper executive's wife. Brothers Arthur and Nizamodeen Hosein were awaiting trial for her murder. The killing of an old man in a tiny village few people had ever heard of did not rate much more than a glance.

Even so, Overton had never seen anything quite like this. An invasion of police officers and their attendant pack of local reporters swarmed everywhere. Mrs Edith Byrne down at the grocer's had a boom time selling sandwiches by the score, while landlords in the pubs thanked their lucky stars. There was a mixed response to the invaders. Mrs Flo Jackson chased photographers from her orchard as they tried to get a shot of the house. Others confided freely with both police and newsmen alike. John Atkinson, a press photographer, recalls: 'One villager burst out laughing, telling me how the police dropped Mr Parkinson's body as they carried it out of the house. It didn't seem particularly funny to me. But that was how many people seemed to think of the old man.'

'Ma' Macluskie, the landlady of the Ship public house, said: 'It doesn't matter whether you like yon policemen or not—like I keep telling my customers, you've got to help them all you can. I suppose some folk would say police were a nuisance, but they're not a bad bunch on the whole.'

Police set up their Murder Headquarters in the nearby Memorial Hall. Conscious of keeping good public relations, they immediately offered to vacate it for a few hours on Sunday to allow the village Catholics to have Mass, as usual. The congregation declined the offer—but appreciated the gesture. They met over the road in the First Overton and St Helen's Scout Hut where they heard a plea from Father Thomas Walsh, who urged full co-operation, stressing the folly of suppressing information 'out of loyalty to any other person'.

News was almost inadvertently suppressed, reported the *Lancashire Evening Post*, when 'a queue of sweating reporters, clutching exclusive copy with deadlines on their minds, almost burst into tears when a GPO engineer calmly closed the kiosk and resolutely proceeded to re-wire a light fitting'. Not everyone, it seems, was sharing the village's new-found sense of urgency.

When the copy was filed, it more often than not contained unflattering remarks about the victim—editors were safe in the fact that they cannot libel the dead. The landlord of the Globe Hotel, Edgar Baxter, said of Harold Parkinson: 'He was a bit peculiar. A lot of people would walk away from him rather than towards him. He was more of a nuisance than anything.'

There were two immediate priorities for police arriving at the scene. First, they had to make sure an inch-by-inch study of the house was carried out by scientists before any potential clues were lost under the trampling feet of visitors. This was the job of Dr Alan Clift, chief biologist at the North Western Forensic Science Laboratory in Preston. He found blood-stains on the hearth, carpet, wireless set, and the legs of a stool. He also dropped some buttons into little plastic bags for further study. Second, they had to determine the exact medical cause of Harold Parkinson's death. Home Office pathologist Dr Brian Beeson, based at the Royal Lancaster Infirmary, made a lengthy report. But one supposition stood out. Death was caused by strangulation from the calico bandage—a pressure which was 'maintained for several minutes at least'.

'The evidence indicates the material was applied to the neck very tightly . . . pressure was transmitted to the wrists in a downwards direction, thus tightening the figure-of-eight white calico ligature.' Dr Beeson said facial bruises could have been caused by punches or 'chops'. The old man had suffered five fractured ribs in the attack and other internal injuries consistent with 'rabbit punches' or even kicks. A fracture to the lower jaw could have happened after death. The report ended with what might be termed an under-statement: 'In my opinion the general picture of the injuries and tying indicated that the deceased was subjected to rough treatment.'

After the police photographer, Detective Sergeant George Brogden, had taken eighteen black and white photographs in the living-room of the house and more in colour later in the mortuary, detectives were then free to start examining some of the books, diaries and other documents without fear of contaminating evidence.

It was obvious from the outset that this was not going to be the easiest crime for the Lancashire constabulary to solve. There seemed no clear motive, no immediate and important witnesses and no high-profile suspects. But the young detectives who streamed to the north of the county from many parts of the north-west of England took up the challenge. They couldn't fail—they had Joe Mounsey.

3

Joe Mounsey:
the Means to an End

There weren't many policemen in the country with a reputation like Joe Mounsey. His tenacity, single-mindedness and shrewd interpretation of criminal psychology were legendary. Here was the model professional whom young detectives everywhere would emulate. For there was one quality which Joe Mounsey never seemed to lack—his ability to get results.

Strangely enough, he started his career patrolling the same Morecambe streets that were my beat as a young constable. For three years PC Mounsey dealt with the mundane trivia, the hard-drinking holiday-makers and the shoplifters that plague every busy trading centre. But after a few months' duty in Lancashire's traffic department, he was transferred to the branch which dominated most of his working life—the Criminal Investigation Department. The Lancashire branch was at that time one of the biggest in England, outside London's Scotland Yard, and not the easiest place to break into the big time. But Joe Mounsey's rare qualities of initiative and total dedication began to get him noticed.

Promotion inevitably came in 1957, following an event best likened to a 'boy's own adventure', when Mounsey, a former Guardsman, was drafted on an assignment to Cyprus. Seconded to the British Police, he joined anti-terrorist officers on the trail of 39-year-old Nicos Sampson, the most wanted EOKA gunman on the island. At 3 a.m. one January morning, Joe and two other officers stormed into a hideaway cottage fifteen miles from Nicosia and seized Sampson as he fumbled to load his Sten gun. A burst of machine-pistol fire into the ceiling from one of the policemen persuaded their prisoner to come quietly. Sampson admitted twenty 'political' killings under the late General Grivas, some of them British servicemen in the notorious Ledra Street, known locally as Murder Mile. Years later, Sampson was appointed President of Cyprus after a coup.

Mounsey had some happy memories of the island, where he was married to Margaret, a former policewoman. Later that year he was switched back to more routine work at Widnes in Lancashire. Within seven years, he rose two ranks in the constabulary to Detective Chief Inspector and was posted to Ashton-under-Lyne. There he faced the biggest challenge of his life, in the course of which his name became known to millions of people in the UK. It happened while investigating the blackest series of outrages committed in Britain in recent times—the Moors Murders.

Soon after taking over in Ashton, Mounsey had become intrigued by the dossier on missing 12-year-old John Kilbride. He had left a local fair just before 6 p.m. on 23 November 1963 to go home for tea. He never made it. Mounsey decided to visit the boy's home one day and came away with the resolution that this was *the* case he must crack, he *would* crack. Soon, John Kilbride's own identity became almost submerged in police circles. He was re-named 'Mounsey's lad'.

The desire to put an end to the mystery of the missing Ashton schoolboy was never far from Mounsey's mind. But it was a whole year before there was any positive hint of a breakthrough. On 6 October 1965, teenager Edward Evans was found murdered in a council overspill house in Hattersley, near Manchester. The two people being questioned were Ian Brady—a Scot—and his lover, Myra Hindley. While interviews were under way, a search of their home revealed a notebook with names doodled in it. Clearly legible were the words 'John Kilbride'. The officer-in-charge telephoned Mounsey—in whose office a poster of the boy had remained for two years after the disappearance. Mounsey's response is well-documented. In *Beyond Belief*, Emlyn Williams describes how Mounsey arrived to interview Brady at Stalybridge

34

police station: 'Five minutes early, the bull-dog with something between his teeth which he would never let go. He had the exact mind of a watchmaker or a miniaturist, the sort of man who can stare a jigsaw puzzle into creeping together.'

The Police Review magazine was also later to sum up Mounsey's innermost feelings during the dramatic meeting with Brady. He 'knew, as all good detectives know, that this was the man he had been looking for'.

Getting little information from Brady and Hindley, Mounsey spent hours poring over photographs from their 'family album'. He became almost obsessed by two of them: both showed Myra Hindley in coat, trousers and boots, her dog inside her coat, looking at an unidentified spot of moorland ground in front of her. There was little to distinguish it from the many square miles of moors in the area. But Mounsey relentlessly organized massive searches and digging operations at different places. Meanwhile, he drove miles trying to place the photographs with the skyline. Eventually, by hard graft and determination, he settled on a remote area. The body was found soon after. In May 1966, Brady and Hindley were both jailed for life, at Chester Assizes. They are still behind bars.

Mounsey's career took off at speed. By the end of 1967 he had risen from Detective Chief Inspector to Detective Chief Superintendent in the Northern District Crime Squad. For the next seven years he was to be head of Lancashire CID, earning a British Empire Medal, two conduct and service medals and a commendation for efficiency in that time.

This was the calibre of the man who arrived on the morning of 26 February in the tiny hamlet of Overton. His task was to take charge of a homicide which seemed insignificant in comparison to other cases he had dealt with. But Joe Mounsey was the sort who would consistently apply the same effort and vigilance in solving every case.

Dressed in a thick overcoat and wearing a trilby to keep out the biting salt-winds of Overton, Mounsey first of all visited Harold Parkinson's seventeenth-century cottage in Main

Street. Having seen all he wanted, he was off a few hundred yards down the road to the Memorial Hall where his 'control post and enquiry organization' had been set up. He was pleased with the local response and commented: 'More often than not, we find ourselves working in an area which is more highly populated than this where the goodwill is perhaps not as strong as is evident in Overton. The degree of public co-operation here is very good indeed and we are grateful to everyone for helping our enquiries.'

This was typical of press statements from Joe Mounsey. Like many other high-ranking officers, he knew how to deliver a carefully prepared statement which gets the point over without offending anyone. He had cultivated press contacts for years and knew whom to trust and whom to avoid when quotes were given out. Reporters loved him. He would shower photographs like confetti whenever possible. He would also impart 'off-the-record' information. This would improve a newsman's understanding of the case and ensure that the information would remain unpublished until Mounsey okayed it. It was a crafty example of news management, but one which journalists willingly agreed to. The words actually printed in newspapers seldom sounded like the man whom close friends and associates knew, but he realized that the printed word would always be scrutinized far more closely than any throwaway remark in conversation, and so he took care to choose his words.

Mounsey's authoritative manner and experienced handling of all the immediate tasks set him apart from any other officer. The Murder HQ was soon packed with policemen and women, all with their own specific roles to play. They worked as a team, striving towards one common aim. There was a taxi squad, a house-to-house squad, a background squad and many others. They were all instructed to file reports and statements back to the control room where they would be analyzed by Mounsey, his superintendent and a 'researcher'—a middle-ranking officer with a fresh mind who would monitor everything. The bosses would then underline significant or ambiguous phrases which would need following up or clarifying.

The important thing was to talk to everybody and find anybody who might know something about the victim. The difficulty was this: Harold Parkinson may have been heartily disliked by many people in the community, but this was Overton, not Chicago. Grudges had never ended in even the mildest form of violence before. It seemed likely that robbery had been the motive. Yet it looked as if nothing had been stolen. Certainly none of his splendid coins had gone.

'Trussed Up Body: Mystery Deepens' the headlines said on 27 February. The newspaper report said that police had admitted they were baffled why anybody would want to tie up and kill a 67-year-old pensioner. It also said that the victim was last seen alive at 4 p.m. on Tuesday 24 February.

This is significant because the three acquaintances of Mr Parkinson's mentioned in Chapter Two who had seen him alive the following day were to tell Mounsey's men a different story.

Charles Ramsey, the barman from Queen's Hotel, spotted Mr Parkinson at 1.35 p.m. on the 25th walking along Queen Street in Morecambe on the opposite side of the road. 'His coat was buttoned and he had his hands in his pockets.' They didn't speak but Ramsey was sure he had the day right— Wednesdays were his day off. He was also certain this was Mr Parkinson. 'Although he was about twenty yards away from me I easily recognized him.' Mr Ramsey had served the old man with drinks most lunch-times for the past eight years.

Richard Luke, a bus-driver, had earlier been driving the 8.30 a.m. to Euston Road bus station when he saw Mr Parkinson on two different occasions. The second time, 'he lifted his hand to me in acknowledgment—I have no doubt it was Harold.'

Just as convinced about timing was Jimmy Braid, a retired fisherman: 'I last saw him about 10.30 a.m. on Wednesday the 25th when I went to a small shed situated next to the air-raid shelter where I keep my car, at the rear of Parkinson's house. I got some bolts out of the shed and as I was walking back I saw Parkinson and he asked me if I was going to Morecambe.'

Three different sightings, either morning or early afternoon. But all on the 25th. Lack of hard information meant Mounsey was somewhat coy with his public announcements on the crime. It was Saturday before he declared conclusively that the coin dealer had been strangled. But he refused to go one step further and confirm it was murder. 'All I can say is that the main cause of death was strangulation and that was the direct result of Mr Parkinson's bonds.'

Police also revealed that the old man was understood to have had a telephone call about his coin collection at 9 p.m. on Wednesday. They did not name their source, but it must have been Lancaster telephone exchange operator Mrs Sylvia Kinnaird—whose critical contribution was later to be cast aside. Her observations were eventually deemed irrelevant for the police, but they certainly would have been a boost for me!

However, Mounsey did develop the importance of this telephone call on one more occasion before it was ditched. The *Lancashire Evening Post*, 2 March: 'The Overton death riddle is now centring on Mr X—the man who phoned wealthy coin collector Harold Parkinson and arranged to meet him on the night he died. Mr Mounsey said: "The identity of this man is very important. I feel that he is a key figure in our investigation." '

There was no feedback on this aspect of the enquiry, so it was back to the 'hard slog' of routine interviews, poster distribution and loud-speaker appeals. Detectives in the Memorial Hall were snowed under with paperwork and information, maps and diagrams, all of which needed microscopic attention.

The men on the ground were soon getting a reputation for their thoroughness. Mrs Hockenhull, the cleaner, helped police with many aspects of the victim's character and identified belongings later to be used as exhibits in court. She said: 'There seemed dozens of them coming and going, they never left my doorstep. I told them the last time I had seen him alive on the 24th he had been wearing grey flannels [trousers], a check shirt, an old tweed jacket with a tear near the sleeve, a yellow cravat and a grey pullover. That was different to what he was wearing when he was found dead.'

She was more important to the police than any other single witness in determining where certain of the bonds which were so cruelly wrapped round Mr Parkinson's body came from. She was asked which of the bonds were his and, more importantly, which were not. Her memory and attention to detail were of enormous help to the police, both then and in many years to come. At the centre of the police enquiry was a purple strip of material, used as a gag, round the lower part of Mr Parkinson's face. Mrs Hockenhull was later to make an important pronouncement about this cloth. It is not altogether clear whether she made the same remark in 1970.

An estimated 800 statements were taken over several weeks. In such a community that didn't leave many people out. Because of the New Year's Eve party at the cottage, many villagers had to give fingerprint samples for elimination purposes. This total involvement of the community gave rise to a flood of rumours, innuendoes and scare stories. Overton's last major criminal act, the papers said, was when William the Conqueror wrested the place from the Earl of Tostig. And that was nine hundred years ago. It was not long before this murder began to resemble an Agatha Christie-style 'Whodunnit?'

Not everyone was impressed by the police operation in their midst. Businessman Rex Calverley thought he had a crucial piece of information to impart. But, he claims, they never showed much interest in it. In response to police appeals for information, he told them about a suspicious pair of young men in the village's Ship Hotel pub. On that Wednesday night the strangers had been anxiously awaiting a taxi out of town. 'I kept saying in a village like this in the middle of winter strangers stand out. We were regulars and the pub was always very quiet at that time of the year. But the police just didn't seem to follow up what we had to say.'

Meanwhile, one of Lancashire's own officers had something to offer. PC Alan Knowles had taken a telephone call at 1.22 a.m. on the night in question. An anonymous speaker reported an accident at 17 Main Street, Overton, the house next to Mr Parkinson's. PC Joseph Howarth was unable to find anything on arrival and the call was put down as a mischievous prank. The value of that call was also played down for reasons that again did not become obvious for more than a decade.

All this information was being processed in the Memorial Hall by policemen fast becoming experts in the life of Harold Parkinson. They could tell you how many eggs he had delivered each week with his milk, how many times he had made informal contacts with police with tittle-tattle over neighbours, who he worked for and where he went, night and day. They also knew he was blood group A, as the first results started coming in from Dr Clift, the chief biologist from the forensic science laboratory.

Dr Clift confirmed what Mounsey had suspected from the very beginning—'considerable violence' had been used to break down the pensioner's resistance before he had been trussed up. Several buttons had been found on the carpet and floor throughout the living-room. Some had obviously come from the killer as they did not fit any of the victim's garments.

The pathologist's post-mortem work gave police some lee-way over timing. Dr Brian Beeson put the time of death between 7 a.m. and midnight on 25 February—but it was just possible it could have taken place as early as the evening of the 24th. The strangulating tightness of the white calico bandage had closed veins in Mr Parkinson's neck, preventing proper blood supply to the brain, said his report. The compression had been tragically effective because it had been applied for several minutes. It was considered unlikely that the Overton man had been strangled. Instead the fatal vice-like grip had been an indirect result of pressure put on a lower webbing strap. This perhaps was proof that the mystery intruder might not have intended to murder his victim. Police were left with the opinion that Mr Parkinson may have physically brought about his own death by struggling so much that he tightened the bonds himself.

Although that charge might have stuck, it could also be proved he had been so vicious that he had not cared whether Parkinson lived or died. Parkinson had obviously been punched or kicked in the face while he still had his spectacles on because of bruises caused by the bridge of his glasses. His chest injuries were consistent with him being 'stamped upon'.

Dr Beeson also killed off one rumour going around Overton. Some villagers had heard that Mr Parkinson, bulky as he was, had been powerless in a fist fight and unable to free himself from the ligatures because of the state of his hands. He had no little finger on his left hand and the right little finger was naturally deformed. His 'poor healing flesh' had prevented him from heavy gardening and odd jobs around and outside the house. But Dr Beeson concluded this would not significantly have impaired the function of the hands and remaining fingers.

The officers designated to look into Harold Parkinson's background were told of his boasts about being a private investigator. But they were never able to turn up one single case that he had been involved in, either on contract to any of the private detection agencies or on his own. Detective Constable Ellison, who had known him since 1964, never mentioned it in his statement. Detective Sergeant Harold Bentham, a Lancaster-based crime prevention officer, who had met him occasionally over nine years was more specific, though. 'The deceased was known locally as a private investigator but he was in fact a freelance debt-collector.' Some of his colleagues were to close their eyes to this information.

March 6, 1970. By this time, the newspapers had dispensed with one angle. They no longer mentioned a grey car seen outside the Parkinson home containing two men. Instead it was another telephone call that suddenly assumed elevated importance.

'An anonymous telephone call to police investigating the

Overton death riddle could provide a vital clue,' trumpeted the *Lancashire Evening Post*. 'The caller who rang Morecambe police station late on Wednesday night has given detectives a lead because he appears to have been one of the last people to see Harold Parkinson alive. The man who made the call said he had seen Mr Parkinson getting into a taxi outside the GPO building in Morecambe on Wednesday 25 February at 7.40 p.m.'

'It is very important that any taxi driver who may have picked up a fare corresponding to Mr Parkinson's description should contact us as soon as possible,' said Detective Chief Superintendent Joe Mounsey. 'We are checking with every taxi driver in Lancaster and Morecambe.'

Two interesting points come out of this press release. First, it indicates police were still open-minded on whether Harold Parkinson was alive on the Wednesday. Second, the hunt switches to finding a taxi driver.

At last—a firm lead which Mounsey's boys could get their teeth into! The cabbie could be the prime suspect, or at least one of the last people to see Mr Parkinson alive. The order echoed around the Memorial Hall as detectives attended the daily conference: *Find that driver*.

It wasn't long before two threads of the enquiry fused inextricably together. For the first time more than one fragment of circumstantial evidence fitted into place with another. And there was a name which Joe Mounsey could target: Keith Noel Fellowes.

The first tenuous link to put me under suspicion was that I drove a cab for 'Charlie and Kim's' taxi firm in Euston Road, Morecambe. A big handy-looking lad who never made the grade in the police force, they said. Marriage on the rocks, maybe a bit of a playboy with his looks and tall physique. But there was a flash of huge excitement at the Memorial Hall when they found another name in Parkinson's receipt book —Mrs Castagnini. Thorough detective work had revealed Mrs Castagnini was my mother-in-law. What if she had hired old Parky as a private eye to get grounds for a divorce, one officer wondered. This could not only be a motive, but a crucial breakthrough in the investigation.

Mounsey promptly decided to have me interviewed, while other officers were told to make subtle enquiries about my background and alibis. I didn't know it then, but these enquiries would eventually throw a 22-year-old carefree individual into Britain's waste disposal system. Only three days after the police press release, on 9 March 1970, I was in Lancaster Police Station, charged with the murder of Harold Parkinson.

4

The Nightmare Begins

I had been charged with a murder I knew nothing about. I was stunned. I stood in silence as Mounsey ordered the officers to return me to my cell. My legs were like jelly and my stomach seemed to disappear. All I could think of was that *they had actually charged me with murder*. Before I was charged, the teams of detectives had tried to win my confidence to obtain admission of guilt. Now, the whole atmosphere had changed. There was hostility towards me—verbal and mental. They marched me through the long narrow corridors, down the stairs and slammed me up in the cell again.

As they left, one policeman looked back and said, 'You might as well get used to it. When we are through with you, cock, it will be life imprisonment.'

In that one line I had been tried, convicted and sentenced. I was speechless with shock. I lay on the bed and looked about me—the cell was a mass of concrete and steel with a feeling of death about it. My whole body seemed to be in a state of paralysis. The shock to my whole system was so intense that I was telling my limbs to move but they wouldn't. My breathing became erratic and then I must have passed out. I came to some while later to realize, with surprise, that I was still alive.

A little later the station sergeant came down with a tray full of dinner, opened the cell door, placed the food on the floor and locked the door again without so much as a word. There you have it—the dog had been fed. The last thing I wanted to do was eat. They could stuff their food. Anger started to well up inside me. I felt like screaming or at least smashing hell out of the cell. I considered it, then decided that was one of the very things they would like me to do, just to show them I was violent. It was a real fight within myself to keep those desires locked in. My whole being seemed to be screaming for revenge at what I had endured in the past twenty-four hours. The level of anger that I had reached within surprised me. This was so different from my usual state. I'd been angry many times before, but never at that level. Finally I beat the anger into submission and decided to get my head down. Tomorrow had to be a brighter day.

I awoke to the sound of a squeaking door being opened. A young policeman stood outside and then spoke, 'Breakfast, Fellowes. Time to get up. You have a busy day ahead of you.'

I wasn't interested in food. I had no desire to eat. I drank the mug of tea and prepared myself for the day ahead—a day over which I had no control. Around nine o'clock, after I had washed under police supervision, they led me to an interview room where I was introduced to a Mr McHugh, who was to be my solicitor. We sat down and the police officers left, locking the door behind them.

Mr McHugh looked at me rather nervously and then smiled, saying, 'Now, don't you worry. I am sure we will be able to sort this out.'

The smile was both genuine and reassuring. At long last I had someone to talk to, even if it was someone I had never met before. Mr McHugh was a small, round-faced man, in his late fifties or early sixties, with striking grey hair and a soft, warm, inviting voice. He was well dressed—a 'gentle-man'. He explained that the police had contacted him to act in my defence and said that he would be pleased to do so if I was in agreement. If not, then I could appoint a solicitor of my choice to defend me.

At this point I agreed he could represent me. Besides, I didn't know any other solicitors. Indeed, I'd never had any dealings with them before so he was as good as anybody else. In retrospect, the whole sequence of events leading up to this moment had been quite bizarre. Since my arrest I hadn't had any opportunity to contact anyone myself. It had all been done by other people. Here I was again, confronted with someone the system had chosen for me. The most disturbing point was that I didn't know the man's track record or his pedigree as a solicitor. All I had to go on were first impressions. But, if nothing else, at least he was human. I could sense his nervousness as he gazed at me, trying to assess my reaction to the serious crime I had been charged with. There was a long, pregnant silence, then I fired a barrage of questions at him.

'What have the police told you? Has any of my family contacted you? Have you any idea what they are trying to do to me in here?' And so on.

He remained calm and systematically answered the questions, never varying the level or tone of his voice. The answer to most of the questions was 'No', which did my morale no good whatsoever. Eventually Mr McHugh, looking somewhat pensive, informed me that I was to appear before the magistrates at South Lonsdale Magistrates' Court later that day and told me the police were probably going to ask for a remand in police custody.

'What about application for bail?' I asked.

He replied that he doubted that would be granted in view of the seriousness of the charge. Of course he was right. That was difficult for me to understand, as all I could think of was my innocence. People didn't seem to be interested in that.

By this time my nerves were on edge and I reached for another cigarette that Mr McHugh had kindly brought with him. I was now turning into a chain-smoker. What on earth was happening? My thinking was incoherent, my body was out of control and I was puffing continuously on cigarettes. The press release probably said a man was helping police with their enquiries. The truth of the situation was that I was being mentally and emotionally tortured.

I told Mr McHugh, 'It all seems like a nightmare that won't leave me.'

He said he could appreciate how I was feeling and in fact I was standing up to it very well.

I remember thinking, 'You want to try being inside me for a while, then you would really understand.'

Mr McHugh then asked me to tell him all that had happened since the time of my arrest. I was able to give him a comprehensive account. Afterwards, he asked if I had ever met the deceased or if I had any involvement in the crime whatsoever. I told him of the statement I had made to the police on 5 March 1970, and of the interview with them when they implied Parkinson had been hired to follow me. As for the crime itself, I told him that I had no involvement whatsoever, so they couldn't possibly have any evidence to substantiate the charge.

In reply Mr McHugh said, 'Mr Fellowes, the police couldn't have charged you if they had no evidence. Are you sure you have told me everything?'

'Of course I'm sure,' I retorted. 'Whose side are you on? I can't tell you anything more than I have already told you. This might come as a great surprise, but I am innocent.'

At that point I don't think he was convinced. His face reflected signs of puzzlement. But we talked over other issues and he said he would put the wheels of defence into motion. I signed the necessary forms for legal aid and he left to start work on the case and to contact the people I had asked him to. The interview over, I was taken back to my cell.

Lunch was served and for the first time in ages, or so it seemed, I felt hungry and I eagerly tucked in. What the hell? There was no point in starving to death. My body was in a bad enough state as it was.

In the early hours of the afternoon, three detectives came down to the cell block and informed me I was going to the magistrates' court.

'What about my clothes?' I asked. 'All I have are the rags that you have given me.'

The police had taken all my clothing after I had been charged and had given me a shirt and a pair of trousers which were both dirty and ill-fitting.

'Your clothing has been sent to the forensic laboratories,' they said.

'Well, can't you get my other clothing from my flat?'

'We have already collected that and sent it with the rest to forensic,' they told me.

'I refuse to go to court looking like this. Besides, I haven't even got any socks or shoes.'

With that they grabbed my arms and a struggle took place. They never hit me, just overpowered me onto the floor and handcuffed me. There's not a lot you can do in the circumstances, when three fifteen-stone men decide to take you. I could not believe they would take me to court dressed like that. It was degradation in its worst form. They dragged me outside and put me in the police van and we sped off in the direction of Lancaster Castle.

My heart was thumping again and I began to shake uncontrollably. The vehicle came to a halt and the back doors opened, revealing a glimmer of winter sunshine. It was a cold day and the clouds looked down in angry array. We had arrived at the court round the side entrance. One of the detectives offered me a blanket to cover my head in case photographers tried to snatch a photograph. I refused, saying that I had nothing to hide or to be ashamed of. I told them that they were the ones who had blankets over their heads— blinding them to the truth. Perhaps they would be better removing theirs. As expected they looked totally bewildered at what I had said.

What a spectacle I must have looked—no socks or shoes, a pair of dirty trousers with a forty-inch waist (mine was thirty-two) and a shirt that would have better suited a coalman. They frogmarched me up the steps to the court and into the dock. The court was quite empty, then I realized of course that they had arranged a special court sitting to fit me in.

The magistrates entered, sat down, and the police prosecutor presented his case, asking for a remand in police custody. Mr McHugh stood up and offered no objection to the request and sat down again. I couldn't believe it. There I was, standing before their worships in unkempt clothes, with nothing on my feet and nobody took any notice. *I* was only the person being talked about. This was 1970. Surely magistrates could rebuke the police for bringing a prisoner

48

before them in this manner? What about the Geneva convention on human rights? What about judges' rules? Anger was starting to erupt again deep in the pit of my stomach. I protested at the humiliation of being brought before the court in this fashion. It was a complete waste of time. They merely approved the custody order and I was whisked out promptly. The whole proceedings had taken less than three minutes.

It was deeply disturbing to witness first-hand the power and authority the judiciary have over a person who at the very best has only been charged. The old law, 'innocent until proven guilty', is a flag of convenience the judiciary sails under. At police college *we* had been taught and trained how to treat prisoners—their rights and our role in those rights. We were guardians of the law and employed to uphold it. The crazy thing is, I actually believed it and tried to uphold it in my short encounter with the criminal element.

Perhaps my case was an isolated incident and they had decided to make it hard for me because I hadn't co-operated in their mind-games of chess. They had thought the nut would crack and it didn't. Was this a new form of psychology to degrade me, humiliate me and bring me to a state of total mental collapse so I would confess to the crime? Down the steps they dragged me, as I had refused to walk in bare feet in the wintry conditions. I was put in the van and off we went back to the police station. Nobody said a word to me. I sat there in total outrage when I considered what I had just been put through. It had seemed totally unreal in the court. Everyone had seemed embarrassed at my outburst, yet none contemplated my position. The first doubts about my position started to form. If this was what happened before the magistrates, what would happen at the full trial? Still, I would have plenty of opportunity to sort that out when I saw my solicitor again.

We returned to the police station and I was returned to my cell. In the late afternoon a senior police officer came and told me he was very sorry for the way I had been taken to court and as soon as he could he would find me proper clothing. So someone must have said something, but it was too late. Soon after that I was taken upstairs to a room by two police officers and introduced to another police surgeon. Again, he explained that he wasn't a member of the police force, merely a doctor who was called on from time to time to perform his duties. The police would like certain samples to send away for forensic tests. He went on to explain that I didn't *have* to give the samples, but that they could apply to the court to gain a court order for them.

I thought for a minute and decided, 'I have nothing to hide. They can have whatever they want.'

It was a difficult position. If I didn't give the samples it would show non-cooperation and that I had something to hide, but at the same time I knew they wouldn't gain anything. He began by taking a sample of blood, then a snip of my hair, nail scrapings from under the nails on both hands and finally a scraping of my skin. These were packaged and labelled accordingly. The doctor then asked me to undress so he could check for any cuts or bruising. I said there was no need as the police had not beaten or injured me physically. They had done a far better job mentally.

'It's not for that reason,' he said. 'It's to check if you have any injuries that might show you have been in a fight in recent times.'

Of course I hadn't any bruises as I hadn't been in a fight for a number of years. Having finished, the doctor thanked me for my co-operation in a professional and clinical manner and departed. I went back to the cell, thoughtfully pondering the doctor and the samples. Then it dawned on me that there had been something missing in my recent encounter with the doctor. At the time I couldn't put my finger on it. Then I realized. He had been meticulous in his manner and examination, but at no time had he asked me if I was feeling OK or if there was anything he could do for me. After all, I had been charged with murder, been interrogated for some twelve hours or so, been dragged to court in the middle of winter unshod and he hadn't even offered me so much as an aspirin for a headache or a pill to give me a better sleep. The whole world was turning its back on me, or so it seemed.

Was I over-sensitive or was I now in the early stages of paranoia? The only consolation was the fact it was really happening. It was no delusion of the mind or fiendish nightmare. I was indeed imprisoned in every sense of the word, both body and mind. Now I began to be more rational, with a strong instinct to survive. It was time to take full stock of my situation and plan a new initiative and counter-attack. I knew for certain there could be no real primary evidence—documentary evidence or forensic evidence—as I was innocent. The only evidence they could have was circumstantial—the name in the notebook, flippant remarks I had made to friends. That's all they could possibly have.

I began to feel better. Even the samples taken this afternoon would help to strengthen my case of wrongful arrest. Then I contemplated the worst. What if they already knew they had made a gross mistake and to save themselves had decided to stitch me up? Surely not, they couldn't possibly get away with it. I lay back on my bed, my mind racing from one thought to another, not reaching any single conclusion, just trying to understand how it all happened and how I had managed to get in this position. The only thread of reality was the undeniable fact that I knew I was innocent. That in itself was my strength, my purpose for fighting on. Whatever they planned to do with me, no one could ever rob me of that. My biggest problem was the fact I was locked up and couldn't speak to anyone outside who could prove my innocence. I was on the inside looking out; no one was on the outside looking in.

The cell was beginning to have a sense of familiarity about it, as though I had lived there for some considerable time. Yet it had barely been three days—the worst three days of my life. It seemed I had been locked away for months.

I tried to rest for a while, only to be awoken by a policeman who said there were some visitors to see me. I raised myself from the bed and looked through the steel bars to see my father and mother entering the cell block. I decided to be brave and hold myself together. That would make it easier for them. But when I saw them I just broke into an uncontrollable bout of crying, and I cried like a child. It was a total release of all the hurt and anguish I had stored up over the past three days.

I managed, after some time, to pull myself together and looked my mother and father in the face. They too had tears in their eyes and I could see the inner struggle of trying to hold the emotions back. They both looked ashen and tired. At first we looked at each other, expressing the hurt through our eyes. My mother stretched forward a comforting hand on to mine. At last contact had been made with my family. The police were present but that didn't matter. This was a precious moment to me. It wouldn't have mattered if the whole world looked on.

'They've charged me with murder and I am totally innocent,' I said.

'We know, son,' my father replied. 'We're here now. Don't worry, son, I will take care of things.'

My mother echoed my father's assurance. It was just good to see them. They had travelled all the way from Bracknell in Berkshire as soon as they had learned of my arrest. The first they knew of it was a telephone call, but no details were given. I could still see the shock-waves in both their faces and voices. It was a strange feeling, talking to people you loved through steel bars with policemen listening to your every word. There was obviously much they wanted to ask but didn't considering the company we were in. There were silences when we just looked at each other, then an attempt to strike up conversation about other matters. That failed absolutely and I asked my father to contact my solicitor, who would be able to tell him what the present situation was.

Shortly after that, the policeman told them their time was up and they left. My mother kept looking back as she walked away, tears flowing down her cheeks, and my father wrapped his comforting arm around her shoulder. It was distressing to see them leave as the precious opportunity to talk had gone. There seemed to be so much I hadn't said to them. I slumped on my bed trying to understand how they must be feeling, having just seen me locked up. My suffering and torment had now extended to my family. I felt utterly dejected when I thought about the day. Everything seemed to be going against me. There seemed to be no light in the torture chamber of my mind. Indeed, the visit had exhausted me. My emotional defences had been opened and now I felt totally drained. I momentarily considered what was happening in the world out there. Everyone was probably moaning about the weather or arguing over which TV programme to watch and here I was in this lock-up.

Although I felt drained, my mind refused to rest and I spent a very long time fighting to get to sleep; having no watch or clock in the cell one lost the sense of time. At some point I must have dropped off to sleep as again I was awakened by the sound of the cell door being opened as the duty policeman served breakfast. I was hungry and I eagerly devoured a good helping of eggs, bacon, beans and toast, finished off with a large mug of tea. That over in about five minutes, it was time for the daily ritual of the supervised washing and shaving procedure.

At about mid-morning Mr McHugh came to see me again and I challenged him at not making any comment about appearing before the magistrates without socks, shoes or any of my own clothing. He seemed a little embarrassed and disturbed about the incident, then said he hadn't noticed my demeanour until I mentioned it. By that time it had been too late as the police were hurriedly taking me out of the court. He assured me that he had made representations to the senior police officer at the station and was sure I would have proper clothing for my next appearance. We then got down to the more serious matter of my case.

All the legal aid forms had been sent off and already he was active in trying to check out my movements from Tuesday 24 February 1970, late afternoon, until Thursday morning 26 February 1970. Mr Parkinson had last been seen alive on the Tuesday afternoon and was found dead in his home on Thursday morning. I had difficulty in remembering all that I had done on those dates, but I knew the taxi records would show my movements, and Lynn would be able to fill in the gaps. Mr McHugh informed me that he had employed a firm of private investigators to help him trace and substantiate my movements to build up an alibi and prove my innocence. At last things were moving in the right direction. At least there were people out there asking questions and actively working on my behalf. Then he dropped a bombshell.

The police had informed him that two men who worked at the Beach Club in Heysham, a Mr Thornton and a Mr Bamborough, had made statements to the police that I had told them that Mr Parkinson had been following me and I had beaten him up in Morecambe around the time of the death. I just sat there dumbfounded.

'Did you beat him up, Noel?' Mr McHugh asked.

'Never ever met Mr Parkinson in my life,' I said.

'Why would these men have made these statements?' he asked.

I thought for a while, trying to get over the initial shock, and then replied, 'I think the police must be having you on, Mr McHugh, because they're nothing but lies. I made a few jokes about being interviewed by the police, but never anything like that.'

He assured me that the police were serious about the statements—they were one of the main reasons for my arrest in the first place. I confirmed my earlier statement that I had never said such things.

'What else have the police given you?' I enquired.

'That's about all of it—except for the fact that your mother-in-law's name was found in Mr Parkinson's diary. They must come up with something more substantial to hold you on this charge at the moment. It seems to me they haven't got a case,' he said.

'They cannot possibly come up with anything, Mr McHugh. I didn't do it and I have no idea who did.'

'Well, we shall continue to establish your defence as quickly as we possibly can and try to get you out of here.'

With that Mr McHugh departed.

Back in my cell I thought about what Mr McHugh had just told me. What was behind the statements of Carey Thornton and John Bamborough? I knew them. In fact, I had often taken them to work at the Beach Club and sometimes home again in the early hours of the morning. I couldn't remember ever having done anything against them. Why were they trying to implicate me in the murder—if indeed they were? It just didn't seem to make any sort of sense.

Memory recall revealed a possible answer. Carey Thornton was the manager of the club and on several occasions after dropping him off I used to pop in the club for a quick drink. On a number of occasions I had seen plain clothes detectives drinking there and they knew I had left the force. Perhaps they had questioned Thornton and Bamborough about me and asked them to help with a couple of statements. The whole subject didn't make any sense at all. Either the police must have had some hold over them or Thornton and Bamborough were trying to make a name for themselves. Either way I was the victim. Still, looking on the brighter side of things, I would soon be out—then I could find out for myself what had really happened.

By this time the police had stopped questioning me because since seeing my solicitor I had decided to keep quiet. A couple of detectives came down on a number of occasions and tried to engage me in friendly conversation, but I was having none of it. I completely ignored them.

My parents returned to visit me and we chatted quite openly about things. The good news was that they brought me some clean clothing. My father confirmed he had spoken to Mr McHugh and they were going to keep in close contact about the case. I found that quite reassuring. At least I could count on that. Both my mother and father looked better since their last visit, which was another encouragement to me. It must have been heartbreaking for them driving back home two hundred and fifty miles away, knowing their son had been charged with murder. What an agonizing journey, trying to think of a way to tell my younger brothers and sister. My elder sisters, Brenda and Carol, were married and had families. It would be perhaps easier breaking the news to them.

Two more days crept slowly by without any visits or communication from anyone. Then I was taken back to the magistrates' court. This time I felt more human as I was wearing proper clothing and socks and shoes.

The court went through its usual formalities. Then the magistrates informed me I was to be remanded to Risley Remand Centre. Shock enveloped me and the familiar feeling of fear started to rise inside me again. Why were they sending me to Risley? Hadn't I been through enough? Or were they set on destroying me?

5

On Remand

The very thought of Risley Remand Centre sent a chilling shiver down my spine. Not so long ago I had been escorting prisoners to Risley as a matter of course. The thought of ever being there myself had never entered my head.

We left the court and drove back to the police station. Within minutes Mr McHugh arrived and I was ushered into the interview room. He tried to reassure me that his enquiries were progressing well and I wouldn't be in Risley long.

At that point I felt sickened as I began to imagine what life was going to be like there. After all, I was an ex-policeman. Utterly dejected, I told Mr McHugh to hurry his enquiries and get me out as soon as possible. He left me shortly afterwards to await the dreaded journey to Risley.

Alone in my cell I considered my position again. I came to the conclusion that things were going from very bad to worse. It was difficult even trying to think straight. I seemed to drift into a very low depressive state. I had no reserves, no mental strength left to pull myself out of it. From sheer frustration and distress tears slowly ran down my cheeks, tears of immense fear. There was no one to talk to and nobody who could reach me. The system had me totally incarcerated—body, soul and mind. The police had controlled everything from the very beginning—when I washed, ate, slept, who I saw, the length of the visit and so on. At no time had I ever been asked if I wanted to make a decision. Everything I had requested had been rejected outright.

The policemen came to escort me to Risley and within a short space of time I said goodbye to my cell and we were on our way. The journey in the back of the Ford Transit van was uncomfortable as it was a cold day and, being handcuffed, it was difficult to keep my circulation going. Besides, the handcuffs were so tight it was painful trying to move my hands. I complained to one of the policemen, but he just shrugged his shoulders and said I shouldn't have such fat wrists. After that, I was totally ignored. The two policemen talked about their respective families, cars and other meaningless subjects. At no time did they ever consider including me in their small talk.

It was a long tiresome journey. Risley was some seventy miles from Lancaster. But at least I was breathing fresh air again. It was obvious the two men were rather disgusted at the thought of escorting one of their former colleagues to prison. In their eyes I was not merely charged but undeniably guilty. Was this the judgment I had to face in every contact I made, or was it solely reserved for the police? The van drew to a halt and I heard the unmistakable sound of large gates being opened. My heart began to thump louder and louder. We had arrived.

We drove on a little further and the van stopped. The engine died to the sound of the van doors being opened. I was escorted to the reception area where the policeman handed over a piece of paper to the prison officer, saying, 'One ex-copper for you to sign for and look after.'

With that everything seemed to stop. I was aware of eyes coldly staring at me. I noticed there were a number of prisoners cleaning up. With their gaze firmly fixed on me at that point, the prison officer signed the receipt for my body and now I was under their care. It is amazing to think that one day you are a person living in a democracy with free speech, freedom of movement and all the benefits that system offers, yet at any given moment you can lose the lot on the premise that you have committed a serious crime or *may* have committed a serious crime. While the charge remains yet unproven in any court, you can lose everything you hold dear to life.

The handcuffs were taken off, allowing blood to flow through my hands again, and revealing bruising to both my wrists. I remained silent. Then the prison officer ordered one of his staff to lock me up until I could be processed. With that I was taken to a long line of cubicles, shown the inside, and locked up. It was similar to a cubicle provided at a swimming pool to change in—about five feet deep by three feet wide, the ceiling was approximately seven feet from the ground. There was a plain wooden bench seat across the back of the cubicle and a small light-fitting on the ceiling.

This 'sweat-box' was enough to give anyone claustrophobia. It was very warm and I noticed a number of holes had been drilled in the door for ventilation. I could imagine people going to the door, wrapping their lips over the holes and drawing in great gulps of air. I sat on the bench rubbing my wrists, trying to get the circulation going again. My fingers looked quite white and bloodless.

'Hey, Fellowes,' a voice whispered through the holes in the door.

'Yes,' I said.

'We're going to have you, boy, when you come out. When the screws aren't looking, we'll have you.'

That was it and the person left. Why did they want me? I hadn't done them any harm. Then it struck me. They knew I was an ex-copper. I was filled with a new fear. While the police had treated me badly, the people in here were free agents. They didn't have any rules or regulations to restrain them. Perhaps they were just trying to frighten me. Surely the prison officers would protect me from any hint of physical abuse?

I had been cooped up in the cubicle for two hours or so, when a prison officer came and took me to a room where I was introduced to a senior prison officer sitting behind a desk. He started to ask me questions and fill in a form. After I had answered his questions he told me the procedure for remanded prisoners. It all went in one ear and straight out of the other. There was no way my brain could take in such information—it was still totally locked on red alert. The questions over, he instructed me to strip off as they were going to supply me with new clothing while I was remanded in their custody.

I stripped off down to my underpants but he told me to take those off, which I did. It was a degrading experience as all the prison officers looked on. There I was, standing before them, stripped of my pride, my dignity and my name. As I stood there in my nakedness he informed me that from that moment on I was 811168 Fellowes. My forenames were redundant. It was cold and calculated in its delivery. Now I was a number, not a name. What more could the system do to me? This was a total humiliation. My nakedness revealed a greater insecurity as I was exposed to the sniggers of my audience. One prison officer eventually threw me a towel to cover myself and informed me in a stern, crisp voice that I was to have a bath before my medical examination. With that they led me to the bath parlour and told me I had five minutes to bathe and get dry again. A trustee prisoner handed me a small tablet of white soap with the inscription *HM Government Property* engraved on it and led me to a vacant bath cubicle. The water had already been run into the bath and I was about to get in.

Without any warning I felt a heavy blow, first to my head and then my body. As I keeled over with the pain I felt more and more blows descending upon me. As the blows raged on my hands and arms instantly covered my head. In the midst of all this violence I managed to scream out for help. Immediately the blows ceased and I was left in a crumpled state on the floor. Excruciating pain engulfed my head and the upper part of my body. At the same time I trembled with shock and a deep feeling of nausea crept through me. It was then that I realized that I had been beaten up.

'What happened, Fellowes?' an unfamiliar voice demanded. I glanced upwards, looking through the barrier of my protective arms, to see a prison officer standing over me.

'Come on, lad. Tell me what happened. Did you slip off the bath or something?'

Still dazed, I drew myself upwards and looked at him in utter disbelief. Surely it was obvious to anyone what had happened? He pulled me up towards him as I clung to his trousers, trying to help myself up. There was no strength in my arms at all. It was useless. Within seconds other prison officers were at hand lifting me bodily to my feet. They sat me on the edge of the bath and asked me again what had happened.

'I don't know,' I replied, which was true. I had no idea who had beaten me up.

'You'd better get in the bath then, lad. The doctor is waiting to examine you. I will leave one of my officers with you until you're ready.'

I slumped into the tepid bathwater, still half-dazed and aching from the assault. There was no time to consider my dilemma. The shock of it was still occupying my head and body. I automatically scanned my body for signs of cuts or blood and thankfully found no traces. My head and face seemed all clear, too. Whoever had done me was quite an expert at hitting in the right places. The prison officer looked on as I washed but that only seemed to add to my security. Only a few minutes ago I had despised them for the humili-ation they put me through and now they represented protec-tion. It was a sharp contrast within such a short time. It was remarkable how quickly my body seemed to recover from the onslaught. It was as if to prepare me and encourage me to face the stark reality of my new environment.

After bathing and drying myself off, the officer led me out of the bath parlour and I noticed the two trustees busily mopping the floor, at the same time looking at me with expressions of joy and pleasure. They had been my assailants —it was clearly written on their faces. We arrived back in the reception office only to be ushered into another room where I was confronted by a doctor. He examined me and scribbled notes down periodically. At the end of the examination he asked the officer how I came by the bruises on my head and body. He replied that these had been an accident in the bath area, saying that when he arrived he had found me on the floor. The doctor asked the same question of me.

'I was attacked,' I said.

'Sir,' the officer shouted. 'You call everyone in this establishment Sir.'

The doctor gave the officer a long hard look and said, 'There are too many accidents in the baths for my liking. It's about time someone supervised that area.'

The prison officer looked slightly bemused but remained silent. He turned his attention to me and said that due to the seriousness of the charge I was remanded on I would be allocated to the hospital wing for observation, medical reports and, not least, my protection. The last phrase echoed in my ears—protection, what a wonderful word! Next I was taken to the clothing stores where I was to be fitted out for my stay in Risley, or so I thought. Two inmates (prisoners) were behind the service hatch. They looked me up and down, then produced a pair of trousers, jacket, shirt, socks, shoes, pyjamas, underclothes and a toothbrush. The uniform was brown and the shirt was a heavy cotton blue and white striped one with a great deal of starch added.

'Try them on, mate,' the inmate said.

Everything was too big and the shoes were obviously secondhand.

'None of it fits,' I said.

'Looks all right to me. It isn't Burtons you know,' the inmate said.

'Come on, Fellowes. Let's get you to the hospital wing,' said the officer. After recent events my position seemed very vulnerable, so I decided not to argue the point over the clothing. I kept my mouth tightly shut. We arrived at the hospital wing, where I was allocated a single cell and locked up.

It resembled the police cell I had so recently left, although there were some differences. The cell was a little larger and there was a large window to the rear, giving a panoramic view of what I was later to know as the exercise yard. The yard was heavily overlooked with several storeys of cell blocks on all sides. My furnishings included a bed, chair, small table, wash bowl, water jug, small plastic jerry and a booklet on prison rules. Needless to say, the window was one mass of bars. It certainly didn't give the impression or feeling that it was a hospital. Still, at least the door was locked and could only be opened by a member of staff. Bearing in mind recent events, that was a comfort.

The clothing allocated to me was both dirty and ill-fitting, with the exception of the underclothes. They at least were clean. I looked a sorry sight. The shoes were so tight that they crippled my toes and carried the odour of the previous owner. I hoped that when I had settled in there would be an opportunity to make representations to the powers-that-be about my treatment thus far in their custodial care. In the space of a few hours I had been degraded, humiliated, beaten up and put in isolation for my own protection. It seemed ludicrous. Surely everything they were going to protect me from had already taken place. I lay on the bed, still hurting from the beating I had endured. My head was sore and aching; my ears still rang from the heavy blows they had taken. Was there to be no escape from the avalanche of abuse that had continually rained on me since my arrest? Indeed, would I ever see life again outside of four walls of a cell? Imagine your worst nightmare. It was actually taking place hour by hour, day by day. There was a jingling of keys, then the cell door opened. In walked a prison officer, accompanied by an inmate carrying a metal tray.

'There's your dinner, Fellowes. Eat it up, lad,' he said. The door closed again and I looked upon the steaming dinner before me. At best it looked repulsive, besides which my stomach showed no signs of desire for food. I took one sip of the tea and instantly spat it out. Someone had laced it with salt. Again I found myself the victim of their petty games.

It had been a long, gruelling and painful day. In utter despair and total mental and physical fatigue, I crawled into bed. It was incomprehensible the amount of hostility, physical abuse and mental anguish I had been subjected to in one day. At that point my mind switched off and I drifted into the protection of sleep. Whatever I dreamt that night would surely be more advantageous than the reality of my conscious hours.

The next morning I was wakened by the cell door being

opened and a prison officer instructing me to slop out. I didn't even know what he was talking about, so I asked him.

'Empty the contents of your jerry,' he said.

Not having drunk anything, mine was still empty, so he promptly shut the door again. The injuries I had received to my head and body were now apparent. My head, chest and upper back were bruised and painful to the touch, the pain restricting movement. Again the door opened and an officer instructed me to go for my breakfast, so I walked down the corridor following other inmates heading in the same direction. There was a queue outside a servery where other inmates were dishing out breakfast under the supervision of prison officers. My turn came and I picked up the metal tray with compartments for food. I was served with porridge, bread, a small block of margarine and a mixture of corned beef with potato. Then I was allocated a plastic knife, fork and spoon, together with a plastic mug into which I poured tea from an urn.

Returning to my cell I was aware of whispering as the inmates talked about who I was and what my previous employment had been. I quickened my steps back to my cell where I could hide behind a locked door. I breathed a sigh of relief as I returned unharmed to the safety of the cell. The food was appalling. My stomach heaved after each mouthful. I forced the food in, trying to convince myself I had to get used to it. The porridge had salt in it—there was no way I could eat it. As for the meat and potato, I put it between two pieces of bread and ate it. If I was to survive I had to eat. At least the tea hadn't been laced this time—if you could call it tea.

After breakfast I lay on the bed considering the day ahead, only to hear the door being opened again and the familiar sight of a prison officer standing beside it. He angrily informed me that beds were for sleeping on at night, not in the daytime. I wasn't allowed to lie on my bed between the hours of early morning call and lights out. If I was caught doing so in the future I would be put on governor's report. I explained that this was my first day in Risley and nobody had told me the dos and don'ts. It was all in the prisoner's rule book, he said, so I had better read it and digest it. With that he promptly gave me a razor, brush and shaving stick with the direct instructions to shave. 'What sort of a place is this?' I thought to myself. There certainly wasn't any understanding or consideration of my ignorance of rules and regulations. I was horrified at the prospect of spending any length of time in their custody. Surely I had some rights?

I had my first ever shave without hot water. It was a cutting experience in the true sense of the word, as only men who have actually shaved with cold water can understand. The hallmarks of a cold shave were there to be seen—small lacerations to the face. Coupled with the other injuries, I looked a sorry sight. They returned for the razor shortly afterwards and I made the bed and sat on the chair. Unsure of what else I should do, I decided to read the prison rules.

The rules were set out in typical civil service language—precise and offputting to the reader. Nowhere did I find the rule about lying on the bed. Obviously the prison staff had also made up their own local rules. The key to survival was to learn and act fast, otherwise the system would destroy me in whatever way it could. I considered for a moment what the prisoners I had brought to this institution had gone through in their terms of incarceration. I had never ever considered their plight—just handed them over and left, having completed my role in the procedure of the judiciary. Here I was gaining first-hand knowledge of the other side of the fence.

A small flap opened on the top of the door and an inmate peered in.

'Hey, Fellowes, come over here,' he said. I nervously approached the door and he said, 'Don't be scared. I just want to help you.'

I stood a couple of feet from the door and he asked me if I had any snout.

'What?' I said.

'Cigarettes, tobacco. You know,' he said.

'Oh, yes,' and I produced my cigarettes for him.

He took a couple out and said, 'If you want to live, mate, you better learn about this place.' He went on to inform me of the rules of the prison jargon. Officers were screws, inmates were cons, people who had done several sentences in prison were old lags and so forth. It was an education just listening to him. He was on his eighth sentence inside and had another five months to serve on this sentence. It was my first contact with a con who seemed human towards me. Trying to win his confidence I offered him the rest of the packet of cigarettes, but he refused saying that wasn't the reason he was talking to me. He wanted me to understand the system and the screws so I could protect myself, as he and all the other cons knew I was an ex-bobby.

'Don't let them know you're frightened,' he said, 'or they will make your life hell in here. And don't speak to the screws or the cons will think you're one of them.' He made a lot of sense. I heard the sound of footsteps in the corridor. He said he would have to go, picked up his mop and bucket, closed the hatch and carried on cleaning the floor. I felt a small flicker of excitement at the prospect of having someone to show me the ropes. Now at least I knew some of the jargon so I could speak as they spoke. At that point I determined that in future I would ignore the screws, even if they tried to converse with me. It was obvious that to gain the cons' confidence I would have to prove to them I was in fact one of them—or so I thought.

At about mid-morning I noticed what seemed to be hundreds of cons in the exercise yard, four or five abreast, walking in a clockwise direction round the concrete path laid in a circle. My door was opened and a screw asked if I wanted to go out for exercise. The sheer number of cons outside convinced me that if I joined them perhaps I would be much the worse for wear on my return. Without further consideration I declined the offer. I could hear the sound of feet trudging round the exercise yard and voices in heavy conversation eagerly exchanging views. Within a short space of time the noise diminished and the cons vanished back to their respective living quarters. I sat on the chair reflecting on my own circumstances. It seemed to me that I had been locked up for a long time and no one outside seemed to appreciate what I was going through. If they had, I was sure they would be all the more active in securing my release.

The day drifted slowly by. Lunch was followed by another opportunity to take exercise in the afternoon, which I again declined. Dinner followed in late afternoon and resulted in a severe attack of indigestion. My system hadn't come to terms with prison cuisine. In the early part of the evening, I was visited by the medical officer who briefly asked about my health and welfare. He informed me that at some stage he would be examining me in more detail but that in the meantime I would be under observation. Then he left to continue his rounds.

Night fell and at 'lights out', at about nine o'clock, I lay thoughtfully in bed. It had been a long, boring, tiresome day with nothing to do but try to kill time. Day after day the same monotonous routine continued as I remained locked up in my cell, still refusing to take the option of exercise both morning and afternoon. The only respite from the monotony was the con who shared more of his jargon and prison life with me.

At least I was beginning to learn how to live in the confines of prison walls. The food was still lousy and for the first time in my life I experienced the peril of trying to use a plastic chamber pot some six inches off the ground. It was degrading and difficult to function properly. To add to the insult the toilet tissue, which was both coarse and somewhat sharp, had *HM Government Property* painted on every leaf. I doubted that anyone in prison had ever contemplated stealing such an item.

The following week I was taken back to reception, given my own clothing and then banged up in the sweat-box until the police escort arrived to take me back to Lancaster Magistrates' Court for a further hearing. They arrived, handcuffed me and off we sped to Lancaster. Again there was no conversation —just the now-familiar pattern of their small talk and my silence. The small comfort was that the handcuffs were at least tolerable this time. Within one minute of arriving at the magistrates' court I was back in the police van, having been remanded for a further week. All the expense of the seventy-mile journey for a one-minute hearing! We stopped off at Lancaster Police Station, firstly to change escort for the return journey and secondly, to see my solicitor.

Mr McHugh arrived looking quite cheerful and I asked him how the defence was progressing. He informed me that they had nothing new. Everyone they tried to interview had already been interviewed by the police. It seemed the police were one step ahead all the time.

'What about the taxi records?' I asked. It was then that his cheerfulness disappeared.

'The police have already been to the taxi office and discovered that your records for the relevant times are missing.'

I couldn't believe it. What had happened to them?

'Surely someone knows where they are,' I said.

He looked at me seriously and said, 'The police are saying you got rid of them to cover up your movements. Did you?'

I told him I hadn't and reminded him of my absolute innocence. He accepted my word. When I told him of the treatment I had received at Risley, he listened to my account of the events and told me he would look into the matter with the authorities. I very much doubted that this would achieve much, considering the way the police had treated me when I was in their custodial care. I explained to Mr McHugh that I felt totally isolated at Risley, being more than seventy miles away from friends and family, and worse still, from any contact with him. I wanted to be kept informed of the daily happenings of the case. Mr McHugh told me that there was no remand centre any nearer to Lancaster and that he would see me each week when I was brought back to the court. This conversation did little to build up my confidence. In fact, quite the reverse. I felt dejected—there seemed to be nobody willing to fight for the injustice I was suffering daily. Every ear on every side of the case seemed to be tightly shut to my cries for help.

As we travelled back to Risley, I felt depressed about the seeming lack of concern for my welfare. Also the startling revelation concerning the taxi records disturbed me. Either someone was trying to help me or someone had deliberately destroyed them to implicate me in the killing. It was a mystery. Surely no one would do such a thing? There had to be a mistake. All I knew was the certain fact that I had not taken or tampered with any record sheets.

When we arrived back at Risley the screws signed for me and locked me up in the sweat-box. After an hour or so I was re-allocated to the hospital wing. There was the usual procedure of changing into the secondhand uniform. The only difference from the last remand was that there was no need to have a bath or medical. To my astonishment the set of clothes fitted far better this time. The screws escorted me back to the hospital wing. Then came the shock.

We passed my cell, then carried on upstairs to the first landing where I saw a ward full of remanded cons. Fear welled up inside me. Surely they weren't putting me inside with that lot? They certainly were. Another screw opened the large barred gate and we entered.

'One on, sir,' the escort screw said to the other. My whole body was trembling inside as I looked at the twenty or so cons in the ward. The screw in charge of the ward pointed out my bed and storage cubicle and then told me to put my things away. I walked nervously to the bed and unpacked my belongings. Then I sat at the side of the bed and one of the other cons nonchalantly wandered over to me.

'Hello,' he said. 'You look very frightened.' I looked up and instantly recognized his accent. He was a Liverpudlian.

'Well, it's been a long hard day,' I said.

'What's your name?' he asked.

'Noel,' I replied.

'Mine's Swannie. At least, that's what everyone calls me. What you in for, Noel?' he asked.

'They've charged me with murder,' I said.

'Same here,' he replied.

'I didn't do it. In fact, I don't know anything about it,' I said.

'I hear you're an ex-copper.'

With that I broke into a cold sweat, fearing the worst. He had engaged me in conversation and now he was going to attack me. I took a deep breath.

'Yes, I am. But I resigned before all this happened to me.'

'I've heard you've had it pretty rough since you've been in here.'

'Yes I have.'

'Well, don't worry, Noel. I'll show you the ropes. After all, we're all in the same boat.'

What a relief. At last there was going to be someone to talk to. He chatted on for a while about his case and then it was time for lights out. I got into bed feeling somewhat better as the result of Swannie's kindness towards me. However, I couldn't sleep because I feared someone might attack me whilst I was sleeping. I tried to convince myself that it wouldn't happen—the security screw was at the end of the ward and would be there all night. When morning dawned I had been awake all night and felt exhausted.

I went through the usual procedure of washing and shaving before breakfast with the added security of knowing the ward screw was always at hand. At least there were sinks, toilets and a bath in the ward, unlike the archaic facilities in single cells. Swannie came and ate his breakfast with me on the side of the bed and continued to tell me about the privileges one could have as a remanded prisoner.

You could have food parcels sent in, buy things out of your private money, have visits daily and write as many letters as you wanted as long as you bought the stamps. He was a mine of information. No one had told me of all the things I could do, so it was a complete revelation.

After breakfast everyone made up their beds and cleared the ward up. Then they started playing cards, chess, dominoes and other table games. I was invited to join in the domino school. Feeling more secure I joined the three other cons and learnt the game quite quickly. After all I had suffered recently, it was a relief to be accepted by other people, even though they were remanded prisoners like

70

myself. We soon got round to the usual topic of conversation—the fact that I had been a policeman. They all seemed to think I must be an expert at law. One of the cons, called Jim, had stabbed his girlfriend who later died.

'Do you think I'll get life or less for diminished responsibility?' he asked me.

'It will depend on your lawyers and medical reports,' I said. The truth was I didn't have a clue what would happen. Still, it satisfied him. The exercise bell went and I decided to join the others for exercise. After all, it seemed I was more accepted following my introduction to the hospital ward.

Outside I tasted fresh air for the first time in days, walking round the exercise yard in convoy with what seemed like a hundred or so cons. We were about six abreast and were tightly packed in rows so the line in front determined the step and pace at which we walked. The screws were dotted about at strategic points watching over us.

Suddenly I felt a blow to my lower back in the kidney area and instantly seething pain shot through my body. It was so intense that I found myself fighting for breath. At the same time I heard someone behind say 'Bastard copper' and then felt another blow strike me in the same area. With that I fell to the ground reeling from excruciating pain—the result of yet another cowardly attack. I lay on the ground still fighting for breath, the other cons either walking over me or kicking me as they passed. Everything inside myself was telling me to get to my feet. I tried to muster up the strength to force myself to stand up, but the sheer weight and volume of cons walking over me kept me pinned to the ground. At last I could breathe again and I swallowed great gulps of air. Then I felt a pair of hands on my shoulders.

'Get up, Noel. Come on, la, get up.' Someone was pulling me up with all his strength. Then another hand grabbed me and I was on my feet. My legs buckled under the shock and pain that still raged in my body and I could sense myself swaying from side to side, still not aware of my rescuers. They had me tightly in their grip and we were moving forward.

71

'Keep going, la.' It was then I recognized the voice. Swannie. It was Swannie and another con holding me. They walked and I stumbled. The bell went for the end of exercise and we returned to the ward. I sat on my chair shaking all over and still feeling pain all over my body. 'How much more can I take?' I thought to myself. The screws hadn't even noticed the attack and if it hadn't been for Swannie and Jim, what would have happened to me? I nervously pulled on a cigarette, trying to come to terms with the jungle behaviour of my contemporaries. How stupid and naive I'd been, thinking I was safe going on exercise because a few people had talked to me. This was a different world altogether from the one I had left outside. I had never imagined there could be so much hatred and bitterness towards authority, whether it be the police or prison officers. All I knew was my incarceration was worsening by the day. The cons had been very calculated in their attack, hitting and kicking me in the right places. No blood was shed. All I was left with was horror, shock, immense fear—and bruising. Swannie came over and asked how I was feeling.

'Lousy,' I said.

'You'll have to fight back,' he said.

'How can I when they attack me from behind? They always have the element of surprise.'

'You'll have to learn quickly, Noel. If you sense trouble, hit out first.'

'OK, I'll try to remember that in future.'

I thanked him for helping me and we continued chatting. Swannie was an expert on how to survive in prison and the laws of the jungle. I learnt that he had grown up in the backstreets of Liverpool and had served his apprenticeship in personal survival techniques. He was the same age as me— twenty-two years old—but he had far greater maturity and much more experience of the judicial system than I, having been paraded through the courts on numerous occasions in his life.

The week passed by and after a few days I went on exercise again. This time I stuck very close to Swannie and the exercise period passed without violence. Cons still made provocative remarks but I ignored them. It was obvious to me that Swannie was respected by the other cons and he wasn't to be tangled with.

Monday came and again it was the usual procedure of going in the sweat-box and off to the magistrates at Lancaster for a further remand. The only consolation was I would be out of Risley for a number of hours. After the short hearing I saw Mr McHugh for a few minutes. He had no new information about the case or any indication that I would be released. He told me I would have to wait for the committal proceedings, when the police would present their case to the court, who in their turn would decide whether to send me for trial.

'When will that be?' I asked.

'When the police have gathered all their statements together and finished their enquiry,' he said.

My heart sank. 'Well, you had better start making noises because I'm the victim of constant attacks in Risley and I can't take any more. It's destroying me,' I said. He again tried to assure me that he was doing all he could in the circumstances. 'What's the point?' I thought to myself. 'Nobody believes anything I tell them.'

We returned to Risley with the usual silence from the police. I felt dejected and depressed knowing that I would have to spend more time at Risley than I had at first envisaged. Back to the sweat-box, then back to the ward.

The days seemed to get longer as prison routine ground on—the same boring daily existence determined for you minute by minute. I wrote to my parents and friends, trying to make things look better than they actually were, but after a time I got short of topics to write about. They even controlled your writing. If you told the truth the censor sent it back to be written again. Even the screw on the ward used to write up his report on everyone's daily behaviour pattern. One was a prisoner in every sense.

Later that week I was escorted to see the senior medical officer—a convenient title for a psychiatrist. He introduced himself and informed me that everyone remanded on a murder charge had to have a medical report to present to the court. He began by taking down my history, then onto the more subtle questions regarding the charge of murder. I told him I was totally innocent and could not therefore give him any information. He accepted my reply but continued questioning me about the case. It was like a game of mental chess lasting two hours. As always I totally denied any involvement in the case. The thorough and systematic sophisticated questioning left me mentally exhausted. It was ironic to hear the doctor tell me that the finished report would be impartial. I wondered how it could possibly be impartial when the interview had taken place inside prison and I would never be given access to it, nor would my defence lawyers.

At last the interview came to an end.

'Would you like something at night to help you sleep?' the doctor offered.

I shook my head. 'No thank you,' I said. 'My conscience is clear. Sleep is only interrupted by the nightmare of this place.'

I had seen lots of the cons on the ward getting their tots of Valium or Librium at night. There was no way they were going to turn me into a junkie. Besides, many of the cons were bleary-eyed during the day, incapable of rational speech. I wanted to know everything that was happening to me, not escape from it under drugs.

The following afternoon Swannie was lying on his bed. The ward screw noticed and commanded him to get off his bed and sit on his chair. Swannie told him to get stuffed. An argument began, each trying to out-shout the other. Swannie just lay there shouting obscene abuse at the screw and refusing to get off his bed. The screw pressed the alarm bell and within seconds ten more screws arrived on the scene. They grabbed Swannie and carried him bodily out of the ward to the continuous cries of abuse as Swannie tried to free himself from their grasp.

One screw shouted to another, 'Get the padded cell ready for this bastard. We'll show him who's boss here.'

Everything in me felt the injustice of the place. All Swannie had done was lie on the bed in the afternoon. The screws obviously couldn't imagine—or couldn't care about—what it was like living under the pressure of such a regime month after month, endlessly waiting to go to trial. To me Risley represented oppression and demonstrated a total lack of human care or understanding of the unbearable position of prisoners on remand.

The weekend arrived. I was informed that my parents had come to visit me. My heart leapt at the news—it was their first visit since being in Risley. I was escorted to the visit room where I greeted my parents. They looked well after their long journey and I sat down opposite them to chat. Much to my disgust the discipline screw who had escorted me pulled up a chair and sat in the corner of the room. We were not to enjoy any privacy together. Again, I had been denied private conversation with my family. We couldn't discuss the case openly for fear that the onlooker would put it down in his report and pass it on to the police, who in turn might try to undermine our intent. It's possible that all this was speculation on my part, but the system breeds paranoia at an early stage.

My father told me that Mr McHugh said he had engaged a top barrister on my behalf to conduct the defence. There was no more news, except that Mr McHugh was trying to get the police to fix an early date for committal proceedings. I found the visit difficult as there was so much I wanted to ask my parents but couldn't in the presence of our uniformed guardian. I felt frustrated and irate.

I turned to the screw and said, 'We would like some time on our own.'

'Sorry, I don't make the rules. It's not allowed.'

My mother said it didn't matter and not to worry about it. I knew there was no way I could tell them of the treatment I had suffered to date. Besides, it would only add to their worries. I put on a brave face, as one does to protect others from sharing pain, anxiety and the cold reality of inner turmoil. From what my parents said it seemed they were as much in the dark as I was regarding the case. They were still bewildered by it. As far as they knew no primary evidence had come to light, in spite of the intensive police activity—as indeed it couldn't. It was simple—they had got the wrong man and by now must have realized it. Just before the end of the visit my father casually mentioned that my younger brother, Paul, had been interviewed several times by the police. He said that Paul seemed to be deeply disturbed following the interviews but couldn't talk to them about it. The only thing he had talked about was the fact that I had borrowed a jacket from him and returned it around the time of the murder enquiry—the police had taken the jacket for forensic tests. Paul had made a statement to the police about the jacket and that was all they knew.

The visit over, I returned to the ward, a little dejected at seeing my parents leave. It had been a refreshing hour talking to them. I thought over what they had told me. I was a bit baffled about why the police had to interview my brother and take his jacket away with them. Then it dawned on me. It was obvious my clothing had revealed nothing, so they were looking for anything that might tie me in with the crime. I felt rather excited at the prospect of the police having egg on their faces and myself sueing them for wrongful arrest. At long last it seemed the truth was beginning to surface and I would be exonerated.

Since Swannie's departure from the ward I had kept myself in voluntary isolation from the other cons, only allowing myself the luxury of conversation when it was offered to me. I passed messages and cigarettes to Swannie via the hospital orderly (another con) when I had the opportunity. Swannie was out of the strip cell and had been allocated a single cell on the ground floor. Later on I saw him taking exercise again, so that was my cue to exercise again in safety.

Weeks drifted by, the routine never changing. Every seven days I was escorted to the magistrates' court at Lancaster and remanded again. But on 6 May 1970 I learned that the committal proceedings were to take place the following week.

After the magistrates had remanded me for another week I was taken to Lancaster police station where I met Mr McHugh for an extended interview. He showed me statements and depositions from the prosecution and questioned me on the contents. This was a staggering and painful experience. For the first time since my arrest I had the opportunity to read statements made to the police and, more to the point, the police statements. Although the statements for the committal were limited in number, they had obviously been selected and scrutinized carefully. The civilian witness statements were factual and speculative, with the exception of Thornton's and Bamborough's from the Beach Club, and to some extent Mr Lingwood's from the taxi firm, which were damning to me.

Having read the statements, I sat there in absolute despair. I couldn't believe what I had read. Why was the truth not coming out? Mr McHugh raised questions about the content of the statements and I answered as well as I could the details of times, circumstances and events. It was an arduous task trying to remember things which had taken place some nine or ten weeks previously. But when it came to the police statements about my interview at Lancaster, I had instant memory recall. Mr McHugh drew up a statement of my answers and I asked him what he thought of the prosecution case.

'It seems to me, Noel, that they have nothing more than circumstantial evidence,' he answered.

'Well, they couldn't have as I never did it,' I said. 'What's going to happen now?'

'The prosecution will present their case to the magistrates next week and they will decide whether to commit you for trial.'

'But most of these statements don't tell the truth,' I protested. 'Surely the magistrates will see through them?'

On the return trip to Risley I wrestled with my memory trying to recall the detail of the statements I had seen. The way the police had knitted their statements together was unbelievable, each confirming the next one's account. *Why me? Why me?* That's all I could think.

I spent the following days locked in heaviness and depression as I continued trying to untangle the web of lies that had been finely spun around me. What's more, I was anxious about the way the case was going. My frustration was immense—I was confined to Risley, cut off from the outside world and all I could do was rely on my solicitor's professional opinion that all was going well for me.

At last the thirteenth of May arrived and I left Risley under escort for the committal proceedings at South Lonsdale Magistrates' Court in Lancaster Castle. I was excited at the prospect that this could be my last day in custody.

We arrived at about two o'clock and, prior to the hearing, I had consultation with Mr McHugh. He was optimistic about the outcome of the proceedings. The police hadn't released any further statements to him, so they could only use what we had seen the previous week—or so we thought. The proceedings started with the prosecution handing in statements from twenty-eight prosecution witnesses to the magistrates, with a further five who were to give evidence at the proceedings.

After the opening address the prosecution called Paul Fellowes. My heart sank. Why on earth were they calling my younger brother? Paul took the oath and began to tell the court how I had borrowed his jacket and returned it to him some time around the date of the murder in Overton. He went on to say I had spoken to him on the telephone, saying someone was pestering me and I was going to have him. His evidence ended as he told the court that he had seen me wearing a purple-coloured cravat on occasions. As Paul replied to the questions of the prosecutor, he was white with fear and stuttered. My heart went out to him. I felt strongly that the police had set him up with the statement he had signed—the last two elements of his evidence were complete fabrication. Not only were they trying to stitch me up, now they had implicated my brother.

Other civilian witnesses testified: Dr Beeson, the pathologist; Mrs Hockenhull, the deceased's cleaner; Mrs Barrett, a friend of the dead man and finally Mrs Lingwood, wife of the manager of the taxi firm I worked for. She gave evidence about the missing taxi records for my work on Tuesday 24 February. Mr McHugh challenged all the witnesses in a proper manner but there was little he could do as none of the police were to give evidence. The magistrates didn't hesitate in committing me to trial at Lancaster Assizes to answer the charge of murder.

I saw Mr McHugh after the hearing. I was furious at what the police had done to my brother. 'It's absolutely devastating!' I said. 'Paul's only nineteen, and the police have conveniently tied him into the case.'

Mr McHugh told me to calm down. The trial would expose the police to cross-examination and the defence lawyers would be able to get to the truth of my accusations, he told me.

I returned to Risley in a state of utter despondency. What I had witnessed in court was a farce. I was back in the nightmare. There was no freedom, mental or physical; no let-up in the constant remarks and threats from the cons and no hope of release before the trial. Whichever way I looked or turned I was completely fenced in. I felt totally insecure. Risley had damaged me deeply. Once carefree in my attitude to life, I was now introverted, fearful and depressive. The system had turned me inside-out. All I could do was try to hold myself together until the trial—that was the only thing I had left to look forward to.

6

Expert Witnesses

The morning of 22 June 1970 arrived to the usual sound of screws bellowing 'slop out'. This was my big day and there was a deep feeling of nervous excitement in my stomach. 'This is surely the beginning of the end of my nightmare when the truth will finally be told and my freedom will be won,' I told myself.

Following a rushed breakfast, I was whisked away to reception where I changed into my normal clothes. I wouldn't have won the year's best-dressed man award but at least I looked presentable. After all, I wasn't being tried for the garments I wore. The great disappointment about my appearance was my hair. The previous night I had decided it would look better in court if it had been trimmed. The ward screw cut it—and I could see in the mirror now that I had been well and truly sheared. The screws locked me in the sweat-box to await transport to Lancaster. As I sat there, I considered the possibilities of the day ahead with renewed optimism, thinking it would soon all be over. Before long the discipline screws arrived and within minutes I was cuffed and led into the prison van. I passed the time away during the journey listening to the gossip of my captors.

My optimism took a sudden jolt the moment the van rounded the last corner and began the steep uphill climb towards Lancaster Castle. The sight of this 700-year-old castle reminded me of its history. Being a local, I knew some of the fearful legends surrounding the place. They were of little comfort to me, for Lancaster Court had the dubious distinction of sending more people to the gallows than any other in the land. Back in the fourteenth century, the first Duke of Lancaster had been given absolute powers to wield the sword of justice right across the north of England up to the borders. His daughter married John O'Gaunt, who inherited the land and title and continued to dispense justice in the most barbaric fashion. The castle became the property of the Crown in the next generation when John O'Gaunt's son became King Henry IV.

Perhaps the most famous trial at Lancaster was that of the Pendle witches—ten women from the hills of East Lancashire who practised strange, pagan rites. They paid with their lives, and one is still thought to be buried outside the gateway. The trials of Timothy Burke, the last man to be publicly hanged in Britain, and Richard Peddar, the last to die on the particularly gruesome 'short-drop rope' technique, both took place here, in the 1850s. There had been two areas of execution—the hanging corner clearly visible to passers-by—and a yard on which the sun was said never to shine. The grim building lent itself to these sorts of myths. It was said that gas board workmen uncovered one skeleton during routine work near the hanging corner. All this was great for tourism, but only served to increase my growing sense of unease.

I was shepherded from the vehicle into an ante-room, then they guided me into a sweat-box even more confined than those at Risley. For an hour I sat there with only a glimmer of natural light piercing my gloom. I could hear the chinking of cups as the screws settled down to a cup of tea—I was, of course, excluded from the tea party.

Suddenly the door opened. 'It's time to go, Fellowes, you're going to meet your QC now,' shouted a voice. Trying to adjust my eyes to the light, I ascended a flight of stairs with my wrists still handcuffed together in front of me. Then I met for the first time Mr Ernest Sanderson Temple—the man my destiny depended on. Also present were Mr McHugh and junior counsel. But it was the QC who captured my attention. He was renowned to be one of the top men on the northern circuit of the law courts and his early comments displayed benevolent efficiency. He had a wealth of experience behind him. Educated at Queens College, Oxford, he had later reached the rank of Lieutenant-Colonel in the Border Regiment in

India and Burma and had been mentioned in despatches. During his service he became a barrister-at-law and took on his first case in 1946. Within two years of our meeting he was to be appointed an Honorary Recorder at Kendal.

After the initial pleasantries, the bombshell was dropped in seven carefully selected words: 'Have you considered pleading guilty to manslaughter?'

My jaw dropped in amazement. Before I could mutter a reply he said: 'Possibly you'd get as little as five years.'

I told him that I could not possibly plead guilty to a crime of which I was totally innocent. My bold words carried false confidence for his suggestion had undermined my strength of purpose. Upon hearing this, he pledged full support, but my confidence was shaken. As he disappeared to take his place in the well of the courtroom I felt like a pawn in a game of legal chess. The stakes were high—and yet I did not know the rules of the game.

I was summoned to the dock by the court usher. The familiar feeling of nervousness gripped me once more. The four steps led into the centre stage of the courtroom—a dock fringed by daunting metal spiked rails. It was a massive room, with old oak panelling. Every seat in the court seemed occupied—by barristers, solicitors and police, while the public gallery was full. An excited chatter filled the air until I became clearly visible . . . then a hush crept over the courtroom.

All eyes were upon me, some in pity, others in persecution. It all added to my continuing sense of vulnerability and insecurity. Flanked by screws, I sat down, awaiting instructions. The court rose as His Honour Mr Justice (Bernard) Caulfield took his place underneath the large court crest. I stood too—with the unsolicited help of my two minders. The court clerk's deep voice echoed around the chamber:

'Keith Noel Fellowes, you are charged that you at Overton in the County of Lancaster, between the 23rd and 26th days of February, 1970, did murder Harold John Driscoll Parkinson, against the peace of our Sovereign Lady Queen, her Crown and dignity. How do you plead? Do you plead guilty or not guilty?'

My legs trembling and voice faltering I responded: 'Not guilty, my Lord.'

I resumed my seat as the prosecuting counsel, Mr Godfrey Heilpern QC, opened the case against me. In spite of the fear, a strange feeling of detachment enveloped me. Could this really be me they were talking about? My thoughts flashed to a previous committal hearing when the prosecutor had been forced to admit there was not a single conclusive fact which associated me with the murder. He had stated that there was purely circumstantial evidence against me. But Mr Heilpern's opening address had no such content.

He quickly produced what he considered was the motive. I had been under a 'very strong impression' that I was being followed by a private investigator, he said. My marriage had broken up and I had been 'carrying on' with another woman. He described how my romantic activities were being charted by a private detective, probably employed by my mother-in-law. That man was Harold Parkinson. Having suggested a reason for the killing Mr Heilpern went into grim detail of how the body was found. He detailed the different bonds which embraced the corpse and the general battered state of the body.

As he spelt out the full horror of the way Harold Parkinson had died, many eyes in the courtroom returned to me to detect any give-away expressions my face might betray. There were none. I had no shame over a killing I was not involved in.

The jury—seven men and five women—were first given a description of how the body was found at the Overton cottage by Mr Parkinson's friend, Mr Darby. There was no reason for my counsel to take this witness to task, as I had no dispute over the finding of the body. But his graphic description of the scene of the death must have touched on the emotions of the jurors. Mr Darby had last seen Parkinson alive at 9.30 a.m. on Tuesday 24 February when he called at his home.

Another caller at the cottage, Mrs Hockenhull, the cleaner,

had an even later sighting of him. She had been cleaning there when her daughter, Patricia, called at 3.30 p.m. 'She came in and Harold gave us both some whisky, Benedictine and damson wine to drink. At 4 p.m.—I remember the time because he set his clock right—I left the house with my daughter.'

Mrs Hockenhull was able to recall the clothes he had been wearing that afternoon—an old jacket, a pair of old grey slacks and brown suede slip-on shoes. She added that the house was in a tidy state when she left—not the tip later discovered by Mr Darby.

Evidence of three further sightings on the following day, the 25th, was brought to the court's attention—although the prosecution did not put much conviction behind it. The information from Messrs Luke, Ramsey and Braid was relayed to the jury, but they were urged into disregarding these statements in preference to others.

One came from the pathologist, Dr Brian Beeson. His post-mortem analysis came up with the firm opinion that death had occurred between 7 a.m. and midnight on 25 February. Having established that, he then dismantled the precision of his own argument by saying it was 'possible that death could have occurred as early as the evening of the 24th.'

The underlying reason why the prosecution was leaning towards Tuesday 24 February as the day of death was that I had a cast-iron alibi for the 25th and 26th. Mr Heilpern stressed this by saying 'the deceased was dead by Wednesday morning'. Why was he so certain of this when Dr Beeson—an expert in his field—could not be? The answer was simple: I had been alone for most, though not all, of the time from 6.30 p.m. on Wednesday evening until 2.50 a.m. the following morning.

Police had relied heavily on my taxi firm boss Gerry Lingwood to highlight potential areas of doubt. He told investigators: 'I arranged with Fellowes that he would look after the office that night (24th) up to midnight; he was there at 6.30 p.m. I returned to the office at 12.05 a.m. to do the night-time office work. Fellowes was there then. I believe he was stood up answering the telephone. He was wearing my fawn Gannex raincoat and I told him to take it off. He told me to hang on while he took his money out of a pocket. He then hung it over the office partition. I cannot recall what reason he gave for wearing my coat.'

Lingwood then told how I left in a taxi to pick up fares in the Morecambe area. 'As far as I can remember Fellowes returned to the office about 2.50 a.m. and would remain there until about 5.30 a.m. when according to his log-sheet he went to pick up the ICI duty driver.' The prosecution would later say that I had had ample time during those hours to commit the crime in the neighbouring hamlet of Overton.

Lingwood was 'useful' to the police in several other important areas. He outlined the system of how each of his drivers would fill in his own log-sheet for fares taken. When the driver returned to base, the details would be transferred to a daily record-sheet by office staff. It was then suggested that some of these office-sheets had been deliberately removed from the premises. I was the obvious offender. The prosecution claimed I had destroyed them so that my movements could not be monitored hour by hour. They scored points over their 'convenient' disappearance.

Lingwood's memory was becoming more and more helpful to the police case. 'I remember one day just after Fellowes had left his wife a man came to my home—I presumed he was a private detective—and asked where Fellowes lived. I later told Fellowes about this and I seem to remember in the conversation that he said there was a private detective at Overton and one at Lancaster. Fellowes also said that he thought for a long time that someone had been following him.'

He also recalled: 'I have been shown a purple-coloured silk scarf and it is very similar in colour and material to one that I have seen worn by Fellowes. The last time I had seen him wearing this scarf was about three weeks ago, before the Overton incident.'

If I had actually been involved in a bloody struggle with

Harold Parkinson, the onus was on the forensic scientist to come up with conclusive evidence. Dr Alan Clift was in the witness-box a long time. First he gave evidence on blood-stains found at the house—all group A, resembling the victim's, not mine. Then he told of his intricate analysis of nail scrapings, material matching and all the bindings used on the old man. Despite thorough research, he could produce nothing which connected me to the victim, or *vice versa*. But there was one fibre—which my defence could easily explain away—which left a major doubt in the jury's minds.

Dr Clift had found one opaline green wool fibre in the hand-nail scrapings taken from Mr Parkinson. This did not match any of the clothes he was wearing at the time of death—but was similar to fibres in the lining of the Gannex raincoat I had worn occasionally at the taxi office.

Under cross-examination, this important find did not stand up to close scrutiny. Dr Clift was forced to admit that a green jumper found under the stairs—near the body—contained the same fibres. What significance the attentive jury placed on these words is difficult to imagine.

Dr Clift also submitted in evidence one wool fibre from the shoes of Mr Parkinson, which he said was similar to one found on a pair of black trousers I wore. Again, under cross-examination from my QC, the biologist confessed that 'similar', in precise forensic terms, stood for little. He admitted the pink fibre was very common and the jury themselves might find a fibre of the same sort on their person at any time.

Mr Sanderson Temple suggested to Dr Clift that he might have expected to find more direct forensic evidence against me, considering the degree of violence used against the deceased. They had checked for fingerprints, hair, skin scrapings and inspected my entire wardrobe of clothes and come up empty-handed.

My defence summed up: 'The deceased was by no means a small man and was a thick-set type of person. It is inconceivable that he would have placidly allowed himself to have been tied up in the manner indicated and indeed evidence shows that considerable violence was used. One would have thought that whoever committed the crime would have shown some sign of injury himself.'

The content of Dr Clift's statement raised the eyebrows of my defence lawyers. One wrote in his brief: 'The surprising thing in the forensic evidence is the large number of matters which it does not mention and which normally are available in a trial such as this.'

He added: 'The absence of identifiable fingerprints is, one would think, a strong point in the accused's favour, even allowing for the fact that he is a former police officer and would perhaps know how to deal with fingerprint difficulties. One would think however that it would be impossible to tie up the deceased in the manner indicated in the photographs whilst wearing gloves.'

That comment touched on one issue that was to worry the jury: a former policeman would know how to cover his tracks. After every contrived allegation against me I could feel the eyes of the jury searching for confirmation.

My expectations of an acquittal began to rise as I realized that, despite the most sophisticated of forensic investigations, they had only come up with two common every-day fibres. Mr Sanderson Temple made much of the fact that the police had taken every single scrap of my clothing for forensic examination, and not a 'pinhead' of Mr Parkinson's blood was ever traced.

Dr Clift said he had attempted to tie himself up in the same manner as Mr Parkinson was found but had been unable to tie the cable around his wrists. In my opinion my QC had professionally and verbally tied Dr Clift up in the witness-box—I felt his contribution to the prosecution case was almost irrelevant.

My confidence was high now, but it took a dive when I saw my 18-year-old girlfriend, Lynn Hazelgrave, walk towards the witness-stand. It was an ordeal for a young girl who had never set foot in court before. And the prosecution were determined not to make life easy for her. Mr Heilpern questioned her on the intimate details of our relationship—although I could not see what bearing that was supposed to have on the case. If he was trying to intimidate her, he succeeded, and some of her answers to his probing questions did not measure up to his expectations. After a gruelling session of firing questions at her from every angle, he applied to Judge Caulfield to treat her as a 'hostile witness'. It didn't make much difference, for Lynn continued to answer queries the only way she knew how—with the truth.

Lynn described how she first met me in the August of 1969 and how we had become fond of each other. She said I was always joking about life and that I had made jocular remarks about the case before being arrested. Lynn said that once, when we were with other people, I had laughingly exclaimed: 'Watch out, you might be sitting next to a murderer!' and, 'Well, I didn't tie him that tight.' She reported another occasion when she and I had been at her home in Morecambe when we heard noises outside. The prosecution suggested it might have been a private investigator. She replied that it could have been anybody.

Determined to get something from her the police had asked her if she had ever seen me wearing a purple cravat—adding that Mr Lingwood had said he had. She knew me better than anybody at that time and she was adamant in her denial. She had never seen such a neckerchief, recently or at any other time.

The Crown tried their best to blacken her character but they could not take away from her the fact that she was from a 'very respectable family' and had talked frankly and candidly about our relationship. She said my flippant remarks about the death were an illustration only of the light-hearted way I looked upon life. She left the witness-box with the same simple dignity with which she had entered it.

Lynn's father, Mr James Hazelgrave, was next in the prosecution firing line. He had welcomed me into the family home and I in turn had assured him about my attitude to his daughter. I had been honest with him about the break-up of my marriage and he respected that. His testimony was further proof that the jocular remarks I had made about the case were perfectly in keeping with my happy-go-lucky style of life. Mr Hazelgrave, a college registrar with an impeccable background, recalled that on the last occasion he had seen me I had joked: 'Don't forget, future address Walton jail.' He hadn't taken it seriously of course and certainly didn't read into it what the prosecution sought to.

My defence was beginning to look sound—even in the early stages of the case for the prosecution. But possibly the most grievous damage against my credibility was to come in the form of two men—Carey Thornton and John Bamborough.

Thornton was the 23-year-old manager of the Beach Club, a gambling den in nearby Heysham. Occasionally I had been the taxi driver who drove him and Bamborough home in the early hours. I was dumbfounded as Thornton began to detail the most alarming accusations against me. A couple of days before the death, he alleged that he and I had met in his club's 'Shell Bar'.

Thornton told the court: 'I asked him about his marriage difficulties and he told me that he had been followed by a man named Parkinson who was a private detective. He had mentioned this man on an occasion about four weeks previously as someone who was following him around. He thought his mother-in-law had employed Parkinson. He said to me, "The other night I saw Parkinson on the promenade by the central pier in Morecambe. I tackled him about following me and then I did him up." '

Now for the first time the jury were given the opportunity to evaluate an alleged link between me and the old man. The motive couldn't be any more clear. But Thornton hadn't finished there.

He talked of another meeting in the same club, along with Lynn and Bamborough, on 7 March. By that time all my clothes had been taken for forensic testing. Thornton alleged I said, 'There seem to be a lot of things pointing at me,' and he replied: 'Aye well, if you duffed him up before it happened he has been following you'.

Thornton startled me with another quotation he attributed to me: 'I made three trips to Overton in the taxi that night.' The jury were now being urged to believe that I had clashed with Parkinson on one occasion because he had been tailing me and that I had been in his village on the night of the killing. During our conversation, Thornton said I had developed a nervous laugh. And there was one more nasty surprise the club manager had in store for me. 'He always wore an open-necked shirt and in place of a tie a purple-coloured silk scarf of an identical colour to the one shown to me' [by police].

Bamborough was a thirty-year-old bouncer at the same Beach Club. He loyally confirmed what his boss had earlier stated, but added: 'Fellowes didn't seem worried, more likely annoyed at being pulled in by the police'. Bamborough's integrity as a witness came in for a battering from my QC when he revealed that he had once been arrested—by a PC Fellowes! It was true. I, along with PC 1410 Harrison, had detained him for an alleged motoring offence, in Euston Road, Morecambe. Mr Sanderson Temple challenged him on previous confrontations with the law. The jury were left to decide for themselves about this man's credentials as an impartial witness.

Counsel had cast doubt on Bamborough, but the damage had still been done. I was shaking like a leaf and outraged by their version of events. At the end of that day's business in court, I returned to Risley with my heart in my boots. Suddenly, the pendulum had swung away from me. Was the Crown convincing the jury I was a murderer?

7

Gagged and Bound

The beginning of the next day's proceedings were taken up with my brother Paul giving evidence. It was doubly distressing to hear what he had said firstly at the committal proceedings and now in the full trial. I suspected he was only standing there because of the intolerable burden of police pressure.

Again he was pale and too agitated to glance in my direction. My defence lawyers had perhaps underestimated the impact on a jury of seeing a suspect's brother giving evidence against him. In their pre-trial brief they wrote of Paul: 'He really did not know very much of what he was talking about. He may very well have had his memory refreshed by the time of the trial but his evidence does not amount to very much.'

On the contrary, Paul told the court that he and I used to tie each other up during games as children. He described me as aggressive and related an alleged telephone conversation we had around the time of the Overton killing.

'We talked about family life and marriage and he said something like, "Somebody is following me but I'll have him",' he said. This perhaps was *the* turning point of the trial. Although his evidence itself was uncorroborated, it seemed to lend credence to the earlier remarks of Thornton and Bamborough. A tide of accusations flooded against me— and still there was all the police evidence to come.

The police case was interrupted before it could get started by Mr Sanderson Temple, who rose to make a legal submission about the inadmissibility of some of their evidence. I did not fully understand what was going on at this point. Mr Justice Caulfield turned to the jury and explained that points of law had to be discussed in their absence, in the interests of a fair trial. Then he ordered the ushers to clear the public gallery and to my astonishment instructed the warders to return me to my cell. This was known in legal circles as a trial within a trial—but to me it was a trial without a defendant.

The object of dispute was the inordinate length of time the police had taken to interview me. I had been at the mercy of different teams of high-ranking officers right through the night. Mr Sanderson Temple outlined how on Sunday 8 March I was first seen in the taxi office by detectives McEwan and Bowe, at 6.50 p.m. After being taken to the Memorial Hall there had been a forty-minute session with detectives Mounsey and Thomas. This was the conversation which culminated in Mounsey's fateful words, 'Wrap it up here. Let's go to Lancaster Police Station. We've got him.'

The gruelling sequence at Lancaster Police Station started at 8.10 p.m. with Mounsey and Thomas again, said the QC. They were replaced three hours and thirty-five minutes later by McEwan and Bowe. Just after midnight, Mounsey and Thomas returned. The grilling continued:

12.20 a.m.–1.05 a.m. Collins and Crompton
1.05 a.m.–3.00 a.m. Mounsey and Thomas
3.00 a.m.–3.40 a.m. Mounsey alone
3.45 a.m.–4.05 a.m. Mounsey and Griffiths
4.05 a.m.–5.30 a.m. Griffiths and Collins
5.30 a.m. Short interview with Howson and Yarwood

Mr Sanderson Temple and his opposite number Mr Heilpern were drawn into open combat over admissibility for most of the Wednesday and the Thursday morning of the trial. When the jury was asked to return to their seats, they were told that a great proportion of police evidence was to be swept away.

'I rule that all evidence subsequent to 9 p.m. on Sunday 8 March to breakfast time of Monday 9 March is inadmissible,' said Mr Justice Caulfield. He added that some of my alleged remarks had been obtained by oppression.

The first officer to get into the box was Detective Sergeant James McEwan, an officer who had been brought in from the other side of Lancashire to aid the investigation. He told how he had first met me in the taxi office and how he had revealed the name and address of my mother-in-law which had been found in the victim's notebook. He said that I had agreed to go to the Memorial Hall with him where I was photographed and fingerprinted for 'elimination purposes'. McEwan had showed me a photograph of Mr Parkinson and I had said: 'I've seen him somewhere, but I can't remember where it was. It may come back to me.'

What I meant by that was that Morecambe was a resort full of retired old folk, and there were plenty of male pensioners who were not dissimilar in appearance. The picture of this man looked like many others—he looked like everybody's grandad.

McEwan had been the officer who had taken my clothes for forensic examination and noted down my one and only statement. The detective mentioned an alleged conversation we had during a car trip to the Memorial Hall. Again I had that familiar sinking feeling as I heard snippets of chat I was convinced I had never said.

I was sure there was little or no conversation during that journey. McEwan had other ideas. He reported that I had said: 'I did see that chap on Tuesday or Wednesday. I remember now. I think it was on the front at Morecambe in the afternoon. There's a few things I know about this chap.' Then I was supposed to have said: 'Do me a favour and I'll do you a favour.' McEwan said I had asked if he could 'do anything about' a speeding offence committed by Carey Thornton. I would certainly have remembered saying that, if I had said it. At the hall, he had handed me over to Mounsey.

McEwan had also played another part in the enquiry which later became an area of dispute. He had carried out time and distance trials in a police Ford Zephyr in the Morecambe and Overton areas. It was an attempt to prove I could have driven to Overton and killed Mr Parkinson in the time between taxi jobs on the evening of the 24th and the early hours of the 25th.

My defence had done their own homework on this aspect

of his evidence. 'Experienced taxi drivers from whom instructing solicitors have sought advice have in practically each case doubled the time to do the journey from that given by the witness,' said my QC.

Joe Mounsey became the next actor on the prosecution's stage. He cut an impressive figure as he strolled to the witness-box, clasping a bundle of statement papers. Not waiting for the usher to pass him the card with the oath printed on, he began to speak. His tones were deep, powerful and authoritative. 'I swear by almighty God that I shall tell the truth, the whole truth and nothing but the truth.'

You could have heard a pin drop in the hushed courtroom as Detective Chief Superintendent Joseph Mounsey introduced himself to the judge. In spite of his outward calm, Mounsey must have had some misgivings. Most of his all-night interview with me had been ruled inadmissible by the judge the previous day.

I listened intently as Mounsey recalled the conversation between us at the Memorial Hall:
    Mounsey: 'Who was the private detective at Overton?'
    Fellowes: 'That was him, Parkinson. He couldn't mind his own business. He's a sadist.'
    M: 'What makes you say he's a sadist?'
    F: 'That came second hand.'
    M: 'Do you know Parkinson?'
    F: 'I've seen him.'
    M: 'How well do you know him?'
    F: 'Not socially.'
    M: 'But you have met him?'
    (Long silence)
    M: 'You've met him?'
    (Long silence)
    F: 'I've nothing to say.'
    M: 'I repeat, you've met him?'
    F: 'I've never met him.'
    M: 'I repeat again, you've met him?'
    (Long silence)

F: 'He was following me, it was her fault.'

M: 'Whose?'

F: 'Her mother's.'

M: 'When did you last have a conversation with Parkinson?'
(No reply)

M: 'I believe you have met him recently.'

F: 'I haven't had a conversation with him that I can recollect.'

M: 'When did you last meet him—was it last week? I think you met him the night he died. I think you went to his house.'

F: 'I don't know—I don't know him socially.'

M: 'I think you met him last week, the night he died. Did you go to his house that night?'
(No direct answer) Short discussion on domestic difficulties.

F: 'He was following me that night. I will speak to my wife before I do or say anything about this. She's the only one I trust.'

F: 'It's all her mother's fault anyway. She thinks it's her kids not our kids. I was lucky to have handed in my resignation to the police force first before the trouble started.'

M: 'Tell us what's on your mind. What was your intention with Parkinson? Why was he following you?'

F: 'You don't understand, he was everywhere.'

M: 'Tell us what your intentions were with Parkinson. I think you went to his house last week.'
(No direct answer)

M: 'Did you kill him?'

F: 'He was following me. My wife will tell me what to say.'
At that stage Mounsey arranged transport to Lancaster.
On the journey:

F: 'You wouldn't have caught me without the help of the public, you've got nothing from my fingerprints and my clothing, have you?'

M: 'Why don't you tell us what you did to Parkinson?'

F: 'If I told you, that would be an admission and I'd sooner talk to my wife first.'

At Lancaster Police Station.

M: 'Now tell me what you did to Parkinson the night he died.'

F: 'He seemed to be everywhere. I saw him when I was in Euston Road—I said, are you following me? He mumbled something and I swore at him.'

M: 'That wasn't the night he died, though?'

F: 'No.'

M: 'Did you hit him on that occasion?'

F: 'No.'

M: 'But what about the night Parkinson died?'

F: 'That would be an admission. I met him that night, it was in the centre of Morecambe. My wife will tell me what to say.'

M: 'What night was it that he died?'

F: 'It is in some corner at the back of my mind. What do I do? I can't tell you until I've seen my wife. I trust her, what do I do?'

M: 'Do you want your wife to tell you whether to tell the truth or not?'

F: 'Yes.'

M: 'I thought you said you didn't know him. Then you said he was following you. What is the story? I believe you went to his house that night. You said you met him the night he died, in the centre of Morecambe. What happened after that? What did you do to him?'

F: (glancing at another detective) 'If he is going to write it all down I'm saying no more.'

The rest of the interview—which took up ten pages of statement paper—was inadmissible.

Mounsey was adamant that the interview had been conducted properly.

'There was no rapid fire questioning and I did not exercise any pressure to induce him to make any admissions,' he said. He added that I had not asked for a solicitor at any time while in the interview room.

Mr Sanderson Temple challenged him on his interview

technique, saying that even one of his own officers had described his manner as 'brusque'. He also took issue over the reason behind showing me a number of harrowing photographs of the dead man. My defence claimed Mounsey had tried to 'frighten' me into making a confession.

Mounsey deflected the barrage of criticism in the manner of a professional detective who had seen and heard it all before. But there were moments when Mr Sanderson Temple's interrogation provoked heated exchanges. Mounsey claimed his persistent questioning had been justified by the seriousness of the charge and the 'strong' suspicions against me.

My feelings of hostility towards this man had not subsided by the time he left the box to take up a vantage point in the well of the court in order to monitor what was to be my defence.

On day four of the trial, Thursday, I finished lunch and was escorted to the by now familiar mid-day briefing with Mr Sanderson Temple. I stared at him with incredulity as he told me that he had no intention of calling any defence witnesses —myself included. I was aghast.

The QC explained that I would appear as a solitary figure denouncing every prosecution witness as a liar. He asked me to consider who the jury would believe—me, in a fragile psychological and emotional state, or police officers with unimpeachable credentials?

Desperately trying to make sense of a situation which had now swung crazily out of my grasp, I at first refused his advice. He countered that the Crown under cross-examination would 'rip me to shreds' undoing all his previous good work. Support for Mr Sanderson Temple came from both junior counsel and Mr McHugh. Three knowledgeable legal tacticians outnumbered me. With a leaden heart, I asked for time to consider. But there were only minutes left before we were all due back in court. The decision had to be made there and then. So I agreed to their plan, even though everything inside told me to do exactly the opposite. It was a decision I regretted for many years.

Now the prosecution case was completed, Mr Sanderson Temple announced to the judge that there would be no defence submissions other than his own summing-up. This was greeted by a clearly audible gasp from the public gallery and a puzzled expression on Mr Heilpern's face.

On Friday morning, before counsel gave their final addresses, I was asked to sign a four-line statement. It read: 'I have been advised that I am entitled to give evidence on my own behalf at my trial and I have decided that I do not wish to give evidence.'

First to sum up was prosecutor, Mr Heilpern. He said he had established a motive—that I had killed Parkinson in a fit of rage because he had been following me as a private investigator hired by my mother-in-law. He claimed that the defendant had had the opportunity to commit the crime on the evening of the 24th or early hours of the 25th. My movements had been shielded by the 'convenient' removal of taxi record sheets, he added. He stressed that a number of witnesses seemed to prove conclusively that the purple material gagging Mr Parkinson had been my cravat. There was also the alleged verbal admissions, jocular remarks and forensic evidence on fibres to consider.

Mr Sanderson Temple's immediate response was to underline the fact that the evidence against me was only circumstantial and it did not stand up to close inspection. Out of the hundreds interviewed no witnesses had been traced who had ever seen me with Harold Parkinson, or even anywhere near his home. He reiterated that the joking remarks I had made had always been taken in the spirit they were given—as jokes, and not serious. He said that in his opinion there had been no reason to call defence witnesses because the prosecution had failed to substantiate 'beyond any reasonable doubt' that I was involved in the crime. His final remark to the jury was: 'Direct evidence against my client disappears like snow in the sun.'

A weekend of hell lay in store for me back at Risley. I knew

98

that on Monday my fate would be sealed one way or the other. As I mulled over every minute of the week-long court case I came to the conclusion that nearly everyone had it in for me.

Visitors tried to comfort me and convince me that all was well and I would soon be a free man again. This was the view shared by my counsel as the judge began his five hours of summing-up on the Monday morning.

Judge Caulfield said: 'I am sorry I have had to go into such detail but in a case where there has been a mysterious death it may be that it is the little bits of evidence and perhaps the little utterances made by the accused which you will find the most important. I know not.'

Mr Caulfield added that his final advice for the jury was to consider all the evidence carefully, everything they had heard and everything they had seen. That included an assessment of all witnesses and policemen. After that they had to ask themselves whether the Crown had proved that I had been hostile to Mr Parkinson in any way—'either alone or with someone else'. If they found in my mind I intended to do grievous bodily harm or kill him then I was guilty of murder.

'My final advice is, don't be satisfied with suspicion. Don't worry if in your minds you have strong suspicions but you find you cannot bring yourself to say you are sure. Just treat your deliberations judiciously, without fear, ill will or sympathy.'

Before the jury retired, they were told that I had no previous convictions for any criminal act.

I was taken down the steps of the dock to the dimly-illuminated sweat-box, my mind in turmoil. I sat down, and placed my hands over my face as time rolled agonizingly by. After about an hour, the escort screw opened the flap in the door and said, 'Someone in there [the jury] must be rooting for you.' He added that my mother had handed him a book to pass on to me. Through the flap I received a small blue hardback book—a Bible.

Although I wasn't a Christian, I was that desperate I thought I would try anything. Clasping the Bible in both hands I knelt silently on the floor. 'God, if you are really there, you know I am innocent of this man's death. If you convince the jury of the truth, then I will believe in you for ever.' It was a crude deal, struck out of desperation but it offered me some solace as the hours ticked by. I put the Bible down and once again covered my face to block out the reality of my dilemma. I repeatedly pleaded, 'Not guilty, not guilty', in the vain hope that the message would somehow get through to the twelve most important people in the world at that time.

The news that the jury had completed their deliberations and were ready to give a verdict brought reality sharply into focus. I laboured with every breath as the jury took their seats. The foreman—a tall dark-haired man with a harsh, expressionless face—stood up as the clerk asked whether the panel had reached a decision. He replied, 'Yes.' I thought my chest would cave in under the pressure of that moment.

'Do you find the defendant, Keith Noel Fellowes, guilty or not guilty of the murder of Harold Parkinson?' asked the clerk.

'Not guilty,' responded the foreman.

Instantly my lifeblood returned to me. I started to turn round and make my way out of the dock. I caught a glimpse of my parents, their faces alight with a happiness approaching delirium. But my progress was halted by the screws on either side of me, who kept an iron grip on my forearms.

Somewhere in the court, the drama was continuing, and I was almost oblivious to it. Suddenly I noticed the foreman was still standing and recording a verdict of 'guilty to manslaughter'.

My elation was wiped away amid an outcry from the public gallery. The judge demanded order in the chamber. My legs suddenly caved in underneath me and my body slumped back towards the bench. The screws struggled to raise my dead weight back on my feet. A silent scream lay trapped in my throat. I felt the full terror—I was going to be jailed for a crime I hadn't done. My glance strayed back to the jury, hoping there had been some mistake.

Meanwhile Detective Chief Inspector William Howson was making his way to the witness-box to give further details of my background before sentence. It was ironic it should be Bill Howson. He had been head of the divisional CID when I had been in the constabulary and had at one time called at Morecambe police station to compliment me for a number of good arrests following thefts and vandalism. At that time he had had plans to recruit me as a detective. Now others were making another set of plans for me.

He described me as a native of Windsor, educated at Morecambe, having left school at fifteen. I had taken various jobs before joining Lancashire police in 1968. I had resigned the following year because of an unsettled family life.

My QC then stood and attempted to argue for leniency. After he had finished, Mr Justice Caulfield, whom I had stared at for six days, ordered me to my feet. His voice was a punishment in itself. I half expected him to don a black cap and despatch me to the gallows. He said the case had been particularly tragic for me. The jury had found as fact that I was 'at the very least implicated' in the tying up of Mr Parkinson. They had also found that I had intended some harm on him and, as a result, a life had been lost.

'It would appear to be your own temper which prompted you to enter into this field of activity,' he said.

Again my legs buckled as he handed out a sentence of seven years. I doubt it would have had more impact if he had said seventy years. As I was hustled away from the court for the last time, I glanced into the gallery and saw my mother-in-law and wife, incongruous among the rest because of the smiles playing on their lips. I burst into tears long before the screws had managed to cage me once more into the sweat-box. Once inside, my sobbing became uncontrollable, and every muscle started to shake involuntarily.

Despair consumed my heart and mind. There was nothing else. My parents were allowed in to see me fifteen minutes later but my mother was unable to speak as she held my hand through the bars of the sweat-box. Her pain made mine even worse, although I had not thought that possible.

'They gave me seven years and I am innocent,' said an unfamiliar voice. It was my own.

My father guided my mother away, all attempts to console her failing miserably.

Only a few months earlier I had been carefree and happy-go-lucky. Now, I felt engulfed by the quicksand of an uncaring and biased system, a system which dared to call itself justice.

8
Seven Years

The twenty-ninth of June 1970 was the blackest day of my life. All my hopes were shattered. My head was thumping like a bass drum—the result of the intense pressure and emotional tension I had endured since the early morning. All my expectations of freedom had vanished in one word—*guilty*. Nothing seemed to make sense. How could I be found guilty of a crime I did not commit? Things like that were reserved for fiction writers who dreamt up stories to catch the reader's imagination.

I sat there in deep shock, unable to control the shaking of my entire body. Tears started to flow again. I tried to force them back but within seconds I was sobbing my heart out. They were tears of distress, insecurity and fear. After a short time I managed to control myself by breathing deeply, spurred on by humiliation and embarrassment as the screws outside looked on at the pitiful sight of a totally broken 22-year-old man.

The only thought in the dungeon of my weary mind was the seven years—'*You will go to prison for seven years.*' I could still hear the judge's voice echoing the words. The impact of both sentences was to stay with me for a long, long time. One of the escort screws asked if I would like a sweet cup of tea before the journey back to Risley. I just looked at him, unable to utter a word. My voice had also suffered under the intense state of shock. The next thing I realized was that the same screw had returned with a cup of tea in his hand, saying to me,

'Now come on, Noel. Drink this up. It will help you over the shock.'

He spoke in a very soft and reassuring voice.

I took the cup in my shaking hands and held it to my lips. I tried to drink but found it difficult to control the cup. I finished up pouring half of the contents over myself accidentally.

The screw watched on and said, 'Don't worry, Noel. It's quite understandable, considering the day you've had.'

This was the first time that anybody in the system had offered consolation.

Shortly after eight o'clock we left Lancaster Castle Assizes for the return trip to Risley. I was driven in a prison van under the personal supervision of two screws. Again I had been handcuffed, but now as a convicted killer—the very thought of the label distressed me. The screws were very considerate towards me, engaging me in conversation and trying to reassure me that seven years wasn't really seven years.

One said, 'You'll probably only do a couple of years and get parole. At the very worst you'll only do four years eight months with good behaviour.'

'I'm innocent. I should be outside,' I said.

'You'll get used to it. They'll probably allocate you to an open nick, you being an ex-copper.'

On they went trying to convince me all would be well and in my heart I really believed they were sincere in their speculations of what would happen to me once inside. I could only think of my past months in Her Majesty's care—months of fear, mental stress and the recipient of physical abuse. What was going to happen now I had been convicted? How would I stand up to the increasing threat of violence and intimidation of the cons? I had heard rumours about life inside prisons for convicted coppers. It would be a matter of personal survival at any price. Having just witnessed gross injustice at first hand, I now understood why the cons hated the police so much. Was I to be the punchbag for the cons to vent their hatred on, or would the authorities be humane and sensitive to my dilemma? All I could do was wait and hope for the best. If the past few months were anything to go on, I was finished.

When we arrived back at Risley, I was in an absolute daze.

The screws escorted me to reception and announced my sentence to the senior screw.

'Not bad, Fellowes. You could have got life,' he said.

I just gazed at him without offering an answer.

'Right, Fellowes. You are now a convicted criminal so you will wear grey clothing.'

I was now a con—easily recognized by the colour of my clothes—greys rather than browns. They fitted me out with grey clothes and then escorted me back to the hospital wing. The night screw was on duty in the ward and immediately I arrived he asked if I wanted a sleeping draught (Librium) to calm me down. I declined the offer as I wanted to be able to reflect on the trauma of the day. I walked through the ward to the sound of whispering voices saying,

'What did you get?'

'Seven years. Seven years.'

All I could say each time was seven years. The more I said it, the more daunting it sounded. I lay awake in bed all night going over the final day of the trial, trying to understand how on earth the jury had convicted me of something I had never done. How could I fight the conviction? It seemed as though everyone was convinced I was guilty. My constant denials of the crime and emotive pleas of my innocence had been brushed aside or had fallen on deaf ears. I was on my own now. There was nobody to trust or count on. I decided never to trust anyone again.

The next day the remanded cons in the ward offered their consolation at my sentence and wished me luck in trying to serve it. They didn't have to say why I needed luck. It was written on their faces. They all knew I was an ex-copper and many knew the consequences of such a label 'inside'.

I was still in a state of shock and despair when the senior medical officer came to see me.

'Seven years is not that bad. Don't worry, it will all work out for you.'

What amazed me was the way he said it, with a smile on his face. The man had no idea what seven years really meant. He obviously thought I had done well only getting seven years. To me it represented a lifetime.

'What's going to happen to me?' I asked.

'In a few days you will be going to Walton Prison in Liverpool.'

'What will happen to me at Walton?'

'Well, it's an allocation prison. The Home Office will decide after you have been assessed where you will serve the rest of your sentence.'

Now I knew I would be going to Walton, I wanted to find out what a prison for convicted criminals was like.

I spoke to Swannie on exercise and asked him what to expect. He told me that Risley was Paradise compared to real prisons and I could expect nothing more than hostility from cons and screws alike, as real prison life was nothing less than a cattle market. He went on to explain the routine of local prisons and the need to show no sign of fear or weakness to either screws or cons. If I did, both would capitalize on them, making my life more intolerable than it already was. Swannie was still on remand, so I wasn't sure whether I would see him again. I wished him well for the coming trial. He just shrugged his shoulders and said,

'What will be, will be.'

What a character! He seemed to take everything as it came, unmoved by the seriousness of his situation. If what Swannie said about Walton was true, how on earth was I going to cope?

On the fifth of July 1970 I was informed that I would be transferred to Walton Prison the following day. This information came as a shock as I had been back at Risley less than a week. I felt physically sick at the news and spent another sleepless night worrying about what lay in store for me.

The next morning I was escorted to reception and, along with other cons, was handcuffed and put onto the prison coach, which had small windows covered in security bars and ventilation fans in the roof. We were instructed where to sit on the wooden benches. As I sat there, I surveyed the faces of the other cons—all looked gloomy and despondent, and there was little exchange of conversation on the one-way journey to Walton. Everyone seemed totally lost in their own thoughts.

On arrival at Walton we were quickly moved to the reception area, and were ushered into sweat-boxes and told we would remain there until we were processed. The graffiti on the walls of the sweat-box represented hatred and violence. Nowhere did I see 'Kilroy was here'.

The walls were covered in comments about rozzers, coppers, pigs and screws. Reading some of the more disturbing comments on the police made my heart sink. Swannie was right. Coppers weren't the best-loved people in prisons. The familiar feeling of immense fear gripped me as I awaited the formality of processing.

I sat on the wooden seat awaiting my turn, desperately in need of a cigarette. How things had changed in one week! Since being convicted all remand privileges had been withdrawn, including the ability to buy cigarettes out of my private money. Now I was paid the miserly sum of four shillings and six pence (22p) per week as a convict, only enough to buy myself half an ounce of tobacco, two packets of papers and a box of matches. I had already smoked the lot. I hadn't yet learned the art of rolling cigarettes properly or allocating myself so much tobacco per day.

'811168 Fellowes,' a voice shouted out.

'That's me,' I said.

The sweat-box door opened and a screw said, 'Follow me.'

I was processed in the usual manner, given clothing, bedding, and so on, and then I was taken to the main prison. The screw opened the door leading into the main prison block and I stepped inside. The first thing that hit me was the volume of noise—cons shouting and their voices echoing through the long tall wings of the cell-blocks. Hundreds of cons were walking about on various landings with chamber pots and jugs, all heading in different directions.

'You're lucky, Fellowes,' the screw said. 'It's slop-out

time, then association.'

Little did he know that I hadn't got a clue what he meant. I just said, 'Oh, really.'

Walton was a Victorian prison, built in the classic star shape, with four wings going off from the centre where the chief screws operated from. Each wing had four landings with cells either side. There was a wire mesh screen covering the open space between the rows of cell-blocks on the second landing, protecting anyone walking on the ground floor (the ones) where association and recreation facilities were located. This wire also was to save anyone who decided to jump off the fours—without it they could easily kill themselves. Lastly, the wire protected the discipline screws who supervised association, as without the wire cons could throw objects at them off the threes or fours, causing serious injury.

The senior screw allocated me a single cell in 'B' wing, saying, 'You're lucky, Fellowes. Everyone is three in a cell here, but seeing you're a long-termer I've given you a single cell.'

Still clutching my bedding and clothing, a screw took me down to 'B' wing and my cell.

'There you are, lad. This is yours. You'd better get yourself organized.'

I entered the cell and the screw banged the door behind me. My first impression was one of utter horror. The cell was about six feet wide by twelve feet long with brick walls painted in appalling colours. The floor was of quarry tiles and the whole place smelt of damp. The furniture included a bed with a sponge mattress, a wooden chair, chamber pot, water jug, plastic bowl and that was it. What a contrast to the hospital ward at Risley! This was definitely the worst living accommodation I had ever set eyes on. 'How could anybody be expected to survive in such conditions?' I asked myself. It was the worst form of human degradation. I sat on the bed, bewildered. Was this to be my way of life from now on?

My first night at Walton was sleepless. I could feel the bed springs through the sponge mattress and whichever way I turned or lay, comfort was not to be found. The pillow felt like a lump of crushed concrete. It was a bad night's sleep.

The next day, following slopping-out and breakfast, I was escorted to the administration block for various interviews. I sat with other cons who had arrived the previous day, who were also to be more closely processed.

First of all I met the social welfare officer who tried to assure me that whilst in custody he would look after my welfare. What a joke! He didn't know what he was promising! Still, the sign on the door must have given him some job satisfaction. At least he could be used by the system to gather information about home circumstances and problems. Next stop was IQ testing and various other psychological tests.

I asked what the tests were for.

The civvy shrink said, 'They are used to assess your educational maturity and what work will best suit you in prison.'

'What a load of nonsense! They must be used for something more devious than that,' I thought to myself. I did the IQ test to the best of my ability but spoiled the rest of the papers. I wasn't prepared to play their silly games. The shrink interviewed me and asked why I had spoiled the papers.

'Because it's bad enough being in here, without you trying to treat me like a guinea-pig.'

That concluded the interview and next stop was the prison chaplain. All he wanted to know was what religion I was— Protestant or Catholic. I said I was christened a Protestant and wasn't a Christian by any stretch of the imagination. The last stop was the Assistant Governor's office. This was an official meeting.

'811168 Fellowes,' bellowed the screw at the top of his voice.

I stood up and the screw told me to march into the office, stand to attention and speak my number and name to the Assistant Governor. I walked in and did the necessary. I was severely reprimanded by the chief screw who said,

'Sir! You always address members of staff as Sir. Start

109

again, Fellowes.'

'811168 Fellowes, Sir.'

'That's better,' said a little wisp of a man sitting behind a desk double his size. 'We'll soon get you used to prison life and terminology.'

He went on to explain my earliest release date with remission would be the end of 1974. However, he told me that in between I would be interviewed for parole. Furthermore, he told me I was only at Walton to be allocated to a long-term prison and to be categorized by the prison department of the Home Office. That was the end of that interview and off I went back to my peter [cell].

I remained banged up for a couple of days, only coming out of my peter to collect meals and to slop out. Apparently this was the system's way of breaking in new prisoners. It suited me as I didn't want to mix with the other cons in case they found out who I really was. Nevertheless, I was going through depression following the shock of being convicted. There seemed no escape from the nightmare of it all. I relived the trial daily. It all seemed so brutally unjust. The same questions flowed through my mind day in and day out. Why did so many people want to put me away?

A few days later a screw opened the door and said, 'Right, Fellowes. You've been allocated to work in the canvas shop. Follow me.'

My heart sank. 'Where on earth am I going? What is the canvas shop?' I thought. I followed the screw, who was locking and unlocking doors, endlessly it seemed. Eventually we arrived at the canvas shop. Inside, I found fifty to sixty cons eyeing me over. My insecurity rose and I started to tremble inside. This was definitely not the best situation to be in. The workshop screw came over and told me to join a group of cons cutting up canvas. They would show me the ropes, he said. I sat down and one con showed me what to do. Then I noticed a con I had been on remand with at Risley. He recognized me and started talking to the other cons in his group.

110

Within minutes heads were turning and eyes were staring at me. It reminded me of the Memorial Hall when I was led out by Mounsey. The same feeling welled up inside me—fear and trepidation. Instantly, danger signals were ringing in my head. He was telling them I was an ex-copper. Before long, the word was out to the rest of the cons, as they passed on the information, one to another.

Eventually it reached the group I was working with. Then a scouse con said, 'Is that right, la. You're an ex-pig?'

'Yes, I was.'

'Well, la, we don't like pigs.'

'Neither do I,' I said.

With that the conversation ended and I was totally ignored. The bell went for the end of the work period. It was lunch-time. All the cons started to leave and I decided to wait until last as I didn't want to be involved in any accidents. They all trooped out, each casting an angry glance in my direction as they departed. Then I recognized another con who had been on remand at Risley with me. He had got life for stabbing his girlfriend in a romantic bust-up. He walked over to the exit door and beckoned me over. I waited until most cons had left and walked over to him.

'Look, Noel. You're in great danger here.'

'Yes, I know that.'

'Listen, mate. They're planning to shiv you this afternoon, so don't come back to work.'

'What can I do? What do you mean—shiv me?'

'Stab you, that's what, cut you up a bit,' he said.

Those were definitely words I didn't want to hear. I feared the worst. 'The animals want to kill me,' I thought. 'How can I avoid such a confrontation? If they're out to get me, get me they will.'

I followed the procession back to the cell-block, picked up my dinner and made for the safety of my peter. I couldn't eat. I was sick at the thought of what would happen in the afternoon. The screw came to bang us up for the dinner break and I asked him if I could have a quick word.

'What is it, la?' he asked.

111

I told him what had happened in the workshop and asked him if there was anything I could do.

'Leave it with me, la,' he said and banged me up. Some thirty minutes or so later the door opened and a screw instructed me to follow him.

'What for?'

'You're off to see the Assistant Governor,' he said.

Upon arrival I went through the usual formalities of number, name and Sir. The Assistant Governor looked at me sympathetically and said, 'I hear you're frightened for your safety, Fellowes.'

'Yes, Sir,' I said.

'Well, we could put you under protection on Rule 43. That means you will be locked up with sex offenders who are on protection. Now you don't want that, do you?' he asked.

'No, Sir. The cons will think I'm a nonce [sex offender] as well.'

'That's right, they will. So you leave us with a problem on our hands,' he said.

I started to apologize, then he stopped me.

'No need to apologize, Fellowes. I am aware of your problem and I will try to sort it out this afternoon.'

I was dismissed and taken back to my peter. The bell sounded for afternoon work and I could hear the screws unlocking the doors on the landings. My heart started to beat faster and faster as I heard the door next to mine being unlocked. What was to happen to me? Would they send me to work? A sense of relief flooded through me as I heard the screw pass my door without unlocking it. At least I would be safe for a little while longer. I lay back on my bed, the thumping of my heart slowly returning to normal.

Mid-afternoon the door opened and the Assistant Governor entered. I sprang to my feet immediately.

'Well, Fellowes. We have considered your dilemma and we have found a temporary solution. You will be transferred to the hospital wing and kept there until you are allocated to a long-term prison. OK?'

'Yes, Sir,' I said.

He left and another screw said, 'Pack your things, Fellowes. You're going now.'

I quickly grabbed my things and off we went to the hospital wing where I was allocated a single peter and banged up. The facilities and the bed were far superior to those I had just left. Besides, now I was safe again. How long could I keep avoiding what seemed inevitable—a real encounter with the cons who wanted to get at me, at any price?

In the evening I felt really low. I considered how I could possibly survive the daily torment, fear and mental anguish. I had no expectations of life. All was lost in despair and deprivation. Everything I had treasured in life was gone for ever. Mine was indeed a hopeless existence. There was no purpose or inner strength left. I had given my all.

I wallowed in self-pity for a while. Was this my destiny—a life of insecurity and fear? I knew there was no way I could stand it for another four years. I lay on the bed, filled with distress, and the tears started to flow again. There I was, my knees up to my chest, crying my heart out, biting the end of the pillow in sheer desperation. I decided there was no future in being locked away. It was not just the physical prison, but, worse still, the prison of my mind. I decided the easiest way out was to top myself.

It was then that I noticed a conduit attached to the ceiling. It seemed very well secured, so I managed to tear a sheet up and make a noose, then I tied the sheet to the conduit by standing on the frame of the bed and attached the noose to my neck. With tears running down my cheeks, I jumped off the bed. Just my luck—the conduit came adrift from the ceiling and I ended up on the floor with nothing more than a ricked neck. Even the noose hadn't worked.

Now I was in an even worse situation. I had damaged prison property and would probably lose some of my remission. The stupidity of the situation brought me back to earth with a bang—pardon the pun. I detached the sheet and hammered the conduit back into position with my fist. To my surprise it held, the plugs going back into their original holes. At least something was going right. The sheet was a definite problem. I wasn't sure how I was going to get over that one. I lay in bed trying to work out a way of changing the sheet without the screws finding out how it had been damaged. There was no way I wanted to be put in the padded cell or—worse still—lose remission. Still, if nothing else, the attempt to top myself had broken my emotional crisis. Now at least I was thinking more rationally. Only a few minutes before I had been trying to end it all. Now I was trying to save myself from being charged with damaging prison property.

The next morning following slop-out and breakfast I was visited by the senior medical officer who was doing his rounds on the wing. It was the usual introduction—number, name and Sir—even in a prison hospital! One could imagine a dying convict lying in his bed with only hours to live, uttering his last words in this life—number and name. Prison rules, regulations and procedures are no respecters of persons.

'How are you today, Fellowes?' asked the SMO.

'Very well, thank you, Sir.'

'No problems then?'

'No, Sir.'

With that he left, under the escort of the senior hospital screw. An hour or so later the door to my peter opened and in walked the senior hospital screw.

'You feeling all right, Fellowes?' he asked.

'Yes, Sir.'

'What happened to the conduit then?'

'What do you mean?'

'Looks to me as though someone has been tampering with it.'

My stomach turned over. Eagle eyes had spotted my misdemeanour.

'Look, Fellowes, why don't you tell me what happened?'

I told him about my emotional distress the previous night and my circumstances since my arrest, which took at least ten minutes to explain.

He looked at me, unmoved, and said, 'Look, son. I am

114

fully aware of your circumstances. That's why you're in this hospital wing. I'm here to help you. If you get any more inclinations of a similar nature then ask to see me. OK?'

'Yes, Sir. Thank you, Sir,' I said.

'We will keep the incident to ourselves. In the meantime give me the sheet and I will see to it.'

He left with the two strips of sheet bundled up in his arm and banged me up again. What a relief! At least there was one screw who showed signs of compassion and understanding. There was hope for me yet. Just sharing my anxiety with him for a few minutes had made me feel that much better. At least he listened to me and acted in my interests instead of the authority's.

Since my arrival at Walton, I had kept up my letter-writing to my parents and my solicitor, Mr McHugh. In those early days the mail censor must have been fed up, continually reading my pleas of innocence and injustice. Whilst in the hospital wing I received an application form to appeal against conviction and sentence. I eagerly filled in the form and sent it back to Mr McHugh. At least this was something to look forward to. But weeks passed with no word back.

At last I received a letter from Mr McHugh saying he had sought counsel's advice. Their conclusions were that I couldn't appeal against conviction on the grounds that there had been no new evidence. He added that I had been given a fair trial, all things considered, and said I could, if I wished, appeal against sentence. But they felt seven years was not a harsh sentence considering the severity of the crime. In my disappointment I found myself drifting into a very low depressive state once more. The appeal had been my last hope—now even that was lost. I would have to do my bird and also live with the injustice of my conviction and sentence. There was to be no freedom or liberty this time. The faceless judiciary had closed my file.

I went through the motions of appealing against sentence, but, as expected, I received a refusal. Once more I wrote to Mr McHugh, stating that all I could do was to continue protesting my innocence and—however long it took—one day I would clear my name. I never heard from Mr McHugh again.

Three months into my sentence a crime took place 100 miles away in the small town of Warsop, Nottinghamshire. I knew nothing about the place, the crime, the victim or the villains. If somebody had given me the details it still wouldn't have meant a thing to me. But, like so many other factors in my case, its importance only came to the surface later.

In a small wages office in Warsop Town Hall, council clerk Mr Neal Hunt was sitting at a desk, making sure employees would receive their weekly pay on time. He was sitting with his back to the door as three men crept in. A gloved hand suddenly covered his mouth and a voice said: 'Don't struggle and you won't get hurt.' The clerk was dragged into a corner where his ankles and wrists were tied together with pieces of calico bandage. The men sellotaped his mouth to keep him from raising the alarm. Then they rifled £660 in wages from an unlocked safe and left.

On the train back to Manchester the haul was split into three. Two of the men—Lenny Pilot and Billy Clark—decided to get rid of the evidence during the journey and hurled the empty wage packets from the windows of the train.

Pilot—a salesman obsessed with making money the easy way—and Clark—a small-time crook with a string of convictions for petty crime—had plenty to celebrate. The information about the Warsop job had been spot-on. They decided they would use the source again. The three had worked together efficiently. With £220 each, it was not bad pay for an afternoon's work. The beer would flow in Manchester's city centre pubs that night.

The days locked in my peter seemed to get longer and longer. Already I felt as if I had been locked away for years, yet it had only been a couple of months. Being banged up as I was for twenty-three hours a day, week in, week out, only added to the torture of my mind. There were few welcome breaks in

116

the monotony of killing time.

I did receive regular visits from my parents. Those visits brought me back to the reality of life for a couple of hours, but the cost was heartbreaking. It was a reminder of all I had lost and it used to take me days to get over them.

By September 1970 I had become thoroughly introverted and isolated. I never spoke to anyone and all I could think of was revenge. I used to spend the best part of every day reliving the arrest, the remand at Risley and the trial. A small cancer of hatred for all the witnesses who had, in my view, deliberately concealed the truth, formed deep inside me. I kept on feeding the hatred with evil thoughts and the desire for the day of revenge. At least I would have the pleasure of making them all suffer for stitching me up. I just wanted them to have a taste of what I had suffered mentally and physically since my imprisonment—fear, violence, intimidation and mental torture. Then they would realize the cost of their carefully selected words.

I was totally embittered against all those who had robbed me of my freedom and put me inside—the police, courts, prison authorities and everyone else who had taken a part in my incarceration. I was changing from a passive individual into an aggressive monomaniac whose sole purpose in life was to survive the sentence and fulfil an ambition of revenge.

On the fourteenth of October 1970 I was informed by the Assistant Governor that my allocation papers had arrived and I would be leaving Walton for Wakefield top security prison the next day. As I returned to my peter I asked myself why they were sending me to a top security prison. I remembered the screws on the way back from the trial saying I would probably go to a semi-open nick, seeing I was an ex-copper. Once more I was the victim of the system's callous approach to my safety. I had been in solitary for the last three months. Now they were going to put me amongst top security prisoners. There was no arguing with the authorities. All you could do was go where you were allocated. I was only a faceless number. While in its custody the system decided my every move.

Wakefield was some two hundred miles away from my family, but that wasn't a point to be considered. I knew in my heart the system had dealt me a raw deal—all because I continued to plead my innocence. The public have the notion that all cons protest their innocence. The truth is that the majority admit their guilt and get on with their bird. For me, Wakefield represented yet another challenge. I sank on the bed in nervous anticipation of what tomorrow would bring.

9

Doing Bird

The fifteenth of October had arrived. This was the day of departure from Walton. I packed my personal belongings and gave my peter one last look over. For the past three months it had been the scene of much personal anguish and thought. In my isolation I had become accustomed to my surroundings. Only the walls knew my innermost thoughts and fears.

The senior screw opened the door to my peter and announced it was time to go.

'Best of luck, Fellowes. I hope you succeed in the future,' he said.

'Thanks.'

He was the only screw who could have said those few words to me, as he had been the one who helped me through the early weeks at Walton. In reception I changed from prison clothing back into my civvies. It was really quite strange to wear my own clothes again. They had been kept in a cardboard box and smelt of dried sweat and damp. Once dressed, it was into the sweat-box to await the escort. The artistic graffiti reflecting Liverpudlian humour hadn't changed. Every inch of the sweat-box was covered in it. Some forty-five minutes later, the escort arrived and I found myself being handcuffed and escorted to the prison coach, similar to the one I had travelled in from Risley.

To my surprise I found myself with about twenty other cons who were also being transferred. I learnt that we were dropping some off at Manchester nick—known among the criminal fraternity as the Strangeways Hotel—then on to Wakefield. There was much chatter among the cons about their experiences in Walton. I listened intently to their conversations, trying to gather information about Wakefield.

There was little to learn as nobody on board had done time in Wakefield. We dropped the majority of the cons off at Strangeways and continued to Wakefield. By early afternoon we had arrived.

I felt very nervous disembarking from the coach. The first thing I saw was the high external security walls mounted with closed-circuit television cameras. We were escorted to reception where again I relinquished my civvy clothes for the standard prison uniform. At least I was given new clothing and shoes this time. They fitted me perfectly. The scene at reception was different from what I had encountered at both Risley and Walton. The screws seemed more relaxed and chatty. Also there wasn't the usual facility of sweat-boxes. Perhaps it was because there were only five cons to be processed.

Fully equipped, we were led to another room where we were individually photographed. For this procedure they chalked my number, 811168, on a board and I had to hold it across my chest while being photographed. This again was mandatory. Following this, a senior screw welcomed us to Wakefield Prison by giving us our allotted wings and peter numbers. Mine was to be a shared cell on the ones 'C' wing. Like Walton, Wakefield was built in a star shape with four wings. It housed over 600 inmates—all long-term cons doing a minimum sentence of four years and a maximum of life. The screw told us that we would find the regime more relaxed than that of local prisons, because the majority of cons were doing life sentences.

So now I knew the reason for the authorities putting me here. *They wanted to destroy me totally*, I said to myself. I did not look forward to doing my bird with a few hundred convicted murderers. It was bad enough at Risley and Walton, but this place had to be hell on earth. My stomach turned over at the thought of the cons finding out about my career in the police force. I broke out in a cold sweat and my insides started to shake. Was it to be a long time in solitary again? Introductions over, we were led into the main cell-block area. The first impression was one of immense activity and noise, and I experienced a great feeling of insecurity. A screw directed me to 'C' wing, where I was introduced to the senior screw in charge. He in turn told another screw to show me to my allocated quarters on the ones.

I was taken down to the dormitory, which was two peters hashed into one and bedded four cons. Inside I met three other cons—two Geordies and a Scouse. I quickly learned they were doing six years each for various robberies. Then came the question.

'How long you doing?'

'Seven years,' I said.

'What you in for?' another asked.

'Manslaughter.'

'That's all right, as long as you're not a nonce [sex offender]. We don't want to be banged up with nonces,' he said.

'Don't they have a special wing for nonces here?' I asked.

'No. There is no Rule 43 in this nick. Everyone is a long-term prisoner. They mix everyone together,' said the Geordie.

I was feeling my way.

'Don't they get attacked then?'

'Yeh, of course they do, la, but you gotta be careful or the screws bust yer and put yer in the cooler [punishment block] for a stretch.'

At least I was going to be safer in this nick than the last two, I thought.

The rest of the evening was taken up with conversation about the merits and demerits of Wakefield prison and the more I heard, the more assured I felt about the place. Apparently this was a more relaxed prison as far as discipline went, because the lifers would do anything between nine and twenty years inside. So the screws were more tolerant in stretching the rules to make life easier for themselves. The other good point was that haircuts were left to the individual con rather than the usual practice of being sheared every two weeks—something I had endured since being convicted.

'Why are the ones split into small dormitories with four in each dorm?' I asked.

'It's a case of allocation. The lifers get the single peters first

121

and so on down the line until your name comes up,' said the Geordie.

Sounded a fair system to me. After all, anyone serving life deserved a single peter.

My first night's sleep at Wakefield was a good one. It seemed like years since I had enjoyed conversation with anyone. All the time I had spent in solitary at Walton seemed to be washed away in one evening.

The next morning I went through the usual formalities of slopping-out, washing, shaving, tidying the dorm and then breakfast. The food was still the same stodgy rubbish that only a cast-iron stomach could cope with. The bell went for work and the other three left. I was to stay in the dorm until I had been processed again. It was the usual procedure—welfare officer, education officer and the Deputy Governor. I entered the Deputy Governor's office.

'811168 Fellowes, Sir.'

'Well, Fellowes. It says here you are still protesting your innocence.'

'Yes, Sir,' I replied.

'Good. We don't want any trouble with you here, considering you're an ex-policeman. You should be able to cope with the system and you will have opportunity to study if you want to.'

'Thank you, Sir.'

'Any questions, Fellowes?'

'No, Sir.'

The interview over, I was told that until more suitable work could be found for me, I had been allocated to the mail-bag shop. Upon arrival at the bag shop I was given a long thick needle, beeswaxed thread and canvas and was told to join the other cons on the hard benches. The final instruction was that I had to sew the bag nine stitches to the inch. The target for the week was five completed mail-bags. After about an hour I had managed about one-and-a-half inches. My problem was that I kept stabbing myself with the needle.

Lunch-time arrived and the screw checked the morning's work. He informed me that my stitching was wrong and I would have to unpick it and start again. After lunch we returned to the mail-bag shop. I noticed some of the cons were working feverishly, so I asked the con next to me why they were working so hard.

'If you complete more than the five a week, you get a bonus in your wages,' he said.

'How much?'

'Anything up to four shillings,' he said.

I couldn't believe my eyes. These men were working their fingers to the bone for four shillings (20p) extra. I'd heard of slave labour but this was ridiculous. At the end of the afternoon I had managed to complete about three inches of work, so I owed them money.

The screw called me over.

'Call this a day's work, do you, Fellowes?'

I didn't answer.

'If you carry on like this, lad, you'll never get out of this shop.'

'There are machines that can do a far better job than I can,' I replied.

'Machines aren't doing bird, though, and you are. We'll soon knock you into shape, Fellowes. I will be keeping an eye on you in future.'

I left the shop, picked up my tea and returned to the dorm. The lads asked how I had fared in the afternoon and I told them the bad news. We all had a laugh over the incident I'd had with the screw. They agreed I would probably be in the bag shop for a number of years.

The door was opened at six o'clock for association. Association meant you could play darts, table tennis, cards, board games or watch the television all on the ones. Usually you had to try to break into the cliques if you wanted to join in, as many of the leisure activities had been shared among the prison élite for years and most were lifers. I stayed in the dorm to read. At least I could enjoy a bit of peace and quiet.

Some twenty minutes later three cons entered the dorm.

One stood by the door. He pushed it nearly closed and stood there on guard. The adrenalin started to flow through my body. I knew instantly they weren't paying me a social visit.

'We're the reception committee,' one said.

'Now we're going to protect you from all the other animals in here,' said the other.

'Why do I need protection?' I asked.

'Because the news editor on 'B' wing has read up your case.'

'So what?'

'You're an ex-copper and cons don't like ex-coppers, do they, lads?'

The other two nodded in agreement.

'What do you want then?' I asked.

'Well, you pay us your wages in tobacco every week and we'll make sure no harm comes to you.'

'And if I don't?'

'Well then, we'll have to give you a lesson in manners.'

I sat there trying to weigh up my chances of escape and quickly realized there weren't any. I was shaking inside and I was petrified of what they might do to me. I noticed my metal meal tray was on the bedside locker so I eased myself off the bed and said, 'You seem to have me in a tight corner. Whatever I do, it seems I lose.'

With that the three of them started laughing to each other.

'You sure do.'

I leant over the cabinet with my back to one of them and wrapped my hands tightly round the food tray. In one continuous movement I swiftly turned, crashing the tray into the con's face. He went down, the blood streaming down his face. I stood there, shocked at what I'd done for a moment, and before I could gather myself I was seeing stars. Blows raged around my head and body and I heard something crack loudly on my face. The next thing I saw was the floor coming up to meet me. The blows raged on and again I felt the impact around my head. I was still semi-conscious and heard one of them say,

'I'll get you for this you bastard.'

With that comment still ringing in my ears they left. My head felt as though it had been used as a football. I lay there in a daze. I could not focus on anything. I tried to get off the ground but I couldn't. I started to vomit quite violently, which only aggravated my breathing. At that point I thought the end had come. I was definitely going to die.

Some time later I heard an echo in my head.

'Noel, Noel,' the voice said.

I stirred a little and recognized the cold brick walls of the dorm.

'You all right, mate?' asked Joey, the Geordie.

'Yeh, sure I am,' I said.

He picked me up off the floor saying,

'Wow, you do look a mess. Hang on, I'll get the other lads.'

Within minutes all my cell-mates were present. They washed me up and then asked me what had happened. I told them the story, including the reason for their visit.

'You might as well know, lads. I'm an ex-copper but I had left the job before they stitched me up with this.'

'We already know about that,' said Alan. 'It makes no difference to us.'

'In future, till you've learned the ropes, stick with us,' said Joey. 'If you injured one of them they will try to get you again.'

That was the last thing I wanted to hear. I checked my face out in the metal mirror and already I could see bruising starting to show itself around my eyes. My nose felt really sore and when I touched it pain went reeling through my head. On closer examination I could see that it was leaning towards the left side of my face. I remembered the crack I had heard during the attack and realized my nose was broken.

Joey said he would find out who the cons were who beat me up and then we could plan a counter-attack. I told him I wasn't interested in that as I had to fight my own battles from now on. All I wanted was the names and peter numbers.

'It's not as easy as that,' said Joey. 'You're living among some real animals in here, Noel. They will shiv you for a dirty look, mate. You'll have to learn fast.'

I already knew that but I was determined to survive at any cost. If I couldn't do my bird the easy way, then I would have to do it the hard way. I was growing up fast. I knew the law of the jungle—the fittest and the strongest survived. Now I needed to become both super-fit and strong. The lads told me that you could go to the gym twice a week to do fitness work. Also there were weightlifting classes twice a week in the evenings. I decided to join both. At this stage of my sentence I was six foot one inch tall, weighing in at twelve stone six pounds.

I woke up the following day, hardly able to open my eyes. My whole face and head were tender and painful. I looked in the mirror which reflected something of a horror story—two black eyes and the bridge of my nose was deep purple. What a sight! I skipped breakfast and rested a while longer. The lads in the dorm made a number of jocular comments about my looks, all in good fun, trying to snap me out of my sullen mood. The bell went for work and off I trundled, my head kept down, to the mail-bag shop. I doubted if I would be able to thread the needle, let alone sew a mail-bag.

On my arrival, the workshop screw gave me the once over and I took up the task of trying to sew a mail-bag. The other cons were glancing at my injured head and passing comments to each other. The screw called me over and asked how I came to have the injuries.

'I fell down the stairs,' I said.

'There must have been a lot of stairs. Come on, Fellowes, pull the other one.'

I remained silent as all the other cons looked on, waiting for a reply.

'Better take you over to the sick-bay, lad. Let a doctor look at you,' he said.

'No thanks. I'm fine. They're only bruises.'

'Bruises or not, lad, you can't work. Come with me.'

I returned to the main prison and into the medical room. I refused the doctor but took some aspirin for the headache. The screw banged me up in the dorm and I fell asleep on my bed. At lunch-time the lads came in and offered to get my lunch for me. I still felt rough so I declined the offer. After being banged up for some fifteen minutes, the door opened again and I was informed the Assistant Governor wanted to see me.

Upon arrival I said, '811168 Fellowes, Sir.'

'Now what happened to you, Fellowes? I hear you told one of my officers you fell down the stairs.'

'Yes, Sir, I did.'

'I find that rather hard to believe, seeing you're located on the ones. There are no stairs there.'

'I was on the twos going down to the ones and I slipped.'

'There's another inmate with a large gash on his face. You wouldn't happen to know anything about that, would you?' he asked.

'No, Sir.'

'This particular person is known to be a bit of a bully and a hard case and I think he had a go at you, Fellowes.'

'No, Sir, I fell down the stairs.'

I knew if I grassed him up my life would be hell. I had to stand my ground so the other cons would see me as one of them.

'Very well, Fellowes. On your way and take note—my officers will be keeping an eye on you in future.'

'Thank you, Sir,' I said.

'By the way, I have instructed the senior officer to allocate you the next single cell that becomes available.'

Special treatment, I thought to myself. He really does mean to keep an eye on me. I left his office feeling somewhat proud of what I had achieved. Soon the cons would learn I hadn't grassed and I would at least gain some respect. When I got back I told the lads what had happened and they were as pleased about the result as I was. This had been the first day of my fightback campaign and already I was feeling better for it.

During the remaining days of that week I found out about the rest of prison routine. A weekday in Wakefield looked like this:

127

6.40 a.m.	Unlock/slop out
7.00 a.m.	Breakfast
8.40 a.m.	Work/education block
11.15 a.m.	Lunch
11.50 a.m.	Lock up (in cells)
1.10 p.m.	Unlock
1.30 p.m.	Work/education block
4.00 p.m.	Tea
4.50 p.m.	Lock up
6.00 p.m.	Unlock/association/evening classes
8.30 p.m.	Lock up

I enrolled on the keep-fit and weightlifting classes. I was still nervous and ultra-cautious, moving about the wing making sure I was always near to a wall and could see what was in front or behind me. The cons who had beaten me up were probably still out for revenge. Joey told me the names of my attackers and their locations. On association one night he had pointed them all out to me. I took a mental photograph of their faces and planned my own revenge on them, for time was on my side. They weren't going anywhere for a while—all three were lifers.

Saturday arrived to the sound of cons busy cleaning out their peters. This was the general procedure on Saturdays, year in, year out. The cons on the fours, threes and twos would shake their blankets over the landings and we on the ones would try and contend with the dust. Most cons kept their peters immaculate, for to them it was home. The rest of the morning was taken up with association, as there was no work at weekends. At about ten o'clock the dart school would start up—anything from fifteen to twenty cons playing round-the-clock darts, which entailed hitting one to twenty, a double, treble, 25 and finally bull. The first one to finish won the prize which was a cigarette from all the other players. To listen to them you would have thought they were playing for the World Cup.

Then there was the table tennis school. The winner always stayed on the table. Some of the cons were semi-professionals.

Over the years they had perfected their game. When new-comers arrived at the table, they would be given a fifteen-point start and usually end up losing 21–15. The trouble with table tennis was the noise. The sound of the ball striking the table would echo throughout the wing and you could hear cries of anguish and profane comments from the old lags (cons who have done a number of stretches inside) who were trying to have a lie-in at the weekend.

After lunch everyone used to gather round, waiting for the highlight of the weekend—the football match. Wakefield, I learned, had a very good football team, made up mostly of lifers. The only problem was, they only played home matches. Visiting teams used to enjoy coming in and playing because it guaranteed a capacity gate of 600 spectators, whereas the usual gate at their own outside matches was just a handful. The spectators always voiced their opinion as to the quality of football being played in colourful language, which added to the escapism of the weekly event.

The tobacco barons were always active on a Saturday afternoon, usually giving odds of three to one, depending on the strength of the opposition. The odds were better if you wanted to predict a player who would score the first goal. As in all prisons, tobacco was the currency that cons lived by, although the rules only allowed any inmate to have two ounces maximum in his possession. On a good day the barons could win up to thirty or forty ounces. Their runners collected the winnings and dispensed the tobacco among the wings to minders. It was a highly organized business and if a con tried to welch on his bet, the baron would send in his heavy mob to persuade the offender to pay up. They always did. Another facility in their operation was to loan out tobacco with interest. Many cons lived beyond their means and mounted up large debts to the barons. The barons in turn would demand that the con, on his next visit, should have money sent to the baron's personal account or to his dependents outside. This was a way of building up useful collateral to be used on release.

Sundays were a repeat of the Saturday routine, with the

exception of the option of attending church services. Only a tiny minority of cons went to these services and then most of them only went to promote their chances of parole. That was the general opinion, anyway. In the afternoon there was an inter-wing football match, which always offered incident as the teams were not always chosen on merit, rather on performance in the rankings of muscle power. Many duels were fought out on the pitch because the screws would take offending players back to their respective wings and bang them up. The good news was that you were never charged if it took place on the pitch, so many grievances were resolved there without penalty of loss of remission.

Sunday evening always produced a long line of cons outside sick-bay with various injuries acquired in the afternoon. Bruised heads and black eyes were the pattern and all received the same beneficial treatment—a small tot of aspirin water. There was an unwritten rule among the cons—whatever happened on the field was never taken up again on the wings, for nobody wanted to lose the privilege of the football matches. So intense was the competition in inter-wing football that 'B' wing operated a system of scrutinizing cons at reception and if they were potential players, the trustee would try to get the con allocated on to 'B' wing. The barons even tried to operate a transfer market, offering inducements to players so they would ask for a wing transfer. Big business prison football, so some people thought. But the barons were parasites, living and feeding themselves off other people's efforts and weaknesses, and they were despised in reality. Every few months a baron would fall and a new one emerge in a constant power struggle that no one ever really won. The trouble with being king of the jungle is that there is always someone else who wants the same power and supremacy. Natural leaders seemed to stay in office a far greater length of time than ladder-jumpers.

My eyes and nose returned to normal and I felt quietly confident that if trouble arose again I would be able to handle it myself. I joined the gym classes and weightlifting course. It

130

proved tough at first. I had always considered myself a rather fit person, but the first time I donned shorts and trainers and started the gym routine, I thought my lungs were going to collapse. Every muscle in my body ached for days. The physical training instructor, Don Hemingway, certainly put you through the paces. Yet I warmed to him. Although he was a screw, he was never out of his track-suit and he seemed to encourage everybody, however unfit or uncoordinated they were. The cons had a nickname for him which was H. He didn't mind at all—at least he never showed it.

When I first started weight training it was all I could manage to lift the barbell with fifty odd pounds on the end. Some of the cons around me were pumping a couple of hundred pounds repetitively. I felt like the guy who had sand kicked in his face. Still, you can only start at the beginning, as H. said to me on the first session. The hatred I had stored up against all my enemies was enough to keep the adrenalin flowing. I was determined to be fit, strong and healthy. When the muscles in my body screamed out, a result of painful fatigue, I reminded myself of all the past injustice and violence I had been exposed to and kept pumping iron. I learnt fast and did every bodybuilding exercise to clinical perfection. The more it hurt, the more I liked it, as I realized that only breaking the pain barrier achieved the result I was looking for—more strength and fitness.

During the early weeks of my fitness campaign, I was allocated a single peter on the twos, very near to the wing office where the senior screw for the wing resided. I was pleased at the move, even though the lads in the dorm were warm and friendly. It was good to be on my own again. I could do what I wanted in my peter without having to consider anyone else. Much to my dismay, I had been transferred from the mail-bag shop to the loom shop, where they wove prison blankets on dated mechanized looms. I felt it was punishment dished out to me because I had never completed one mail-bag in the two weeks I was there. In fact, the mail-bag screw was most upset as I had been the only con he could remember who hadn't produced a mail-bag.

'You have a large chip on your shoulder, Fellowes, and someday someone is going to knock it off,' he told me on my last day in the bag shop.

'Well, I doubt very much it will be you,' I said.

By this time I was totally embittered and didn't give a damn for anyone in authority. I had endured enough and was willing to give them as much as they gave me. It was all a psychological game inside—who dares wins.

The loom shop was, if anything, worse than the bag shop. The noise was deafening, and you left with the sound of the loom still ringing in your ears. The instructor had shown me how to operate the loom, loading and unloading the shuttles and how to start and stop the machine. My problem was, I didn't intend to learn how to operate it, because if I did I knew they would keep me in that shop. My loom spent more time being fixed than actually working. The yarns kept getting twisted and the shuttle would get stuck in the machine.

On the second day in the shop the shop screw said to me, 'How is it, Fellowes, that yours is the only loom that isn't producing anything?'

'I've got no co-ordination and I'm left-handed. This is a right-handed loom, boss,' I answered.

He looked thoughtfully at the loom for a minute and said, 'You could be right. I've never thought of that before.'

'It really frustrates me, boss. I'll never be able to master it.'

He walked away, still pondering over what I'd said and I knew I had pulled a fast one. I'd convinced him it was a right-handed loom.

In the middle of that week my interview with the senior education officer took place. He wasn't a screw, but he had all the hallmarks of a civil servant. At first I listened to his introduction on the educational facilities they had at Wakefield with my mind already made up. I wasn't having any of it. He was talking about the courses they were running for illiterate and semi-literate cons. If nothing else I could at least read and write.

Following the introduction he said, 'Well, Fellowes, what can we offer you?'

'From what you've already said, nothing.'

'That was to give you a feel for the work we are doing here. As for you, it would be beneficial to use your time in building for the future.'

'What with?'

'You're an ex-policeman, so you must have had a reasonable education behind you. We can help you build on that.'

He went on to explain the facility they had for full-time education and recommended that I start an Ordinary National Diploma course in Business Studies. The study subjects were accountancy, commerce, British Constitution, statistics and English.

'There is a price to pay if you go on full-time education,' he said.

'What sort of a price?' I asked.

'Because you're not producing anything, you would be paid a minimum wage for the privilege.'

Those on full-time studies are the lowest-paid cons in the prison. But I decided there and then that whatever the cost, qualifications were essential for any rebuilding work I had in mind once outside.

'I'd like to take up the challenge,' I said.

He smiled and said, 'I don't think you will ever regret your decision of today, Fellowes. I will arrange for your transfer from the loom shop to the education block.'

I left the interview feeling quite excited at the prospect of studying for qualifications and expanding my education.

I was informed on the Friday that I had been accepted for the OND course and I was to start the following Monday. The screw in the loom shop couldn't believe it.

'You've worked your ticket, Fellowes,' he said. 'Nobody gets on a full-time education course that quick. You've only been in the shop a week.'

'They offered it to me and I have taken it,' I replied.

'They shouldn't even allow it. Cons should be made to work,' he said.

'It sure will be better than working in this noise trap.'

It turned out that none of the discipline screws on the

wings liked cons being educated. They would all have preferred stricter discipline with the cons being made to work harder in the shops. The more a con suffered, the more they liked it. Most of the screws seemed to have been turned down by the police or fire service and had ended up in a prison uniform. They stomped around with their chains and rattling keys like a band of martinets.

There was a senior screw on our particular wing who took an instant dislike to me—not that I had done anything to upset him. I was his target and that was all. Whilst cleaning my peter out one day he came up to me and said in a loud voice, 'Hear you're going to be doing full-time education, Fellowes.'

'That's right,' I replied.

'Think you're a cut above the rest doing time, do you?'

'Not at all,' I said.

'You had your chance and blew it, Fellowes.'

'What do you mean?'

'Ex-copper. You could have made a good career for yourself but you turned to crime instead.'

'Really?'

'Yes, you're a rotten apple, aren't you?'

'If you think that, it's your problem not mine. Besides, I tried to join the prison service,' I said.

'Really? What happened? Did you fail the entrance exams?'

'No, I passed all those. It was when I produced my birth certificate I failed.'

I could see the effect my last remark had on him. He was steaming with anger. I just smiled at him and walked away. In the future I knew I would have to watch myself as he really wanted me badly, even though I had won the first round. Since being in my single peter the cons either side had not spoken to me. It was obvious the word had been put out that I was an ex-copper, so everyone was reluctant to speak to me. After the initial reception committee had done me over, the screws had kept a close eye on me and the cons knew anyone caught doing me over again was going to be in big trouble. So they ostracized me instead.

I still took care moving about the wing, in case someone wanted to prove a point and jump me. The strange thing was that I already had a distinct awareness of who was behind me or to the side of me at any given moment. Not that I had practised the art—it was more a case of natural instinct. Hatred had its full hold on my life as I continued to produce mental pictures of all the people I held responsible for my incarceration. I would dream up better and more sophisticated ways of returning to each of them and fulfilling the promise of revenge I had made to myself. All of them would suffer and none would escape my fanatical wrath.

The OND course started on the Monday morning and with it came the realization that I hadn't done any serious studying for a number of years. It was hard work initially and I had to discipline myself to concentrate. All the tutorial staff were civvies and professional teachers. Prison is not the most conducive place to study at the best of times and it's even worse when you're innocent. I still hadn't come to terms with my conviction and sentence, which meant that I sometimes lapsed into moments of remembered pain during the lectures. I would find myself drifting back into the reality of my situation, having missed the major part of what the lesson was about. Each week ended with an examination of the things we should have learned and recorded and the results were given out the following Monday. Needless to say, mine weren't too impressive.

The course leader called me into his office one Monday and said, 'I'm a little concerned at your results so far, Fellowes. You are not working to your full potential.'

'Well, I have a lot on my mind and I find it hard to concentrate,' I said.

'So does everyone else in here, so get on with the job in hand,' he said curtly.

I felt disappointed and embarrassed at his comments and left the office chastising myself. 'If you're going to come through, Noel, you'll just have to fight all the way and prove to these people you can make it,' I said to myself. From that point on I worked like someone possessed, all day and all night. So much so, that soon I was achieving the standard required of me. Better still, I really started to enjoy the course.

The other cons on the course—there were about ten—used to share their understanding of subjects with each other, helping the weaker ones out. They offered me nothing, and neither did the other cons on the wing who kept me at arm's length. I wasn't one of them, so I was on my own. That made me all the more determined to succeed, so really they were doing me a favour.

It was strange, how the cons' catalogue of acceptance worked. If you were a murderer you were OK. Same for robbers, thieves, violent crimes and so on. However, if you were a nonce then you were the worst kind of criminal, hated by all cons. Policemen or ex-policemen were only second to nonces. It was quite easy for me to accept that anybody convicted of sexual offences against women or children was scum, but I couldn't understand why I was only second to that category. Worse still, the very people who supported this code of ethics were themselves sexual deviants. They were the ones most active in the homosexuality stakes.

I used to see many of the so-called hard men and nonce-haters going down to the visiting block all spruced up and cleanly shaven to see their wives and children. They would return, saying how much they adored them and how lucky they were their wives had stuck by them. But during the week I would also observe them visiting the wing queens to fulfil their own lusts. What's more, they paid for their deviancy with tobacco. The amount depended on their particular preference of services offered. As with the tobacco barons, the queens were part of another racket operated by pimps. The screws knew it went on and probably knew all the queens, but never stepped in to close it down. More horrifying was the pimps' strong-arm brigade, who used to intimidate young cons or physically weak cons to go on the game for them.

One day a young con on the twos near me had slopped out

and returned to his peter to clean it out when he was visited by two pimps. I passed his cell after slopping out and heard an angry exchange of voices coming from the cell.

I stopped for a few moments, then heard a voice say, 'We're going to have you whether you like it or not.'

With that I carried on walking, as it sounded like trouble and I didn't want to be part of it.

Some while later the young con entered my peter, tears running down his face and struggling to walk properly.

'What's up, Stan?'

'They've raped me,' he said.

'What!'

'They came in, one held me down and the other raped me.'

I just sat there, feeling physically sick at what I had just heard.

'Go to the screws, Stan,' I said.

'I can't. They'll kill me if I grass them up.'

I was helpless. There was nothing I could do for him, only listen to him continuing to pour out the sordid details. He was only twenty-one and was doing life. What a start to his sentence, I thought. He was one of many who had endured the same treatment. I lay in bed that night utterly devastated at what I had witnessed that day. I thought my life was hard, that I had been badly treated, yet my treatment was nothing compared to this. Prison undeniably housed most of society's worst animals and I was living with them. It occurred to me that this type of behaviour must have gone on unchecked for years. What chance did Stan have in trying to serve his sentence normally after being subjected to that sort of attack? They had all but destroyed him.

A few days later I learned the answer to my questions. Stan had attacked one of his assailants with a shiv and was down the punishment block waiting to be weighed off [tried before the governor].

Months of dedicated gym work and weight-training resulted in my becoming extremely fit and strong. Considering the prison diet, it was incredible what one could achieve. My reflexes were finely tuned and I could see muscle definition in every area of my body. The first stage of my survival plan was well on course and I felt secure that I could now handle violence if it came my way again. I didn't have long to wait.

One day I was washing in the wing toilet block when two cons walked in. I recognized them immediately as two of the reception committee. They started throwing cynical comments at me about my build and looks. I knew it was a ploy to wind me up. I surveyed the toilet area—it was clear. Both of them showed clean hands, so they weren't carrying weapons or at least, not in their hands. I tried to leave the area but they blocked my way. As I did so, my right boot found itself lodged in the groin of one of them. He fell to his knees with an expression of excruciating pain on his face. Then my knee connected with his head and he was out cold. The other one tried to make a run for it but I caught him by the hair and smacked his head against the wall, at the same time giving him several heavy blows to his stomach. He finished up on top of the other con on the floor. By that time a small audience of cons had gathered to watch. I grabbed both of their heads and turned them to face me.

'Don't you ever try and mess with me again or next time you won't even walk again.'

The adrenalin was still flowing as I pushed my way through the crowd of cons to return to my peter. I decided it would be best to strike while the iron was still hot in case the third member of their little gang decided upon revenge. I ran up to the threes and my luck was in. He was lying on his bed with the door to his peter half open.

As I walked in I said, 'I have just had another meeting with your mates and they're not feeling too well.'

He looked at me, rather puzzled at what I had said.

'Now I'm going to finish the job,' I added.

'I don't want no trouble with you.'

That was his last remark as my fists engaged his head several times.

'You or your cronies come near me again while I'm here and I promise you will live to regret it.'

138

I left, banging his peter door behind me. The job was done. Back in my peter that evening I considered my actions. I was rather disgusted at the realization that I had joined the very club which had caused me so much hurt and anguish in the recent past. I had met violence with violence. All I had achieved was to set myself up for some other crony who wanted to make a name for himself. All the inner hatred I had stored up had been discharged in my frenzied attack on the three cons. Still, I had never made the rules of the jungle. All I was doing was to live by them.

I lay awake trying to analyze my changing attitudes. Having spent a lot of time on my own, there were numerous flaws in my character I didn't like, weaknesses that had let me down in the past, conflicting moods which left me with no real direction or balance. Prison had only encouraged and multiplied these flaws and now they were eating away all the good points of my personality and character. The system was destroying me by changing me into another one of its violent conscripts. The cancer of hatred had grown out of my control and I was falling into the system's trap of self-destruction. Everything I had said to convince the system that I was innocent had failed miserably. You can't beat the system, someone had said. I knew how true that was. Or thought I knew.

After much thought I decided I could beat it. There was a growing sense of realization that if I were to educate myself, strengthen my body in every way I could, keep out of trouble and gain the earliest possible release date, then I would have used the system to my advantage and reversed the present trend. My decision was made. I would take up the new blueprint for rehabilitation whatever the cost.

10

Life Inside

Christmas 1970 arrived to the sound of screws jangling their keys as they opened the long corridors of peters. This was Christmas Day—my first one inside. I wished myself a happy Christmas because nobody else would this year. The atmosphere on the wings was understandably heavy. Christmas should be a time for celebration and family reunions. It was outside. Everyone inside Wakefield was thinking of their loved ones and the futility of their own mistakes, which had separated them from freedom and happiness. Everyone kept his own thoughts and feelings to himself—one wrong word to a fellow con could start a chain reaction throughout the prison. The screws maintained a low profile, keeping a discreet distance from the cons, only responding to a request to open a door or give a con a light for the one cigar he had saved up for all year in order to have something special for himself on Christmas Day.

The only good thing about Christmas inside was the effort made by the chef. The meals were the highlight of the day. I asked myself why the food couldn't be of a similar standard all the year round. Pet lovers fed their animals more nutritious food than we had all year. Like most other cons, I had saved up a couple of pennies a week to treat myself at Christmastide. I was looking forward to opening a couple of Mars bars and half an ounce of tobacco. All the effort of saving had been worth it for a few moments wallowing in luxury.

Christmas was a long drawn-out affair inside as the workshops and education block were closed until the New Year, which meant cons spent all day on the wings for over eight or nine days, days which were predominantly spent in self-pity at being locked up. Both cons and screws breathed a

140

sigh of relief when Christmas was over, knowing both sides had come through without any trouble or injuries.

If Christmas was somewhat subdued, New Year's Eve was a time of great merriment and excitement—another year gone and one nearer release and the outside world. It didn't really matter which month you had been sent down, another calendar year had passed by. At the stroke of twelve the whole prison erupted. Everybody would kick their peter doors for five minutes, as well as screaming at the top of their voices. We must have been heard in half of Wakefield.

After joining in the celebrations that first New Year, I lay back on my bed and said to myself, 'Noel, this has been one hell of a year. It's gone for ever.' I turned on my mental video recording of all the horrifying happenings of 1970 and shed a few tears. 'Let's hope '71 will be a better year,' I told myself. I wrote to my parents on New Year's Day, telling them of my expectations for the coming year. Since being inside my mother had written every week, sometimes twice. This was very important to me, as her letters were the only contact I had with the outside world. Many cons had been deserted by their families over the years and longed for a letter from anybody.

Since my last encounter with the three cons I had been left alone and enjoyed far more security than I had for months before. I sensed a softening towards me from a number of cons who from time to time started to engage me in conversation.

One day a lifer stepped into my peter and asked if he could talk to me.

'Sure,' I said.

'I don't know how to say it.'

'Say it as it comes to you, Joey.'

'Well, I can't read or write and my bird has written to me. Could you read it to me?'

I felt a deep sadness inside as I looked at the letter. It was dated some six weeks earlier. It had taken all this time for the poor man to ask someone to read it to him. I read the letter to

141

him four times. He just wanted to hear it again and again.

'If you like, Joey, I'll write a letter back for you.'

'You won't tell anyone, will you?'

'Of course I won't, Joey. You're safe with me.'

The next day I wrote the letter for him and after reading it back to him my reward was to see an expression of excitement and satisfaction on his face. Within a month I found myself reading and writing letters for five more cons. The word had been passed around by Joey that I would help. Reading their letters and answering them was a pleasure to me, until one day I sat down to read a letter for a con and immediately realized it was a Dear John [a letter telling you they had found someone else]. I scanned the letter and felt a lump deep in my throat as I looked at the con eagerly awaiting the contents. How do I handle it? I thought to myself. I can't lie to him, how will he take it? he might throw a wobbly in my peter.

All these thoughts passed through my head until the con asked, 'What's the matter, Noel?'

The expression on my face had given the game away.

'It's, er, Dear John, I'm afraid.'

He looked at me for a moment and said, 'I'd still like to hear it.'

'You sure you're OK?'

'Yeh, man.'

I read the letter to him as written, feeling just as devastated as he obviously was.

'That's it,' I said.

'It's understandable. She has stuck with me for six years. I've been luckier than most.'

'Maybe she isn't serious and already regrets having sent the letter. I can write one back straight away,' I suggested.

'No, she has acted different to me on visits the past few months. Thanks anyway, Noel.'

I didn't know too much of his history as another con had read his letters until he had been released. He left under a cloud of gloom. It was the first con I'd seen leave this way after my having read his mail. A few days later I learned that he had tried to top himself by slashing his wrists with a razor blade. He was alive but the screws had just caught him in time and rushed him to prison hospital. I wrote to him and within weeks he was back on the wing again, no worse for the experience. He was one of the lucky ones. Many cons who received Dear Johns took it far harder and would continue to mutilate themselves year after year. To them the only escape was death. That was rarely achieved. Usually they were ghosted [taken away] to a mental institution. For them there would be no escape.

I continued the letter reading and writing facility, although at times it interfered with the studying I needed to catch up on for the OND course. After a number of months of gentle persuasion, Joey and Chas joined the remedial classes for reading and writing. I had convinced them both it would open a whole new world to them if they stuck it out. Thankfully it did.

My studies were going well. They demanded a lot of dedication and personal discipline on my part. The screws didn't help by constantly reminding me they would be useless outside as my record would nullify any qualifications. The truth was, they were jealous. They resented cons on full-time education as the cons became more highly qualified than they would ever be. When the screws took this line I used to conjure up a reply containing long philosophical words to baffle them. It usually worked, and they would storm off knowing they had lost the initiative.

I maintained my crusade for fitness by continuing the gym and weight-training classes, with satisfying results. I was lifting weights I would never have dreamt of lifting and my body reflected definition and power. H. had taken an interest in me as I relentlessly pressed on in his classes. He engaged me in conversation from time to time, asking about my past and my case.

When he learned I was an ex-copper he showed far more interest in my well-being. Needless to say, I warmed to H. as he was genuine and always showed a balance between what he was employed to do and the way in which he exercised it. He was a fair man who always had time to listen to a con's grievance, however petty it was, usually directing the con to make a right decision. If the discipline screws had a con whom they saw as a hopeless case, always in trouble or violent, you could be sure it was H. who would be given the task of knocking him into shape. More often than not he was successful. Not by physical persuasion, but by understanding the con and redirecting his energy into more fruitful pursuits such as weight training, gym work, boxing or any other sport. The few hopeless cases were transferred to other prisons or institutions for the criminally insane. If H. couldn't manage them, they had to be hopeless.

It wasn't long before I was asked to join the élite group of weight-trainers which consisted of H., Ken, another physical training instructor, and a con who was the gym red band (trustee). The invitation really boosted my ego as now I could work out with the best, using better equipment. I knew the workouts would be harder as they were all accomplished lifters.

I thanked H. for the opportunity. He just smiled and said, 'Not many can stand the pace. We wear them out. We'll see what you're made of.'

I rose to the challenge. All I ever needed was the opportunity. Within a couple of months I had proved my worth, not missing a single session. The reward was that I began to know H. in a more direct way than the other cons. He started calling me by my first name whilst training with him and began to share things about his family. It was a great honour for me as H. was the first man in the penal system to treat me as a human being. H. was a winner all the way. He made the impossible, possible. His philosophy for life was simple. Everything was possible, but you had to want it badly enough or you wouldn't succeed. Success depended on the effort, dedication and discipline of the individual. Any one element missing meant failure. He was always in charge of any given situation—the situation was never in control of him. The prison system needed to employ more people like H. Then it would succeed more often in rehabilitation rather than destruction.

Many of the cons had cell companions. Being a long-term prison, Wakefield afforded its inmates certain privileges. One such privilege was that a con could have a budgie in his peter. There must have been a couple of hundred feathered friends in Wakefield. Some of them were top quality birds. When one of the cons I had read letters for was released, he asked me if I would like his two budgies for services rendered. I thanked him for the offer and became the proud owner of a cock, hen and a large cage with a breeding-box attached.

I read all the necessary books on keeping and breeding budgies and, soon after, three eggs appeared in the breeding-box. Much to my delight, they hatched and I had a family to look after. When the chicks were old enough, I chose the strongest and more colourful one for myself and sold the other two for an ounce of tobacco each, the current price for quality birds. I named the bird Bobby and used to carry him around with me, tucked in my shirt. This gave him security as he could always hear my heartbeat.

After a couple of weeks I started training him to talk and to return to his cage when commanded. This exercise took much patience on my part but the results came slowly but surely. It wasn't long before my companion was welcoming me every time I entered the peter. He would ring his bell and say, 'Hello Noel. Had a good day?'

'Sure have, Bobby,' I replied.

It wasn't long before he attached my reply to his question so I used to get the lot in one go. I became so attached to Bobby that I sold off the cock, hen and large cage for a tiny sum of snout [tobacco] and bought a luxury cage for Bobby. He became a very close friend and companion to me. Whatever my mood, he was always chirpy and happy, which inevitably brought me round to his way of thinking. When I felt low he would know it and as I lay on the bed he would fly around me a couple of times, land near my shoulder and then give me his full repertoire in my ear. If that didn't work he would repeat the exercise until I responded. I loved that bird. He gave me far more pleasure than anything else inside the prison. He never demanded more than simply to be fed.

What an incredible life, uncontrolled by the trappings of society and the painful pitfalls of injustice. He was quite happy to return to his caged life whenever I commanded it. For me, the banging up process still had the chilling reminder of freedom lost behind it.

The first year exams were slowly creeping up on me and so I spent all my spare time revising. Not only was I taking OND Business Studies, but five 'O' levels as well. Not being gifted with a photographic memory, my studies were nothing but a hard slog, trying to force the material into my brain. My student days at school had been taken up by sporting activities, to the detriment of academic subjects, leaving me in the category of average in most subjects. Trying to study for five 'O' levels and OND in one year was a hard enough task without the added handicap of imprisonment.

Studying certainly stimulated my mind but there were times when I felt like putting all the books together and burning them. There was no doubt in my mind that I had taken on far too much, considering my circumstances, and the cost was becoming too much to bear. Unlike people outside, when I felt depressed or low, there was no one to encourage me or help me. I could only turn to myself, and my own feelings, which were usually negative and subjective. I used to give myself all the reasons why I shouldn't do it rather than the reasons why I should. The drop-out rate on the course had been quite high, which was quite understandable, considering the daily pressures and demands of prison life.

Much to my surprise, I stuck it out and in June I sat the examinations. Running true to form, I believed I had failed all but one examination. Still, I reasoned, I had given it my best and that's all I could have done. A couple of months later the results came through and I was amazed to find I had passed the OND in Business Studies and four 'O' levels. Ironically, the one I thought I had passed was the very one I had failed—statistics. I was like a kid with a new toy. At last I had achieved something. All the worry, sweat and endless studying had been worth it. I lay in bed that night contented, knowing that phase two of my overall plan was well on its way.

In the autumn of 1971 I was given the option of continuing my studies, either doing 'A' levels or taking up the challenge of the Open University. I opted for the Open University as the obvious choice, having such wide and varied courses. If the screws didn't like cons studying for 'O' levels, they absolutely hated the thought of cons doing Open University. Many tried to block it, intimidating the cons. When they tried it on me, I didn't take the bait. No one was going to stand in my way. I swallowed my pride and took all their cynical comments on the nose, refusing to react to them.

I decided upon humanities, studying the Renaissance in art, Kafka in literature, philosophy, logic and history. It was a case of proving the cynics wrong as the few cons selected for OU were 'guinea-pigs'. Ours was the first OU course, a pilot scheme, being watched closely by the authorities. We could afford no drop-outs this time, or they would close the course down. This was a new approach by the cons against the old enemy. Everyone was determined to succeed. To my surprise, the barrier between me and the others was lifted and I was no longer ostracized. We were pulling together as a team. There were long group discussions on the more difficult subjects and encouragement when any one of us felt down or was struggling with course assignments.

I spent the evenings with my head down reading and learning all the time, much to Bobby's annoyance. He couldn't tolerate being ignored. He would land on the edge of my book and flick the pages with his head until I acknowledged him. I welcomed the break at times as Bobby often had a new trick up his sleeve. One night I was studying Kafka, a jug of hot tea beside me. Bobby flew over and decided to drink the tea. He perched on the edge of the jug, leant forward to take a sip and fell in. He flew out so fast, splashing tea all over me and my books, that I rolled around my peter laughing until I cried. Following my recovery I checked him over for burns and to my relief he was fine—no damage at all.

During the autumn Ken, the PTI who managed the prison football team, said, 'You're playing centre-half on Saturday. Let's see you perform.'

It came as a great surprise to me as I wasn't playing for the wing team that often, only when other players had visits and couldn't play.

'I'm not sure they will accept me,' I said.

'That's their problem, not yours. I select the team and if they don't like it they needn't play.'

Ken had been groomed by H. and nobody questioned his decision, for doing so would have meant being dropped. We won the match and I became a regular member of the team. The cons nicknamed me Gorgon after the Hungarian defender who stopped England from reaching the World Cup finals. My speciality was the sliding tackle, usually taking the man as well as the ball. We played on an all-weather pitch surfaced in red shingle, so my tackles always resulted in cut knees or legs. I used to wear elastic stocking covering my knees, but this only reduced injury, never stopped it. Every Sunday I would wake up with sore, grazed legs, swearing to myself that I wouldn't play again. By the time football training came round I was there once more, ready for the next match. By Christmas we were top of the league, undefeated and well on course to win the championship.

Christmas came round again. Strangely, I felt worse this Christmas (1971) than I had the last. It felt as though I never had a life in the outside world. Last Christmas I had been able to remember people and faces; this year there was a blank. The past was sinking into oblivion. This was hard to understand, as I could recall the trial and witnesses in a flash. It seemed as though my memory had cleared away all the past to allow room for the catalogue of remembered pain, suffering and degradation it wanted to store for future use.

My wife had finally divorced me in the middle of '71, which was understandable, considering my status and circumstances. But it still hurt, especially as it meant I wouldn't see my son and daughter again—I had only seen

148

them once in nearly two years. My written pleas had had no effect and in my position there was absolutely nothing I could do to change her attitude or mind. There was nothing else I could lose. The final chapter of the past had been written. The authors of my destiny had written the last line, ending with a full stop. What was a little more resentment and bitterness? I already had a massive dose and the extra bit wasn't going to sink me. For all my wrongs and mis-demeanours during my short marriage, I still loved my children and to lose them this way was the cruellest blow any father could face.

The New Year brought the usual celebrations, but this time I kicked my door until my ankle was numb with pain. I wasn't kicking in celebration, rather in desperation at all that 1971 had brought me.

My second 'festive season' spent in prison had something else to mark it. When the Queen's Birthday Honours list was announced, one honour stood head and shoulders above the rest. Joe Mounsey, head of Lancashire CID, was awarded the Queen's Police Medal, in recognition of his 'enviable crime-busting record'. In the *Lancashire Evening Post* that day were listed Mounsey's successes, including 'the Southport golf links murder, the body in the car boot murder, the Overton coin-collector manslaughter . . .'

Five months later, Mounsey received the medal at an investiture at Hutton, near Preston in Lancashire. He had the luxury of freedom, his wife and three children around him—while I was gone and long forgotten in a tiny cell across the Pennines.

In August 1972, Mounsey's name hit the headlines again. A Blackpool-based policeman, Superintendent Gerry Richardson, had been shot dead trying to catch robbers at a jewellery store. The incident received wide media coverage. It was reported that two thousand people paid their respects to his memory as they filed past his body, laid in an open coffin before the funeral. A quarter of a million people signed a petition in favour of capital punishment. Near the end of that month, Mounsey left for London in search of the killer. Clutching a .38 revolver, Mounsey and two other officers burst into his secret hideaway in Birnham Road, North London, on the morning of 7 October. It had been an exhaustive 45-day enquiry across the country, but Mounsey had his man again. The following March, Frederick Joseph Sewell was jailed for life—at least thirty years on the judge's direction. He was sent to Wakefield prison.

Early in the New Year I was invited to join the debating society, a team made up of about twenty cons who debated against outside teams. The subjects for debate were on current topical issues. One team proposed a motion; the other team rejected the motion. After debating the subject for one-and-a-half hours, there was a free vote and the motion was either won or lost. The competition was first-class as the outside teams were of a very high quality. I took up the offer and it wasn't long before I was contributing to every debate. It was very stimulating mentally, as one needed to master the art of debate, rather than pushing your own line all the time.

Every debate I attended boosted my confidence and within a couple of months I was invited to be the main speaker: to propose the motion, 'This house believes in capital punishment'. Trust my luck! Every other subject debated that term had been topical current events. They had really landed me in it this time. To say the topic was controversial would be an understatement. After much discussion at the highest level, the governor approved the motion and allowed the debate. Just to make sure everything was in order, he doubled the screws on duty and even turned up for the debate himself. Unbelievable, I thought to myself. After all that I had experienced from the judiciary, I certainly never believed in capital punishment. Neither did half the team who were lifers. But in the debate it didn't matter what you actually believed—the task was to present a good strong case for capital punishment and win the motion. I prepared my address for two solid weeks, collating all the information available on the subject. Then I prepared my opening speech.

On the night of the debate I was very nervous as I started to deliver my speech. Everybody, it seemed, was uncomfortable, including the governor. I launched into my speech with great passion and sat down some twenty minutes later to rapturous applause from all sides, including the governor. The debate had taken off and everyone wanted to make a comment from the floor. Unusually, we ran over the allotted time, but the governor gave the nod for an extension.

The debate ended in the usual manner with an open vote. To my great delight, we won the motion and I was presented with the certificate confirming it. We had defeated one of the top teams in Yorkshire and the word was passed round about the quality of Wakefield Training School's Debating Society. From that day on, teams were queuing up to challenge us from all over the country. The only thing I found disturbing was that the visiting team left at the end of the debate; we returned to our peters.

With the amount of studying I was doing with the OU, my football training and the debating society, I found myself leading a very hectic life. Bobby no longer received the amount of attention he had enjoyed in earlier years, so I decided to make a present of him to my parents. He was fully grown by now and the peter was too small a place for his exercise. As he was such a celebrity, giving his daily performances to screws and cons alike, I was anxious that someone might try to steal him when he walked the wing with me, perched on my shoulder. So I wrote to my mother to arrange for her to bring a cage on their next visit. The day of my parents' visit, I put Bobby in a small ventilated box and bade him a tearful farewell until I met him again on the outside. At the last moment I had second thoughts—Bobby was my closest friend and had given me so much pleasure during my time with him. But I gave Bobby to the visit screw to give to my parents after their visit. It was a good visit, learning about my brothers' and sisters' fortunes in life and catching up on the family news generally. I spent time explaining what Bobby liked and the food and exercise he required. We said our goodbyes and I returned to my peter.

Some thirty minutes later Brian Dodsworth, the chaplain, came to my peter. 'Noel, I have some rather bad news,' he said.

Instant panic set in. My heart started thumping faster. I feared the worst. My parents must have been in an accident.

'It's Bobby. Your father was transferring him from the box into the cage inside his car and he forgot the window was open. Bobby flew straight out of the window.'

'Not Bobby,' I said.

My heart sank. My precious friend was out there some-where, probably frightened, unused to the surroundings.

'What can I do, Brian?' I asked.

'Well, I can take you around the prison and see if he's in the trees anywhere. You're the only one he will respond to.'

I went with Brian and spent a long time walking inside the prison walls but there was no sign of Bobby anywhere. I returned to my peter absolutely distraught, knowing I had lost Bobby for ever. Night-time came and I spent hours looking out of my small window, wondering where he was. It was cold outside and he was probably desperately trying to find his way back to me.

I walked my peter most of the night, repeating his name over and over again with tears streaming down my face. His disappearance affected me so deeply I didn't eat anything for two whole days. I couldn't get him out of my mind. A number of cons tried to console me with gifts of tobacco and condolences. They all loved Bobby the way I did. It was a great loss to all of us. My father wrote a distressing letter explaining what had happened and, reading between the lines, both my parents were deeply upset at the tragedy. I wrote back saying it was an unfortunate accident and not to blame themselves. It could have happened to anyone not used to birds. It took me a long time to get used to the fact that Bobby wasn't around any more. While studying I would look round, expecting to see Bobby pecking at my books or examining the contents of my tobacco tin, but alas he wasn't there.

While I was in Wakefield, I spared little thought for my old colleagues in the police force at Morecambe. My opinion of them had understandably been soured by circumstances. But in the early months of 1972 they pulled off a good 'collar'. Travelling villain Lenny Pilot (mentioned in the previous chapter) had decided to do a 'sneak theft' in the resort and had picked an optician's shop. Pilot and his accomplice attacked Mr Harry Wooliscroft; one of them hit him in the face while the other helped himself to £8 from the till. Minutes after they left the shop, the police launched a town-wide search. The pair had split up to avoid detection, but thanks to a good description from the shopkeeper, Pilot was spotted in a Morecambe cafe and arrested. On 21 March, he appeared before local magistrates.

Pilot tried a sob-story in court in hope of a lenient sentence. He told how he came to the resort looking for work and how he had met the other man who said he knew where work could be found. 'Before I knew what had happened he took it [the money] out of the till and the owner came. I didn't know what he was doing and could not believe it had happened,' he said.

The story—which he later admitted was a lie designed to protect himself and his partner—didn't convince the jury. The verdicts of guilty to theft and assault causing actual bodily harm stood. He was jailed for six months. But the JPs decided against implementing a three-month sentence suspended by colleagues in St Helens a short time earlier.

At the time the newspapers didn't give much space to that petty crime. But at that time they were interested in the common-law wife of police killer Fred Sewell, Irene Jermain. She had been jailed for 15 months at Manchester Crown Court for impeding his capture by driving him through the police dragnet in the boot of a car.

Easter brought the usual inter-wing football competition where each team played a knockout match, leaving two finalists to play on Easter Monday. The winning team won a prize of nine shillings [45p] per man, as well as being prison champions in the cup. We played 'A' wing and won relatively easily. We faced the might of 'B' wing in the final. As always, the cons had backed 'B' wing to win. All the tobacco had been put on them, as they were favourites by a long way. We had only beaten them once in a year, but we planned our strategy to bring about their downfall.

The plan was to try to take out two of their star players early in the game. I was given the job of taking out the centre-forward which I did with a sliding tackle in the first ten minutes of the match. Much to my disgust I was booked for the offence by the referee, while the centre-forward limped off with grazed legs. We eventually won the match 2-1 after the fiercest battle ever witnessed on a football field. I was returning to the wing to celebrate our historic victory with the other members of the team and I was climbing the stairs from the ones when I heard a voice say, 'You cost me eight ounces of snout, you filthy pig.'

I looked up to see a sock filled with a round object descending in my direction. I felt the impact on my head and saw stars as I fell backwards down the stairs.

I came round to the sound of people slapping me on the face. 'Come on, Noel. Let's get you out of here.'

Most of the team were around me and they carried me to the showers. The system of bathing had changed recently. Each wing now had its own shower block. I soon returned to the land of the living under the cold shower. Instantly I knew I was quite seriously injured as blood was pouring from a large gash in my head.

'You're gonna need stitches in that,' said one of the cons.

'How bad is it?' I asked.

'You've got a gash about two inches long.'

'Who the hell did me?'

'A lifer from 'A' wing who lost all his snout.'

'He'll lose more than his snout when I get my hands on him.'

'It's already been taken care of. The screws have got him down the block. He hit you with a snooker ball in a sock.'

My head was aching quite severely and I felt giddy as I

stood up. The screws came in and said I would have to go to the sick-bay, then make a statement about what had happened.

'I'm all right,' I said. 'I slipped on the stairs. The next thing I can remember is coming to in the shower.'

'Everyone saw what happened. You were hit over the head with a snooker ball. Now it's time to get your own back on that maniac before he kills somebody,' said the screw.

'Not me, boss. I don't remember anything.'

'Very well, Fellowes. If you want to be a hero, we can't make you,' said the other screw.

I went to the sick-bay, had a few stitches and returned to my peter. 'All this for a miserable sum of nine shillings,' I thought to myself. I was lucky to be alive to collect it. The con who had sprung me faced the governor and received a few days down the block and loss of earnings. He asked for protection down the block because he owed so much snout to the barons he couldn't pay. We never saw him again as he grassed up the barons. Their peters were raided by the screws and he was ghosted [transferred] to another prison.

Wakefield housed some of the country's top criminals including Frankie Fraser, the Richardson's Gang hard man. I also met Arthur Hosein, the older brother of the Hoseins, who allegedly killed Muriel McKay, the wife of a newspaper magnate. Arthur was my hairdresser in Wakefield and always protested his innocence of the crime he had received a life sentence for. Knowing I was innocent, I wasn't prepared to judge the merits of his case. All I could do was listen to his endless denials as he continued giving me haircuts. Unlike the prison barber, Arthur had a natural talent for cutting hair, so it was to him I regularly went for a trim. Most notorious criminals had been given the label by the press. Inside they got on with their bird like the rest of us. To the professional criminals, bird had to be served as efficiently as possible so they could get out at the earliest possible date to continue their prosperous careers. Being caught was all part of their chosen way of life, nothing more than an inconvenience, serving time for an error of misjudgement on their part. They all shared in common a hatred for the police and ex-policemen. So, except for Arthur, I steered well clear of them.

The past caught up with me again and I fell into deep depression as I couldn't see the end to my sentence. Days seemed to get longer and my sleep was interrupted by long nightmares about the trial and early prison life. I would wake up, my bed wet through with sweat and my lungs gasping for breath. It was a situation I had no control over. The more I tried to suppress them, the worse the nightmares became. There was no escape from the nightly torture.

Eventually I decided to go and speak to Brian Dodsworth, the chaplain. All the cons trusted Brian because unlike the other do-gooders, if he said he would do something about a given situation, he did. As a 'man of the cloth' he was, in the cons' eyes, divorced from the system and an ally to their cause. The truth was, he was a man of principle and deep conviction. If he believed in something, he would fight for you to the bitter end. At the same time, he was nobody's fool. If Brian caught cons out in lies or deceit, he spared no words in pointing it out.

I spoke to Brian about my present state of depression and distress. He said he needed to think it over for a day or two and would see me again soon. He saw me a couple of days later and said he thought I had perhaps been overdoing my studies and I needed a second job to take the intensity out of my situation.

'What sort of a job?' I asked.

'Well, my red band [trustee] is leaving me soon and I would like you to take his place.'

'What about my studies?' I asked.

'The work I require of a red band is minimal and I think you could easily do both.'

'I've only done a couple of years. Usually red bands are given to people nearing the end of their sentence,' I said.

'I choose who I want to work for me and if I want a particular person then I make sure I get him.'

I was delighted with his offer of support and gladly took it. Within a couple of weeks the necessary approval had been given and I collected my red band—made of red material and worn around the upper part of the right arm. This distinguished trustees from other cons. With it came a host of privileges. I could walk round the prison unaccompanied and didn't have to be banged up at lunch-time or tea-time. Generally it was a licence for freedom of movement within the confines of the prison. Not that I took advantage of the privilege in the early months, for I still feared an attack could come upon me at any time.

My duties for Brian included cleaning his office, running messages, making coffee for visitors, general cleaning and preparation for church services. The only drawback to the job was working on Sundays. The church was used to show feature films twice a week and it had to be made ready following the cinema show. Half the prison saw the film on Friday night, the other half Sunday night. The church could seat around 350 people and after cinema night the task of cleaning was quite laborious. But it was an escape from the noisy atmosphere of the main prison, a place where I could spend hours in total silence and solitude, gathering my thoughts and relaxing in complete safety, knowing I was the only person there. I used to take study books with me and sometimes, complete my OU essays. There was nothing spiritual about my time there. I had decided God wasn't a reality back at the trial. I believed in the philosophy of life—'I think, therefore I am'.

Midweek Brian used to run a series of Bible studies for the cons who were Christians and I had to make the coffee for them after their meetings. The holy joes, as I used to call them, resented the fact that I was Brian's red band rather than one of them. After all, they were believers and I wasn't. I used to prepare the coffee and cups, then leave them to get on with it, returning after the meeting to complete my duties. Brian never reacted to my choice of doing things. He just carried on. That was the measure of the man. I respected the faith and trust he had in me and believed the feeling was mutual. However, I broke his trust in one small way.

On certain Sundays in the month I had to prepare Holy Communion—the wafer biscuits and the wine. Temptation being what it was, added to the burden of deprivation, I used to drink half a bottle of the wine, then fill it up with water, knowing they wouldn't notice the difference. Holy Communion was my favourite day. It was wine-tasting day. The holy joes used to do all the business on their knees taking the bread and the wine and I would look on, knowing all they had was watered-down wine. They might get parole but they were not getting their wine, I used to chuckle to myself.

I built up a good relationship with Brian. Now I had two people I related to in prison—Brian and H. Both had different qualities but similar goals—to encourage, guide and direct anyone who responded to their particular brand of rehabilitation in the already badly-warped system of prison life. They were two men desperately trying to fight the tide of archaic rules, regulations and procedures that moved against them. Brian had been right. Having been given a small degree of responsibility as a red band, the dual role of studying and working for him had taken the monotony of daily routine away and replaced it with balance and purpose. It was then that a third person entered my catalogue of acceptable people—Eric Treacy, the Bishop of Wakefield.

He used to visit the prison once a fortnight on a Saturday morning to share breakfast with the cons who attended his informal chats held in the church. He was a tremendous character and would always bring his wife along, affectionately known as Auntie May. They both took a keen interest in cons and their family circumstances. In fact, May used to put up cons' families who travelled from far-away places overnight and feed them.

The Bish, as we all called him, would open up the talk after breakfast with current affairs and everyone was encouraged to participate in the discussion. He always made sure the less articulate had their say on the issue at hand, listening intently to every word. Another attraction to attending Saturday morning meetings was that the Bish always brought in a couple of packets of cigarettes, which he would pass round to the cons. They usually returned to him empty. Unperturbed, he would open another packet a little later and repeat the exercise.

Many stories were told in the prison about the Bish, who had stepped in to help cons in various kinds of trouble, either domestic or concerning punishment that had been dealt out to them while in custodial care under the screws in Wakefield. He would demand to see the cons in the punishment block if he heard a whisper about the screws having beaten someone up. If he found a con in anything other than a normal healthy state, then there was a meeting with the governor to report the situation. It was universally accepted in Wakefield that without Brian or the Bish, many more cons would have suffered under the hands of the punishment block screws. The Bish always headed the Christmas Day and Easter Day services at Wakefield. To him, the prison offered the true meaning of those celebrations unspoilt by modern-day commercialism.

One day, just before the usual Saturday morning meeting, I had collected the breakfast in the usual manner and was awaiting the arrival of the twenty or so cons who regularly attended. Auntie May was sitting by herself while the Bish was talking to Brian. I noticed she was sitting with her eyes closed, so I walked up and sat beside her. She was praying in a very soft voice.

When she had finished, I said to her, 'You always look happy when you're here, Auntie May.'

'Yes, I am always happy when we visit this church,' she said.

What a strange thing to say, I thought, considering all the misery that Wakefield stood for.

'Why is that? There's nothing but bad news surrounding this place.'

'Well, Noel, in all the churches I have visited in the world, this is the church where I feel the presence of God the greatest,' she said with a warm smile. 'You see, considering the history of Wakefield prison and the number of poor men who have been hanged here, and all the men serving life sentences here, there has been a lot of heart prayer offered to my God. I just know that God is in this church.'

She said it with such sincerity and conviction that I believed her. That short conversation never left me. It was fine for her, but I didn't have any experiences of God while I swept out the church or when I used to sit there quietly and study. I just accepted the Bish and Auntie May as genuine, warm, caring people.

My case was due before the parole board in mid-1972 and I eagerly awaited the interviews, hoping my case for parole would be approved. I met the parole officer who explained the procedure of parole: a number of reports concerning my attitude and behaviour inside would be presented to the main parole board, together with the facts of my case, conviction and sentence; the board would discuss my case and recommend their findings to the Home Secretary, who would finally decide whether to grant parole or not.

'What about your conviction, Mr Fellowes? Have you anything to say to me about it?'

'I am innocent of the offence I was convicted for. Nothing has changed,' I replied.

'You're still denying the offence then?'

'Absolutely.'

He went on to ask further questions about the qualifications I had gained in Wakefield and how I proposed to use them if released early. I came away from the interview rather despondent. I had only been questioned for ten minutes; the normal time was about half an hour.

The second interview was with the shrink. Apparently, if you have been convicted of a killing, the shrink makes an independent report for the parole board. It's a reasonable safety factor for the system to adopt—not that I had a choice. If a con applied for parole, they decided upon procedures.

I met the shrink at the prison hospital and again he explained the reason for the interview. 'I see you're still protesting your innocence,' he said.

1 Noel Fellowes as PC 1289 Fellowes in 1968.

2 Mrs Hockenhull, Harold Parkinson's daily help.
3 Detective Chief Superintendent Mounsey, who led the 1970 investigation into Harold Parkinson's death.
4 Harold Parkinson with his famed coin collection.

5 The murder room on 26 February 1970, the day Harold Parkinson's body was discovered.

6 Noel Fellowes in 1985 stands on the steps of Lancaster Castle. He was dragged up these steps barefoot in the winter of 1970 to be charged before the magistrates.

7 Mr Justice Caulfield, the judge at Noel Fellowes' trial in June 1970.

CAR REGIST. No	JOURNEY AND ACCOUNT (EXCLUDING TRIPS)	CREDIT			CASH		
		£	s	d	£	s	d
	Bus to South Coast					13	0
	Depots to Junction					15	2
	Beach Cabs to Lunadine AB					13	2

RECORD FOR DRIVER Noel Fellowes **FOR WED DAY** 25/2/1969

CAR REGIST. No	JOURNEY AND ACCOUNT (EXCLUDING TRIPS)	CREDIT			CASH		
		£	s	d	£	s	d
	LYNN to LUTHER AVE					4	0
	2 JIT to A.L.					10	0
	ARNSIDE CRES to KINGSBANK					3	0
	MINI BUS to LANCASTER					15	0
	MINIBUS to SS POTTS					15	0
	BRADFORD STAFF.		5	0			
	SHOP to SPIRMAS RD					4	0
	HUNES ARMS STAFF.		12	6			
	LOR. BUS STN to PARK ST					15	0
	BRAMPTON DR to 2.V.H.					10	0
	GREAVES SCHOOLCHILDREN	1	16	6			

Nights

TOTAL RUNS FOR CREDIT		£	2	14	0		
TOTAL CASH RUNS		£	3	16	0	3	16	0
TOTAL TAKINGS / DRIVER'S SHARE		£	6	10	0	2	3	4
FUEL ETC. PAID FOR IN CASH (ATTACH RECEIPTS)								
BALANCE OF CASH FROM ABOVE						£	1	12	8
BALANCE OF TRIPS LESS TRIP MONEY (SEE OVER)								
TOTAL CASH HANDED IN						£	1	12	8

RECORD DETAILS OF TRIPS AND TRIP MONEY ON BACK

8 The 'missing' taxi-driver record sheets for Noel Fellowes on 24 and 25 February 1970. It was alleged in the trial that Noel had stolen the sheets to cover his movements at the time Parkinson was killed. But the 1984 investigation turned up the records among the papers on the case.

9 (*Top*) **HM Prison Wakefield in West Yorkshire. Noel Fellowes spent most of his sentence here.**
10 (*Left*) A typical prison cell at the time of Fellowes' imprisonment.
11 (*Above*) Joe Berry; who travelled to Overton with Billy Clark on the night Parkinson was killed.

12 Detective Chief Superintendent Bill Lumsden who headed the initial 1984 enquiry into the Overton killing.
13 Deputy Chief Constable Eric Evans ran the full-scale enquiry on the case in 1984.
14 Detective Chief Inspectors Tom Eyres (left) and Allan Potts (right) re-investigated the killing. Potts had proved himself earlier by obtaining Billy Clark's confession.

15 *(Top)* Fourteen years later, Noel Fellowes visits the house in which Harold Parkinson was killed. Noel said, 'As God is my judge, I have never stepped through that door before today.'
16 *(Left)* The Lord Chief Justice, Lord Lane.
17 Bob Westerdale, the *Lancashire Evening Post* crime reporter, who brought Noel Fellowes the news that the case was to be re-opened in 1984.

18 Noel and Coral Fellowes, after Noel was vindicated from any involvement in the crime, outside the Appeal Court on 12 July 1985.

'Absolutely right.'

'What has happened is that you have never accepted your guilt, Fellowes. The minute you do, the better your life will be. Look at your record. You're a model prisoner with a good background. The sooner you accept your conviction the sooner you will be out of here.'

A real catch-22 situation. If I admitted something I had never done, they would give me parole. If I continued in the truth they would keep me in prison.

'If you keep me here until the last minute of my seven-year sentence, then you will have to release me. If that's how long it takes, so be it. I don't need to admit something I have never done, nor will I ever give up my fight to clear my name,' I said.

'Fair enough, but you must understand that we have to be sure of people we recommend for parole.'

'I understand.'

'Look at the size of you—six-foot-two, weighing about fifteen stone. I sure wouldn't like to meet you in a dark alley.'

Then I blew it. I could contain myself no more.

'I sure would like to meet you,' I said.

With that last remark the interview finished. I knew in my heart my chance of parole was lost. After all, I had shown no remorse for the killing I had never committed. The whole parole episode brought the familiar taste of bitterness flooding back and with it the usual depression. It's quite common inside to go to bed in a relatively normal state and then to wake up in the morning feeling depressed. Your bird seems to get on top of you. The endless, repetitive days drag you down, then your mind just switches off for a while.

Many cons who had done a number of years inside were on sleeping draughts to calm them down—Librium or Valium. I would see them outside the sick-bay every night, waiting for their daily tot. They would get their tot, drink it in front of the medical screw, then leave through the exit door. Once outside they would congregate and spit out their tot into a cup. After collecting five or six tots, one of the cons would drink the drug cocktail. Each would get a turn in time. To see the recipient staggering around the wing, bombed out of his brain, was a very sorry sight. Goodness knows what the long-term effects to the brain would be.

I was called to see the Assistant Governor one lunch-time and I knew it was the parole board's answer to my application.

'811168 Fellowes, Sir,' I said.

'Well, Fellowes, it's not good news. Your application for parole has been refused, I'm afraid.'

I had expected it, but I still felt disappointed hearing it read out.

'It's not surprising, Fellowes. You're still denying the offence and besides, a number of people have written in saying they fear for themselves if you're released.'

'Who are they, Sir?'

'That's confidential information. Besides, it's not unusual. Many write in saying they are frightened of the person they spoke against at his trial. You keep your nose clean—there's always next year.'

I returned to my peter angry at what I had just heard. Who were these faceless people who had written in, fearing my release? They were absolutely right to be frightened. If I could get my hands on them now it would be a long time before they could write again. Only the people with guilty consciences could have written. They obviously weren't satisfied with having put me here, now they wanted to make sure the authorities kept me inside. The shock of the parole board's refusal sent me into a frantic rage. I started kicking everything around in my peter and shouting abuse at the top of my voice.

The emotional outburst worked. After some twenty minutes I fell on my bed absolutely exhausted. My peter looked as though a bomb had hit it. Everything was strewn all over the place. My knuckles and feet were throbbing after using the peter door as a punchbag. At least I had the satisfaction of venting my anger on solid objects rather than cons, which was the normal practice inside.

The following days were spent in a low state of mind, the

inner pain refusing to subside. One lunch-time a regular member of my letter-reading group came into my peter, asking if I would read his letter to him.

I went through the usual routine of reading it to him two or three times and afterwards he said, 'You look really down, Noel. Had some bad news?'

'Yeh,' I said.

'What's up then?'

I explained what had happened with the Assistant Governor and my reaction to the news.

'What you need is a pick-me-up.'

Within a couple of minutes he returned with a home-rolled cigarette.

'There you are, Noel. Smoke that.'

'I've got snout of my own. What's the big deal?'

'It's full of dope, man. It will take you out of yourself.'

Drugs were widely available in Wakefield. Dope [cannabis], acid [LSD] and other drugs were smuggled in on visits. Wives or girlfriends would smuggle them in by putting the drugs in a durex or silver paper, keeping it in their mouths whilst being searched at the entrance gate to the prison. When they arrived in the visit room, the welcome kiss resulted in the transfer of the drugs from mouth to mouth. The con would then swallow the package of drugs. After the visit the con might be selected for a strip-search by the screws, but that couldn't reveal the contents of his stomach. Once back in his peter the con would swallow glasses of salt water, make himself sick and the drugs would be vomited up. I knew that dope was the lesser of all the evils—non-addictive. When taken it supposedly gave a feeling of contentment.

I smoked the joint, which left me floating in a cloud of wellbeing. Gone was the anger and inner hostility. I just felt totally oblivious to everything around me. Colours seemed more vibrant and periodically I would burst into incontrollable bouts of laughter. The effects of the joint lasted well into the night and left me with a real famine-type hunger. The next morning I devoured everything at breakfast, which

163

was unusual for me as I usually only had a slice of bread and tea. It was the first time I had eaten porridge in a couple of years.

Dope was definitely an escape route out of the reality of prison life, a way to ignore individual thoughts, to stifle memory. The only drawback was that once you came out of its influence, the reality of your situation and all its problems hit you with a vengeance. At least, that was true for me. I continued to smoke dope occasionally throughout the rest of my sentence. The few hours' release it gave me were worth the extra 'down' times I endured after its influence. I was lucky in one respect—my supplier had a regular supply and because I read and wrote his letters for him, it never ever cost me a bean. Unlike many of my contemporaries, I never advanced to other drugs on the black market. Dope was enough for me and then only in small doses.

It was examination time again. The end of yet another academic year. Open University had been a long hard slog and now was the time to put another year's work and study to the test. The examinations were gruelling and we all knew failure would result in the authorities closing the OU door for us. Examinations over, we awaited nervously the results. The fateful day arrived and Dennis Nash, the course project leader, came into the study room with a piece of paper in his hand and a smile beaming all over his face.

'You've done it, lads, you've done it.'

Ninety per cent of us had passed, myself included. Dennis' position was safe and so were the OU courses for the future. I enrolled for another year and decided to do a couple of 'A' levels on subjects I had already studied the last academic year. After all, I thought to myself, I still have plenty of time to kill. Why not use it to benefit myself? I was also pleased that the two cons I had encouraged to go on remedial classes to learn to read and write had completed a full year and were both continuing with their classes this year. Now and again they would come to my peter and read small pieces of their work to me, which delighted me no end. Although I still wrote their letters, they were copying them down in their own handwriting and sending them off. Both of them had a real appetite for learning and it wasn't long before they were putting whole letters together by themselves. At least their new skills would give them the opportunity to go straight once they were back in society again.

My third Christmas in prison. As I lay on my bed on Christmas Eve 1972 I wondered how many more there would be before they released me? My only contact with the outside world was when my parents, brothers and sisters visited me. The visits had become less frequent—not that they didn't want to visit me, quite the reverse. My mother used to write just as frequently now as she had done in the beginning and would always ask me to send a visiting order. But the longer my sentence ran, the more difficult visits became and I used to make up excuses for not sending one. Nothing ever changed inside and the family news was interesting, but I couldn't relate to it any more. After a time in prison you only see life through glossy magazines. Just then, my peter door opened and in walked Brian.

'Happy Christmas, Noel,' he said.

'Happy Christmas to you, Brian,' I replied.

I noticed he was clasping a small carrier bag under his arm.

'I've brought you a couple of things to thank you for all your efforts since you have worked for me.'

'Thank you, Brian.'

'Don't tell anyone, Noel, or I will find myself in real hot water.'

'I understand, Brian. Mum's the word.'

He left and I swiftly raised myself from my bed to examine the contents of the bag. There were biscuits, tinned meat, crisps, coffee, evaporated milk and sweets. What a surprise! I never even suspected Brian would do such a thing. To think that Brian had put his job on the line just to give me a better Christmas. The very thought brought tears to my eyes. Only he could have done such a thing. It was in keeping with his beliefs and it showed me something about the true meaning of Christmas. That evening I had myself a private feast, eating food I hadn't tasted for years.

On Christmas Day I prepared the church for morning service and made ready for the communion service. I decided never to drink the wine and water it down again. Brian deserved better for the responsibility he had given me.

The New Year brought ice and snow for quite a long period, which meant that a number of football matches had to be cancelled and we spent a number of weekends locked up in the main prison. Even the screws were pleased when the weather finally broke. By then tension on the wings had approached breaking point, cons were snappy with each other and there had been a number of fights that could have led to small riots. But the danger had passed and we, the prison team, were playing and winning again. We had already won the Wakefield and District first-division championship the previous season and were well on the way to repeating the performance this season. Since August we had lost only one match. Unlike our opponents, our team didn't change every season, as most of our players had signed on for a number of years.

At Easter the usual inter-wing football competition took place and again we won through to the final, to be played on Easter Monday, against our old enemy, 'B' wing. During the first half of the match it was obvious they wanted a physical game and intended to take no prisoners as off-the-ball fouls started to wind players up and tempers started to flare. H. stopped the game at one point and told both captains that if the game didn't clean up he would abandon the tournament and cancel all future competitions. All the players took heed of the warning because if H. said he would do it, everyone knew he was a man of his word.

The second half got under way and the score was still 0–0. When a high ball was kicked near the centre circle, I decided it was my ball, leaping into the air to head it. I noticed two opposing players coming for the same ball. At least, I thought they were coming for the ball. My head connected with the ball but their heads connected with my nose. A loud crack rang in my ears and blood literally poured down my face. I was awash in blood.

As I lay on the ground, clutching my face, I heard one say, 'That's done you, copper. It should have been your neck.'

It took a minute or so to gather myself. H. came over and wrapped a towel over my face to hold back the blood.

He examined me and said, 'The game's over for you, Noel. Your nose is all over your face. It will need an operation to fix that.'

'Is it that bad, H?'

'Yes, I'm afraid so.'

'I can't lose face, H. I'll have to finish the match,' I said.

'OK, but don't even try to head the ball.'

The player who had done the damage was sent off, knowing he wouldn't be charged as it happened on the football pitch. I resumed playing and we eventually won the match 1–0. My head felt as though it had been put through a mangle. The whole of my face ached. After showering I looked at myself in the mirror. H. was right. My nose had been spread all over my face and already two black eyes were appearing. Up to the sick-bay I went and the hospital screw gave me pain-killers and said I would have to see the doctor in the morning. It was a restless night for me as the pain grew more intense. What a relief when morning finally arrived. At least I would be able to ask for more pain-killers. The mirror reflected a mass of bruising to my eyes, nose and lips. What a sight I looked! A mass of black and blue. The doctor arrived at the sick-bay and examined me for about thirty seconds.

'This man needs an operation immediately,' he said to the hospital screw.

'How bad is it, Doc?' I asked.

'Quite serious. Your nose has been badly smashed up and we need to fix it right away. I will arrange for a surgeon to see you this afternoon.'

I saw the surgeon at the prison hospital in the afternoon and after examination he said, 'I will arrange for an operation tomorrow morning at Pinderfield Hospital. Don't worry, you will be as good as new when I am finished.'

The night was spent in the prison hospital. The following day I was escorted to Pinderfield Hospital for my operation. Dressed in prison clothing and handcuffed to two screws, we travelled there in a prison van. Upon arrival we walked the long hospital corridors to the annexe attached to the operating theatre. It was really embarrassing as the public quickly moved out of our way as we walked, whispering and pointing at me. Goodness knows who they thought I was, some arch-villain no doubt. My face didn't compliment my looks and when we arrived at the annexe the nurses looked positively frightened. The screws took off the cuffs and I undressed and donned the white operating gown I had been given. A couple of nurses returned to give me a pre-medical injection. I saw they were shaking as they prepared the needle. As they approached the bed I voiced the word, 'Boo!'

They jumped back, startled, and I started laughing at their response to my little joke.

'Don't worry, girls. He's all right. One of our better lodgers,' said the screw. 'Come on, Fellowes, behave your-self. There aren't many cons who get this sort of day-trip.'

'OK, boss.'

I was given the jab and shortly afterwards they wheeled me into the operating theatre where I met the surgeon who had examined me in Wakefield.

'This won't take long. You will soon be back to normal,' he said.

'I doubt I'll ever be that again,' I said with a smile on my face. He got the meaning and smiled himself.

The next thing, I heard a female voice saying, 'Mr Fellowes, wake up Mr Fellowes.'

I was fighting to breathe and felt heavy weights on my body. I opened my eyes to see the familiar sight of the annexe room. Then the reason for my lack of oxygen became apparent. Two nurses and four screws were sitting on top of my body.

'I can't breathe,' I groaned.

They all jumped off me and the screw explained to me that

I had reacted to the anaesthetic in a violent way. Apparently when I was coming round and started to kick and flail my fists about, the nurses were concerned I would damage my nose again, so they all pinned me down.

An hour or so later I was on my way back to prison, handcuffed and feeling rather lightheaded. Back at base I was taken to the prison hospital where I remained for a week. The surgeon came to see me again to check on his work.

'It's a great success,' he said. 'Take it easy for a month and you won't know the difference.'

I thanked him for his help and the speed with which he had responded to my dilemma. Although my nose had a slight twist to it, the surgeon had done a splendid job on it. H. came to see me in hospital and cracked a few jokes about my looks. He also pointed out that if I didn't get out soon he would have to find a replacement for weight training. Typical of H.— always the motivator.

It wasn't long before I found myself back on the wing again, enjoying the monotony of prison routine. My stay in hospital had interrupted my studies, so I had to get my head down again. Examinations were only a few weeks away and I needed to revise. It was a case of literally burning the midnight oil. The lights were turned out at nine o'clock every evening, but I had access to candles. Brian had given me permission to take the altar candles when they were no longer of use. He usually asked me to change them when they were three-quarters of the way down, which left a good four inches of candle.

Just before examinations began I was told by the Assistant Governor that my annual application for parole had come up. I had a long conversation with Brian about it and told him I had decided not to apply for parole as there didn't seem any point, considering the interviews last year. Brian disagreed and encouraged me to apply on the premise that I had nothing to lose. I applied and met the parole board man again.

'This is your second application for parole, Mr Fellowes.

Has anything changed since last year?'

'Nothing at all,' I replied, 'other than spending another year inside and having my nose broken again.'

'I see. Well, I think we have all we need from our last interview,' he said. 'What about your attitude to the people you say put you in this position? How do you feel about them?'

'All I can say is my hands are tied. Although I still hold them responsible, there is no way I ever want to find myself inside prison again. I have no intention of revenge. What's done is done. I live in the hope that one day my name will be cleared. Besides, I intend to start a new life in Bracknell, 250 miles away from Morecambe, and I have no intention of visiting Morecambe ever again. There is nothing but hurt in my memory of that town.'

'Very well, Mr Fellowes. That's all the questions I have.'

Returning to the wing I felt the same as I had done a year previously—no chance.

Examination time came and again I passed. After three solid years I felt weary of studying and told H. that I needed a break from the books. He told me that one of his own red bands was leaving him to go on full-time education and if I wanted I could have his job as red band for the gym. The thought of working with H. thrilled me. It meant I would be able to use the gym and the weight-lifting facilities all the time. I approached Brian with the proposal and he said he was reluctant to see me go but if I really wanted to, I could. It was a difficult decision for me as I respected both men equally. I chewed it over in my mind and decided on H.'s offer as it would mean a change of scenery and I would have a break from studying. My transfer approved, I started working for H. in the gym and I loved it.

I became very friendly with H. as I worked with him, telling him of my past and my plans for the future. He in turn encouraged me and advised me of situations to avoid once outside again. Under his training and supervision I became super-fit and one of the strongest weight-trainers in the prison. He was the one who advised me not to seek retaliatory action against the con who had broken my nose. I respected his counsel and followed his advice. One of H.'s golden rules was that if you worked for him then you had to keep your nose clean. Otherwise you lost your job. In Wakefield it was generally accepted that gym red band was the best number in the prison. It was and I wasn't going to risk a few minutes of pleasurable revenge for the sake of my job.

Christmas came and I still hadn't heard from the parole board about their decision. Whatever, I thought to myself, this would be my last Christmas in prison as my earliest release date was November 1974. If I kept myself out of trouble, I had ten more months to go.

In the second week of January 1974, I was called to the Assistant Governor's office.

'811168 Fellowes, Sir,' I said.

'Well, Fellowes, you will be pleased to know your application for parole has been approved. You will be released on parole on the twenty-fifth of January.'

I couldn't believe my ears.

'Pardon,' I said.

'Yes, you heard it right, Fellowes. Twenty-fifth of January you're going out.'

I was speechless.

'Fifteen days and I will be out,' I kept saying to myself.

Back in my peter I jumped up and down on the bed like a boy who had just opened his Christmas presents. I couldn't contain my excitement. I'd beaten the system. I had been given ten months' parole. I had done them out of ten months inside. Brian and H. were delighted with my news. They both wished me every success in the challenge to rebuild my life outside.

The process of discharge swung into action—final interviews with the various social and welfare officers concerned with my wellbeing on parole, including the long typed list of dos and don'ts. Then on to the clothing officer, who informed me I was eligible for a set of underclothes, socks, shoes, two shirts, a sports jacket and a pair of trousers. The choice was limited in the prison fashion house. I chose the best of the old-fashioned clothing and awaited the final day of imprisonment to come to an end.

11

First Taste of Freedom

I awoke on the morning of 24 January 1974 excited at the prospect and certainty that tomorrow would bring the ultimate answer. Freedom! My innermost feelings were a mixture of excitement and apprehension as I thought of life outside these cold grey walls of captivity. I reflected for a while on the experience of incarceration and what lasting effects it would have on my outside life. In nearly four years I had hardly made a decision. Everything had been thought out for me. Very soon I would have to make decisions again. Would I be up to it?

The earlier encounters with violence and intimidation had left scars, both in my attitudes and in my personality. I had become an intense and deep person, hiding behind a mask of extrovert behaviour. Behind the façade was a frightened, insecure man, fighting for reality and recognition, whatever the cost. To survive in prison I had had to adjust and live by the unwritten laws of prison life. In society, the rules would be different again and I had long since forgotten them.

In the last four years I had viewed society through glossy magazines. All the houses looked new and comfortable, the clothes were excitingly stylish. Even the women all looked manicured and beautiful. Was this reality or just a toyland in my own imagination? To my credit, I had used the time well in educating myself and the education certificates would at the very least give me an opportunity to secure a worthwhile career. Only in time would I be able to answer all these innumerable questions. In twenty-four hours from now, I would start to find out.

I spent most of the day saying my last goodbyes to Brian, the chaplain, H., and the many other acquaintances I had shared my life with in Wakefield. There were also the usual discharge formalities to attend to and at lunch-time I had my final meeting with the governor.

'811168 Fellowes, Sir,' I said as I stood before the governor. There was a hidden satisfaction in the words, knowing that tomorrow I would be a person again. Noel Fellowes would again emerge into society. No longer would I be a number in a primitive penal institution.

'Well, Fellowes, your final day under our care is drawing to an end. I hope you have learned well and make a useful contribution to society in your future.'

'I intend to do my best, Sir.'

'Many faces pass through Wakefield, Fellowes, but you seem to have used your time productively while here. I wish you well for the future.'

'Thank you, Governor,' I said. He probably gave the same lines to all the cons who were due for release, but at least they were words of encouragement.

In the afternoon I went to the tailor's shop to try on my new clothing, which needed slight alteration before the big day. Having donned the full outfit I felt like a million dollars. The cons in the tailor's shop had done a good job. Everything fitted perfectly. What a great feeling, to be wearing civilian clothing that actually fitted. The mirror reflected a new person. Gone was the drab prison clothing. Now I was looking at a tall, well-dressed man I hadn't seen in years. Just standing there before the mirror triggered excitement. It would only be hours now before I would undress and dress in prison for the last time. I dropped the tailor red band half an ounce of snout for doing such a good job on my discharge clothing, then went back on to the wing.

The next exercise was easy. It was time to distribute my excess belongings to the cons who had served me best during my stay at Wakefield. It's a tradition in long-term prisons to leave all your accumulated wealth and possessions to the cons with time still to serve. I collected together my radio, donkey jacket, sports gear, football boots, books, magazines and other prize possessions. Off I went round to Joey's peter and dropped off my radio and jacket, then on to Geordie's peter with the rest. They were both well pleased with the gifts as they would sell them to new cons for snout. My peter was bare. Just a bed, slop bucket, wash bowl and jug. All the wheeling and dealing over the years to acquire such luxuries had taken less than five minutes to dispose of. After tea I spent my last evening on association, playing table-tennis to try to encourage the clock to move faster. The afternoon had really dragged by. Every minute seemed like an hour.

Table-tennis seemed a good way of killing time as it demanded concentration and took my mind off the dreaded clock. Not that it worked. I was so wound up with excitement that I was thrashed out of sight! The cons laughed their heads off. They knew what I was going through. The last few hours inside are the worst and they had seen it all before. The bell went. It was 8.30 p.m. Association over, it was time to be banged up for the night.

The peter door slammed shut to the sound of the discipline screw saying, 'Best of luck on the outside, Fellowes.'

'Thanks, boss.'

I lay there for what seemed like hours trying to get off to sleep, with no success. In the end I decided to count sheep and after reaching six hundred I gave that idea up. I must have dropped off at some point as I was wakened by the sound of my peter door opening and a screw saying, 'Come on, lad. You don't want to be late for your release, do you?'

I leapt out of bed, my stomach turning over and my legs like jelly. A state of excitement and nervousness had overtaken me.

'I'm going home. I'm actually going home,' I said to myself over and over again. It was like a dream. I couldn't believe it. I remembered my arrest and initial remand. The feelings were very similar, but this time I had everything to look forward to. Within a couple of minutes I was washed, dressed and on my way to reception for the first change of clothing. As I passed Joey's peter I kicked the door.

'See you, Joey,' I shouted. With that remark a whole load of abuse came from other peters, where they were trying to sleep.

'See yer, la,' shouted Joey.

'See you suckers sometime,' I shouted again.

Another load of abuse came flooding back and I carried on walking, laughing at some of the more colourful comments.

'Keep your comments down,' said the screw to me in an angry voice.

'OK, boss.'

We arrived at reception and I gladly changed into my new clothes ready for my release. No longer would I have to wear prison clothes. Now I would be able to wear what I wanted. The reception screw checked my belongings in case I was trying to smuggle anything out. All I had was a box of letters from my mother and my examination certificates. Having searched everything, he parcelled them up into a brown paper package and handed it to me. The time was ten minutes past seven. I was to be released at exactly half past. Another screw beckoned me over and asked me to sign a form, which I did. To my surprise he handed me about £18 which was my entitlement upon release. I looked at it and thought, 'Not bad for four years' work.' I felt like throwing it back at him. What a paltry sum of money to build a new life on! I was overawed at the benevolence of the system. There I stood in new clothing, holding a brown paper package containing my only worldly possessions and £18 in my pocket. I felt sad at the thought of anybody leaving Wakefield carrying the same but having no family or friends to rely on. What chance could they have on the outside? No chance at all.

The clock struck half past seven and the screw ushered me to the picket door inside the main prison gatehouse.

'Your time is up, Fellowes. Off you go, lad.'

The door opened and I took one small step through the door into freedom. Tears formed in my eyes as I saw my mother and father waiting in their car only a few yards away. I walked slowly towards the car, then suddenly stopped, turned and looked at the prison for the first time from the outside. Anger and hatred welled up inside as I surveyed the walls and the cell-blocks behind them. I wiped the tears from my eyes and vowed that no man would ever put me behind bars again for something I hadn't done. I turned and headed for my parents.

My mother greeted me with a customary hug and a kiss. My father seemed lost for words, but his face said it all for him. They were both as thrilled as I was. Within a few minutes we were on our way out of Wakefield, heading for the M1 southwards. Initially there was no conversation in the car. We were all busy thinking our own private thoughts. After a couple of miles we joined the M1 and started our journey proper to Bracknell in Berkshire, some 240 miles away.

My parents both looked tired and I asked my father,

'What was the journey like coming up, Dad?'

'We hit everything possible, son. Snow, ice, fog—the lot. We set off from home at two o'clock this morning and we were so badly held up with the weather that at one stage we didn't think we would get here on time. In fact, when the weather cleared some eighty miles away, I put my foot down and was stopped by the police for speeding.'

My heart sank. 'Don't say you're going to get an endorsement on my behalf,' I thought to myself.

'What did you do, Dad?'

'Well, I told the truth. I told the officer we were coming to pick you up from prison and we had to be at Wakefield for 7.30 a.m. and we were way behind schedule. We were concerned that you would be released and we wouldn't be there to meet you.'

'What did he do?'

'He believed me and let us go.'

I was relieved to hear it. At least there were still policemen about who had credibility. We talked about the family and other day-to-day things for a while. Then I noticed a new anxiety creeping upon me. I started to shake and perspiration formed on my brow and began to run over my face and lips. We were travelling at seventy miles an hour along the motorway: the fastest I had travelled in four years was at running pace. The sheer speed of the car and the other traffic heading in the same direction frightened me. What was normal to my parents and other road users was totally abnormal to me. I couldn't control the fear and anxiety I felt. The further we went, the more anxious I became. Rather than share my feelings with my parents I just closed my eyes and gripped the door handle tightly, hoping we would stop soon. My mother noticed my unnatural state and soon worked out the reason for my silence and perspiration. She offered a comforting hand as if to say, don't worry, we know what you're going through.

'I'm all right, mother, I'll soon get used to it,' I said, trying to sound confident and reassuring. Much to my relief we stopped at a service station. I'd survived the first sixty odd miles.

'Let's get you some real food,' my father said as we walked to the service area. I felt quite excited at the prospect of selecting what I felt like eating. This was a brand new world. Now I could eat what I wanted. My first full English breakfast went down a treat. I savoured every mouthful. It was the best breakfast I had tasted in my whole life. We continued on our journey home and by the end of the motorway I was beginning to relax. It's strange how one's body adjusts to circumstances and situations so quickly. A few hours before I was a nervous wreck. Now I was feeling secure and comfortable.

In the early afternoon we arrived in Bracknell. This was the town where I intended to build a new life. Bracknell was a couple of hundred miles away from Morecambe and Wakefield; nobody knew me here or my history. As we drove through the town, I told myself, 'This is your only chance, Noel. A new town, new life and new opportunity to make something of yourself.' I was pumping positive thoughts into my head. What was past was now past. Take up the challenge of the future. I surveyed my parents' home from the car and it finally sunk in that I was home. This was no dream or figment of my imagination. It was real. The house stood before me. I felt somewhat detached from myself, trying to understand it.

Only hours ago I was in my peter; now I was home. The very thought blew my mind.

Once inside, the first thing that struck me was the size. It seemed so dark and tiny. Wakefield held six hundred cons. This held five people. I had imagined it to be much bigger and lighter from what I had seen in the magazine life of prison. But I soon adjusted to my surroundings and my mind was still occupied with the newness of being free. My brother Paul and my youngest brother, Roger, were still living at home. My other brother, John, had got married when I was still serving time in Wakefield. Kay, my youngest sister, was nursing in Windsor and was living there.

Roger was the first one to arrive home from work. It was tremendous seeing him walk through the door. He was warm and outgoing, sincere in his welcome towards me. I was astounded to see how he had grown and matured in the years I had been away. When Paul arrived he seemed edgy as he greeted me. I sensed a nervousness in his voice and apprehension as I went to hug him. He backed off and I realized he was still carrying inner guilt at what had happened in court four years ago. It disturbed me, as I knew the truth: he had been a mere pawn sacrificed in the game to destroy me and still he carried the burden.

'I'm really pleased to be home again with you, Paul,' I said.

'So am I,' he replied.

Those few words took the intensity out of the situation and the moment was won. We ate dinner together and chatted on about family news. Then Roger told me that he was only working half a day tomorrow and offered to take me shopping in the afternoon. I accepted. It would be good to see the centre of Bracknell and I still had the £18 to spend.

My first night of freedom was spent at home watching the television. It was strange to me. As it was January, the doors to both the dining-room and hall were shut to keep the heat in the lounge. Every time someone left or entered the room, they shut the doors, and I got up and opened them again, just a couple of inches so I could see they were ajar. I learned something else about myself—I couldn't stand doors being closed behind me. The family didn't react. They took it in their stride. I could see by the expressions on their faces that I was going to take some getting used to. As I viewed the television, I kept waiting for the bell to indicate it was time for bed. Such was the confusion of my mind. Ten o'clock came and I was exhausted. I bade goodnight to the family and went to bed. That was an experience in itself—scented, clean sheets and a comfortable mattress. Sheer luxury.

Once in bed, I lay awake for a while, soaking up the memorable day. It all seemed like a dream. I felt so content and happy. I didn't want it to end in case I found myself waking up in prison again. The next morning, my fears were realized. I awoke to strange surroundings—curtains, wallpaper and a strange room. I panicked, trying to understand what tricks my imagination was playing on me. I kept opening and closing my eyes, but still the scenery was intact. Then I realized I was home. I breathed a sigh of relief.

Downstairs I found my mother busy cooking my breakfast. My father and brothers had already left for work. I had to wait for the probation officer to call on me in the morning to give me the rundown on the restrictions of my parole. She arrived at midday—a sincere, friendly woman who asked about my welfare, first impressions of freedom and plans for the future. I answered her questions honestly and then she informed me there were no restrictions other than that I had to report to her office once a week to chat over the way things were going. I had imagined parole meant far more than that, so I felt relieved knowing I had freedom of movement without time curfews. Thirty minutes later she was on her way out.

'Thank you Mrs . . .' Before I could finish she said,

'Norma. You can call me Norma, Noel.'

'Thanks, Norma,' I said.

Roger returned at one o'clock, grabbed a quick bite to eat and off we went to Bracknell shopping.

As we arrived at the multi-storey car park, Roger turned to me and said, 'I've been saving up since I heard you were coming home and I would like you to have this.'

It was thirty pounds. My heart was full of gratitude to my brother. What a gesture! He had only just qualified as a butcher and he had saved his money for me.

'I can't take that, Roger. It's too much.'

'Honestly, Noel. I want you to have it. Please take it or I will be offended.'

I took it with great appreciation. What love.

'What can I say, Roger? Words fail me. Thank you. I will never forget it.'

I felt a deep sense of gratitude and belonging. What a precious and practical gift. We walked through some of the larger stores and I had the strangest feeling that everyone was looking at me. They weren't, of course, it was just my own insecurity. I bought a pair of trousers and a shirt—paying for them was another hurdle. Since my incarceration the currency had changed from pounds, shillings and pence to metric. The assistant rang up the till and I fumbled in my pockets trying to come up with the right amount. I finished up giving her pound notes to try to hide my embarrassment. She in turn gave me my change—numerous coins I had never seen before. Roger explained their value, another lesson learned.

After about an hour I felt very weary. People were rushing to and fro and I felt giddy just observing them. Everything moved so slowly in prison, yet outside it seemed people moved nearly as quickly as the traffic.

'I'll have to go home, Roger,' I said. 'It's all too fast for me at the moment.'

'OK.'

Back in the security of home, I reflected on the shopping trip. I knew things would be different on the outside and certain adjustments would be necessary, but I hadn't bargained for such a stark contrast. The simple task of buying a couple of articles in a clothing shop had revealed my deep sense of inferiority and insecurity. I had felt embarrassed both trying to pay for the articles and—even worse—speaking to the female behind the counter. Coupled with that was the sheer pace of life. Could I ever adjust to it? Only time would tell. For the time being I felt I would be better off at home. I felt secure inside the four walls and I had all the comforts of home life. I didn't need anything else. Both Paul and Roger invited me out in the evenings that followed; I declined the offers, making excuses as best I could.

The following week I started work. My father had secured a job for me as a general labourer on a building site in Paddington, London. He was the site agent on the contract and I was to work under him. Dressed in my working clothes and armed with the lunch bag and flask prepared by my mother, I set off with him at seven o'clock for work. I felt slightly nervous at the prospect of meeting people and hoped I would cope. When we arrived on site, my father introduced me to the men, including the other labourers I was to work with. The contract was to demolish a very large house and build luxury flats in its place. Introductions over, I was given a sledge-hammer and instructed to help knock down internal walls. By the end of the day I was shattered.

During the morning some of the men had started to ask probing questions like, 'How long have you been home?'

'Why did you come down from the north?'

And the funniest of all, 'Are you on the run?'

My defence mechanism sprang into action as I tried to cover my tracks, saying I wasn't sure how long I would stay in the south. It was a trial period.

One cockney said to me, 'It's all right for you. Your bleedin' old man is the gaffer. He'll look after you.'

I knew then that they thought I had a soft number, so I worked twice as hard as any of them.

By the end of the week I had won their respect. Not one of them could measure up to my work performance. The years of weight-training had paid off. Now they accepted me as one of the boys. It was only a small thing but I felt pleased with myself for having jumped the hurdle they had set up for me. Another boost—it was pay day. My first wage for four years. The packet revealed a staggering sixty pounds. It seemed like a small fortune to me. Now I was surely on the road to success. All the physical effort and sweat had been worth it. I had actually earned the money. It was mine. After giving up my housekeeping to my mother, I went to my bedroom and counted the money over and over again. I felt like a child with his piggy-bank, emptying it and counting endlessly. I decided to save as much as I could, then buy a whole new wardrobe of clothes.

On the Monday evening following work I had to report to Norma at the probation office. I arrived on time and she asked me how I was getting on. Trying to cover my real feelings, I put on a brave front saying I was fine and everything was going really well.

'How are you adjusting to everyday life outside?' she asked.

'Really well. No problems at all.'

'That's remarkable, considering your time inside.'

'Well, obviously I have to make minor adjustments as the need arises, but generally things are good.'

'Are you getting out much?'

'Occasionally with my brothers, but that suits me.'

'Good. See you next week then.'

I was relieved when the meeting ended. Norma was a lovely lady, genuine in every respect, but to me she still belonged to the system. Take away the badge of office and Norma was really a very nice, caring human being. My problem was that I didn't trust anybody other than myself and four years on my own had reinforced that belief. The less the system learned about me, my feelings and my life, the more I liked it. During my further weekly visits I learned the art of combating her inquisitive form of questioning by answering in a way that flattered her. My cunning was still intact. The years of listening and weighing people up had paid off again. I knew her strengths and weaknesses. Her training had been formal and calculated; mine was gained at grass roots from the encyclopaedia of life.

The trouble with the system is not that the individuals within it are necessarily at fault but its own tendency to strangle itself through archaic theories and red tape. First it punishes the individual through the deprivation and inhuman existence of prison life. Then, after destroying him, it tries to rebuild him from scratch. The logical thing would be to do the rebuilding right from the beginning of a sentence, not after the sentence has been served. I had long since stopped trying to understand the system and now I was doubly sure I was going to live my life by my own ground rules, not theirs. On reflection, it was an arrogant stance, but I saw it as my democratic right. After all, I was the injured party. It was the system who had got it wrong.

After a couple of weeks staying at home every evening, Roger again asked me if I would like to go out with him. I reluctantly accepted the invitation. We went to a local pub and had a couple of drinks. To my surprise I enjoyed myself. The place was packed and everyone was having a good time. More to the point, the opposite sex was much in abundance and it wasn't long before a couple of young ladies drew us into conversation. I felt awkward, not having conversed with females for a long time.

'Haven't seen you around before,' one said to me. 'Where do you come from?'

'Wakefield,' I said.

'Where's that?'

'Yorkshire.'

'Want to buy me a drink?'

'Why? Haven't you got any money?'

She laughed.

'That's a new one.'

'OK. What you drinking?'

'Gin and tonic, please.'

I returned with half a lager.

'Sorry. Didn't have enough money for the gin and tonic.'

'You really are cheeky, aren't you?'

'Yep, I sure am.' There was no way I was going to spend my hard-earned money on someone else's pleasure. I felt more relaxed as we continued to talk, but the perpetual smell of perfume coming from her direction sent my legs a bit wobbly. The sweet fragrance of femininity had long since been lost, replaced by male sweat and slop-out buckets. She was giving me the big come on and I wasn't playing. Half a pint of lager was the top limit of my intended expenditure. Roger kept giving me the eye. He too felt awkward. He was courting strongly and didn't want female company at all.

'Nice to have met you. Sorry but we have got to go now,' I said.

Relief covered Roger's face.

'Let's go, Roger.'

We made our way out and she followed me.

'Aren't you going to ask me out?'

'Can't afford it, luv.'

She wasn't taking no for an answer.

'OK. I'll see you here at seven on Sunday,' I said.

Satisfied, she returned to the pub and we went home. I had no intention of turning up on Sunday. It was just a way of getting out of the situation. I had enjoyed the company but women were not in my plan just yet. The sweet smell of perfume lingered on as we drove home. That was yet another experience in the short chapter of freedom. It had been a good job that Roger had been there. All my emotions had been responding to her advances, verbal and physical. Inside my head I kept saying, 'Take it easy, back off, you're not ready yet, take your time, enjoy the moment and leave.' It was a relief to know that my head had ruled my emotions. Years before, the reverse had been true.

The following week my father asked if I wanted to ease back into driving a car again.

'I'm not sure I could handle the speed and the traffic,' I replied.

'If you don't try you won't find out.'

That seemed totally logical to me. The plan was that I would drive his car to work in the morning when there wasn't much traffic on the road. I sat in the driver's seat and nervously turned the ignition key. The engine started first time. I selected the gear and off we went. It felt strange as I drove the car along the road, trying to keep it in a central position. At the first junction I braked too hard, panicked and stalled the engine.

'It's no good, Dad. I haven't got the confidence.'

'You can do it, son. Start her up again.'

If he says I can do it, then I can do it, I said to myself. Off we went again and at the next junction I stopped perfectly.

'Take your time, son. Adjust the speed to your confidence.'

After twenty miles I felt as though I had never stopped driving. He had been right—to win, you have to try. I drove to work every morning for a week or two, growing in confidence at every try.

One afternoon my father said, 'You can drive home to-night, Noel, if you like.'

This was my big test. It meant driving through London at the start of the rush hour. In his own way my father had planned the whole driving campaign from the beginning. I rose to the challenge and drove home without a hitch. Now I was capable of driving anywhere at all by myself.

Life was sweet. The early weeks of freedom were paying dividends. I had a job, money, a secure home and, most of all, my freedom. My self-confidence had grown since my early encounters with the outside world. Though I still tended to compare the two lifestyles, inside and out, I was learning to cope with people and situations every day.

One Sunday evening I decided the time had come to venture out on my own. I announced to my parents that I was going down the road for a quiet drink—to test the water by myself, so to speak. They seemed happy with the idea. In a strange way I felt they had been concerned at my always staying indoors. Off I strolled to the Golden Farmer pub and ordered my pint of lager. The pub was quite busy and I drank my lager to the sound of the juke-box in full swing. As I sat on the bar stool minding my own business, a man appeared at the bar, about thirty-five years old, medium build and around five-foot-seven inches tall.

'Give me a whisky, Jimmy,' he shouted to the barman. As he waited with an angry expression on his face, I noticed him looking me up and down. Instantly the adrenalin started to flow. Trouble! I could sense it a mile away.

Drink in hand he came up to me and said, 'See you, big 'un. I don't like you.'

'You don't even know me.'

'I don't like yer and that's it.'

My mind was in overdrive. I was on parole—I couldn't afford any trouble. If I lifted a hand I would be back inside.

'Look, I don't want any trouble, mate. I'm just having a quiet drink,' I said.

'I'll give yer trouble, big 'un.'

Then he walked away.

The barman said, 'Take no notice of him. He's aggressive in drink. Any more trouble and I will order him out.'

'OK,' I said.

I decided to drink up and go. It seemed the easiest way out of the situation. But before I could finish my drink and do the vanishing trick, the mad Scotsman returned, still in his aggressive state.

'How about you and me then, big 'un?'

'Sorry, mate. I don't want trouble. You better find someone else.'

I knocked my cigarettes from the bar onto the floor on purpose. Keeping my right hand on the bar, holding the remains of my drink, I stooped down giving the impression I was attempting to recover my cigarettes. He didn't move an inch. I looked him straight in the eye, then grabbed his private parts with my left hand and squeezed them as tightly as I could. Believe me, I really possessed a strong grip. Instant pain reflected in his face, his mouth opened wide and a deep groaning sound emerged from it. I kept a tight grip for about thirty seconds and when I saw his eyes starting to roll and lumps appear in his throat, I let go. He fell into a crumpled heap on the floor, gasping for breath.

'I told you I didn't want any trouble.'

I doubt if he even heard me. People in the bar hadn't even

noticed what had happened. I'd done a truly professional job on him. I swiftly drank the rest of my lager and left. The Scot was still rolling on the floor. Once outside I made haste to get home in case someone called the police. Luckily for me, it was my first visit to the pub. Nobody knew me there. In future I would give it a wide berth. It was just my luck—to go out for a quiet drink on my own for the first time and end up in trouble.

When I arrived home my mother asked if I was all right.

'Everything's great,' I said.

Little did she know I was sweating with anxiety in case the police should come knocking on the door. After about an hour I began to relax again. The crisis point had passed—I was safe. That one incident stopped me in my tracks. I decided in future that I would only go out at nights in my brothers' company. Then at least there would be safety in numbers.

The first month of freedom had been a series of constant adjustments, of unlearning prison life and routine and replacing them with new rules, decisions, responsibilities and encountering new dangers. I was coping quite well but I remained introverted. Having spent so long in isolation in the past I was happy with my own company, only speaking when spoken to and never offering any explanation of my past life. There was a small security in knowing that here in Bracknell nobody knew my past, other than the probation office and my family. Still, I lived with all the nightmares of the past and the label of being a convicted killer. Whatever happened in the future, I knew I had to protect my new-found anonymity, no matter the cost.

Since my arrival at home neither my parents nor brothers had ever mentioned prison or the case against me. It was obvious to me that they must have discussed my homecoming in advance and decided silence on the subject would be the safest thing. I wasn't too concerned about their decision, but it just meant I had to lock all my hurt and frustration deeper inside myself. Besides, nothing could be gained in sharing the past and trying to understand and comprehend the reality of it all would only put more pressure on them. At least I was one of the lucky ones—I had a family and a home to return to. Many who had been released before me had nobody at all.

I was working hard and saving my money with the satisfaction of knowing that the amount grew steadily week by week. One of the men at work said he was buying a new car and offered to sell me his old one for fifty pounds. After close examination of the Ford Zephyr, I decided to buy it. Now I was the proud owner of a car. It was two-tone—white and rust. Having taxed and insured the vehicle, I was independently mobile. My father was running two other contracts besides the one I was working on, which had meant relying on him to pick me up at the end of the day. Now I could drive myself to and from work with the added bonus of going out at weekends if I liked. It certainly wasn't the classiest car on the road, but it was reliable. Roger helped me fill in the holes and clean it up, which also helped to occupy my time in the evenings.

Norma, my probation officer, was delighted with my progress and extended our meetings to once every two weeks. I was relieved to hear the new arrangement as I always clammed up when visiting the probation office—it reminded me too much of my recent past.

Paul was rarely at home these days. He was engaged to a girl called Linda in Reading and seemed to spend most of his time over there. He used to work, come home, grab a meal, change and out he would go again. I wondered if he wasn't too pleased at my returning home, but Roger assured me it was his normal lifestyle. He was head-over-heels in love. One Friday night, Paul came in and asked me over dinner if I would like to give him a hand over the weekend to finish off a garage he was building for a friend.

'What's the money situation like?' I asked.

'It's good money, Noel,' he replied.

We agreed a sum for my labour and on the Saturday I went with him to work. It was the first opportunity I had had to speak to Paul on my own for any real length of time. He told me about his plans for the future, the forthcoming marriage to Linda and the need to work for extra money to cover all the expenses of the wedding. His whole conversation was preoccupied with his wedding plans and his future life.

'I'm really pleased for you, Paul, and I feel sure everything will run like clockwork on the day,' I said.

'Thanks, Noel. You'll never know how much I love Linda. She really is great for me.'

'Listen, Paul. Now we are alone I need to put a couple of things straight. Since I got home you have been uneasy with me and I think we both know the reason. I just want you to know that I never blamed you for giving evidence at the trial. I hold the prosecution responsible. The police must have put the frighteners on you, saying you committed the crime with me and I was covering up for you.'

'Absolutely right,' he answered. 'They frightened me to death, wrote out a statement and told me to sign it. I didn't know what to do. I was confused. Then in court I tried to tell them that I hadn't said a number of things and the barrister twisted what I said.'

'Well, don't let it worry you any longer, Paul. Both you and I know the truth, so stop persecuting yourself.'

'I just can't forgive myself, Noel. It really haunts me all the time,' he said.

'Paul, I love you as a brother. You know that, don't you?'

'Yes.'

'Then stop carrying this burden. It doesn't belong to you—it never did.'

'I'll try.'

We worked together all day and I could see our short conversation had made a difference. He was more relaxed than at any time I had seen him since my release. I knew he had punished himself mentally since the trial and, seeing the results for myself, I felt even more embittered against the authorities for what they had done to him. We worked all day on the Sunday to finish the job and by about six o'clock we had finished. The man paid Paul and he in turn gave me my share of the greenbacks. Feeling exhausted, we headed home in Paul's car.

'I just want to stop at the Three Frogs and tell Linda I will see her later. That all right with you, Noel?' asked Paul.

'Sure. No problem.'

The Three Frogs was a popular pub in Wokingham where Linda worked part-time. Paul went in to see her and I stayed in the car. A couple of minutes later he returned.

'Linda wants to meet you, Noel. Come in for a quick drink.'

'I can't go in there in my working clothes.'

'Course you can. I just did, it's all right.'

'Oh, OK,' I said, getting out of the car. Paul wasn't going to take no for an answer. Once inside, Paul introduced me to Linda. As we shook hands, I could see why Paul was so preoccupied with his fiancée. She was a beautiful girl. When Linda had served our drinks, I noticed a woman walking towards us. She had striking red hair which was her own natural colour.

'Coral,' said Paul.

'Yes, Paul,' she said in a cultured voice.

'This is my elder brother, Noel. I would like you to meet him.'

'Hello, Noel. Pleased to meet you.'

'I'm pleased to meet you,' I replied.

'Where have you come from?' asked Coral.

'We've been building a garage down the road.'

I couldn't say I had just spent four years in Wakefield, could I?

Coral smiled. Her smile was wide, lighting up the whole of her face.

'I didn't mean that, silly legs. You haven't got a southern accent, have you?'

'I've just moved down from the north,' I said. 'We'd better make tracks, Paul, or our dinner will be ruined.'

Both Linda and Coral said goodbye and we left.

'What did you think of my girl then, kid?' asked Paul.

She seems a very nice girl. I was very pleased to meet her.'

'What about Coral?'

'The sort of woman dreams are made of—sheer class,' I said.

'You can say that again.'

'Sheer class. Sheer class,' I said. We both burst out laughing. The funny thing was, I really meant what I'd said.

12

A Remarkable Woman

In the middle of March 1974, the weather changed for the better and there was a hint of spring in the air. Having only ventured out a couple of times in the evening since my release, I was looking forward to the longer days. At least I would be able to go out for evening strolls if I so fancied. Nearly three months had passed since my release, yet it still felt like yesterday. Although I was free, the torment of prison lived on as every night I recalled the horrors of prison life in my dreams. I hoped the constant dreams would fade with time, but I dreaded the thought that I would continue to be a prisoner of my mind and memory. Much of the past was still locked within me. I never shared the horror of my nightly fears with anyone. I had become an island; besides, I thought, nobody would understand anyway.

One evening Paul came in from work and, in between eating and changing to go out again, he said, 'Remember Coral, the woman you were introduced to in the Three Frogs?'

'The one with the red hair and big smile,' I said.

'Yes, you've got her.'

'What about her?'

'She really fancies you.'

'You're pulling my leg. I don't believe you.'

'Honestly, Noel. No kidding. She really does. Look, there's her telephone number. She'd like you to give her a ring.'

Paul passed me a slip of paper with the telephone number written on it. I just stared at it in disbelief.

'I can't ring her up. I don't even know her.'

'Ring her up. She's expecting you to call and ask her out for a drink. That's all you have to do, kid.'

'I can't do that. I wouldn't know what to say to her.'

'Would you feel better coming out with Linda and me? We could make a foursome.'

'Yes, that would be a better idea.'

'OK, then, arrange it for next Friday at seven-thirty and we'll all go out together.'

Within ten minutes Paul was washed, shaved, changed and on his way out. I paced the hallway quite excitedly, trying to pluck up the courage to pick up the telephone and make the call to Coral. Having only met her for a few brief minutes previously, I tried to think of a way to open the conversation. A quarter of an hour later, I still hadn't made the call. There was a fight going on inside me. I desperately wanted to make the call, but inherent insecurity prevented me from doing so. 'It's only a phone call. She can only say yes or no,' I kept saying to myself. After some time I dialled the number and the ringing tone sent me into a cold sweat.

'Who's speaking, please?' asked a soft, warm, inviting voice.

'I would like to speak to Coral, please.'

'This is Coral speaking.'

My legs turned to jelly.

'Er, hello Coral. This is Noel, Paul's brother,' I said.

'Hello Noel. What can I do for you?' she asked.

'Well, er, I was wondering if you would like to come out with me for a drink next Friday evening, along with Paul and Linda.'

'Where to?'

Now I was really nervous. I didn't have a clue where we were going.

'It's a surprise,' I said, breathing a sigh of relief as the thought came into my head.

'Yes, all right then. What time do you want to pick me up?'

'About seven-thirty if that's all right with you.'

'That's fine by me,' she said.

'Thank you very much,' I said and put the phone down. I couldn't believe it. She had said yes and I had a date with her. I'd cracked it. I soon came down to earth again when I realized I had forgotten to ask her where she lived in my excitement. What a dummy! Fancy arranging to pick someone up you were trying to impress and not asking where she lived. There was no way I could ring back. It would only add to my embarrassment. Maybe Paul would know where Coral lived. I asked Paul the next day. Much to my dismay he didn't know.

'Coral asked me where we were going on Friday and I told her it was a surprise, because I hadn't a clue where you had planned to go,' I said.

'Well, I think we'll go to Boulters Lock on the Thames. It's a really nice bar and restaurant.'

'Make sure it looks like a surprise, Paul, or I'll look a fool.'

I was really excited at the prospect of taking Coral out and Friday couldn't come soon enough for me.

The big day arrived. Having spent the best part of an hour sprucing myself up for the great event I was ready. Paul hadn't managed to find out where Coral lived. The only course of action left was for me to phone her again. Tongue in cheek I phoned, gave my apologies and asked her where she lived.

'I was expecting you to call,' she said. 'I thought to myself after your last call, how on earth can he pick me up when he never asked where I lived?'

I felt a right wally. What on earth did Coral think of me, making such a stupid mistake? It was too late to get out of it. Paul had picked Linda up and was waiting for me to give him Coral's address. We drove to Coral's home and I went to announce our arrival. A teenage girl opened the door and I said, somewhat bewildered,

'Does Coral live here?'

'Mum, it's a man for you,' she said in the direction of the stairwell.

'I won't be a minute. Ask him to come in.'

I stood in the hallway a little confused. Surely Coral isn't married, I thought to myself. Coral came down the stairs. She looked stunning.

'Sorry to keep you, Noel. I had to make sure the baby was settled.'

'That's all right. No problem.'

I felt rather nervous. Did I hear right—a baby?

'This is Danielle, my eldest daughter.'

'Hello Danielle. I'm very pleased to meet you.'

Coral said her goodbyes and we left to join Paul and Linda. Slightly perplexed at the revelation that Coral had a family, my mind was working overtime trying to fathom out how such a situation could have arisen. Was she married? Divorced? Single parent? Or what? It definitely wasn't the time to start asking leading questions. Enjoy the evening and all might be revealed, I told myself.

We arrived at Boulters Lock restaurant near Maidenhead. Paul had been right. It certainly was a classy place. Drinks in hand, Coral and I wandered onto the terrace overlooking the Thames.

Formal pleasantries over, I asked, 'Tell me about your children, Coral.'

'Well, I have three daughters—Danielle, whom you have met, Louise who is ten years old and Olivia who is two. Their father left us when I was seven months pregnant with Olivia. He went off with another woman and consequently we are divorced.'

I felt numbed by what I had just heard. This poor woman was bringing up three children on her own.

'I feel desperately sorry for you, Coral. It must be incredibly hard for you and your girls trying to cope with the impact of it all.'

'On the contrary, we are much happier without him. At times it's difficult financially, but it's all worth it really.'

I detected signs of a defensive screen going up, so I pitched in with my own marriage break-up, leaving out the interim years in prison. We talked about love, marriage and relationships with mixed emotion for nearly an hour. It was the first time since my release that I had spoken so openly and for so long with anyone. I found our conversation both stimulating and fruitful. Through it I had offloaded much of the bitterness I had carried inside myself for years. Coral was a great listener. The way I had opened up to her as if I had known her years surprised me. Not that she asked provocative questions; I just poured out my heart to her. The common denominator was the fact that we had both suffered gross injustice in our past, which we both recognized. Hence the openness.

Paul popped his head out of the terrace door and said, 'If you don't come in soon you'll both freeze to death.'

Having been engrossed in each other's marriage stories, we hadn't noticed the temperature, but as soon as Paul mentioned it we both felt quite chilled.

'Just coming, Paul.'

'You two seem to have a lot to talk about,' said Paul as we joined both him and Linda in the bar.

'Just talking about past experiences. Nothing too deep.'

'Well, that's good. Now you're back, let's order a table and have a meal.'

His remark caught me by surprise.

'Can I have a word with you, Paul?' I whispered in his ear.

Paul made an excuse. He needed to go to the loo and I tagged on behind.

Once inside the gents, I said, 'You told me we were all going out for a drink, not a meal.'

'I thought seeing you were having such a good time with Coral, a meal would be in order.'

'It's my first date, Paul. Besides, I haven't got enough money on me to buy a meal.'

'I've got enough on me and down here it's normal to take girls out for a meal.'

'How much will it cost me?'

'With the wine about twenty pounds.'

'No way I'm paying twenty pounds for a meal,' I retorted.

'OK if that's how you feel.'

We returned to our table and the girls were missing. A couple of minutes passed and they emerged from the powder room. As they approached the table, they both started to laugh in unison.

'What are you laughing about, Linda?' enquired Paul.

With that they burst into more laughter. In between further bouts, Linda said, 'We went to the ladies and they must back on to the gents. We heard everything you two talked about.'

That appealed to my sense of humour and I burst out laughing.

'You'll just have to forgive me. I'm still adjusting to the southern way of life. I give in—let's order a meal.'

'Honestly, Noel, we don't have to eat. I'm quite happy not to,' said Coral.

She was both genuine and understanding, which only added to my embarrassment.

'Coral, I really am sorry. It's such a wonderful evening. Let's finish it in style and eat.'

Following a superb meal, together with wine, we left for home. We dropped Coral off at her home and she invited me in for coffee. I declined the offer as Paul was my only means of getting home.

'Perhaps I will see you in the Three Frogs sometime. Do come and see me, won't you?' she said.

'I look forward to that.'

It was well after midnight when I arrived home. Although I felt physically exhausted, mentally I was fully awake. It had been a wonderful evening—with the exception of the overheard conversation between Paul and myself. Coral had broken through my sophisticated emotional defences and opened up past hurts and feelings locked in the recesses of my mind. I had even surprised myself at some of the revelations I had blurted out. My years in custody had been spent in deep concentrated thought, mulling over problems, bitterness and hurt.

For the first time in years I had actually spoken out my true feelings about my ex-wife and my other relationships. My son and daughter were at the forefront of my thoughts daily. I had not seen them in four years and Coral was the first person

I had really opened up to. Given her circumstances she understood my predicament perfectly. Considering she had experienced violence in her past, as well as being deserted whilst carrying a child, she was incredibly stable and secure. I only had myself to contend with; she had three children to fend for. *What a remarkable woman*—I thought to myself—*warm, loving, understanding, mature, caring and gentle.* On my part, I was introverted, insecure, embittered, resentful, aggressive and broken. She had stirred up something inside me I hadn't experienced in years—compassion. The more I saw of Coral the more I would truly learn about myself, I concluded.

On Sunday evening I went to the Three Frogs about half an hour before closing time. The bar was tightly packed with business-type people—the gin-and-tonic brigade. Coral noticed me straight away and welcomed me with one of her beaming smiles. As I had noticed on our initial introduction, when Coral smiled her whole face lit up.

'Well, there's a surprise. I was hoping you would come and see me,' she said.

'The pleasure is definitely mine,' I replied.

In between serving drinks, we arranged to have coffee together after Coral had finished work. I followed Coral home in my car and once inside her home we continued where we had left off in conversation on Friday. Remarkably, I felt completely relaxed and she continued to talk with natural ease.

'Why do you work at the Three Frogs?' I asked.

'Since being divorced I decided I needed to meet with people again and it seemed the easiest way of talking to people without any ties. Besides, you don't get any medals for staying in and wallowing in self-pity, do you?'

'I've never thought about it but I'm sure you're right.'

'Secondly, there is a need financially. Living on social security really doesn't keep us in the lifestyle we were accustomed to. I work a couple of evenings a week, which enables me to earn four pounds, the maximum I am allowed to earn whilst drawing social security.'

What commitment, I thought. Working for a miserable

199

four pounds to supplement her benefit. She was growing in stature by every sentence.

'What made you decide to phone me and arrange a date?' she asked.

I related the conversation I had with Paul truthfully and Coral burst out in laughter.

'What's so funny?'

'Only that Paul had said to me in the Three Frogs that you really fancied me and wanted to take me out. I told him I didn't go out on blind dates and that if you wanted to take me out you would have to ask me yourself. So he took my telephone number.'

'That's amazing. So we were both set up by Paul!'

'We certainly were. We both fell for the three card trick, didn't we?'

'All I can say is it was worthwhile anyway. Without Paul I might never have met you and I really do enjoy your company.'

'The feeling's mutual, Noel,' said Coral.

I felt rather embarrassed at Coral's last remark as it was so unexpected. She said it with such feeling my heart started to flutter. It was an unfamiliar feeling completely out of my control.

After several deep breaths I said, 'Could I take you out again, Coral?'

There was a short pause.

'I'd like that, Noel, but I must make sure the children are happy. They are my first responsibility.'

'There's no rush. Whenever suits you.'

'Perhaps you could come round in the evening and we could spend the evening here?'

'That's fine with me. In fact I would prefer it,' I said.

I saw Coral a couple of times the following week and we continued to flow in conversation together. The following Sunday, Coral invited me to tea so I could meet all the children. I arrived mid-afternoon, slightly nervous at the thought of meeting them in case they didn't like me. Danielle, whom I had met previously, was a very mature fourteen-year-old and so full of self-confidence that one could have mistaken her for a friend rather than Coral's eldest daughter. Louise, number two in the family line, was a shy quiet ten-year-old with striking blonde hair. She kept her head down as we were introduced. My heart went out to her as it was obvious she was the one who had been affected by her father's departure. Olivia was no more than a bouncy two-year-old baby, with huge eyes. She was totally loved and spoilt by her two elder sisters.

After tea I played with the children whilst Coral and Danielle cleared up. Olivia loved every minute of it; Louise, on the other hand, remained polite and courteous but I could sense her insecurity. Coral told me later that Danielle had suffered with her father's contrasting moods but Louise had been her greatest concern. She still hadn't got over the marriage break-up.

I felt happy in their company and knew that to win Coral, I would first have to win the trust of the children. I decided the best policy to adopt was to be perfectly natural—children have a knack of seeing through pretentious people. After a couple of weeks the children began to warm to me. They would tell me what they had been doing at school, furnishing me with all that interested them. Although I barely knew them, I really had become very fond of them all.

Every time I visited Coral I could sense real love and peace in the house. Here was a family tightly knit together and with absolute trust in each other. It was a family scene I had never set eyes on before. They were openly affectionate and responded to each other's call. It was heartbreaking to see these children surviving on the benefit of the state, the innocent victims of grown-up games.

It was obvious I was falling in love with Coral—I couldn't think of anything else when I wasn't in her company. It wasn't just emotion; it was old-fashioned love. We complemented each other and from the start we had both got on like a house on fire. I lived for the evenings when I could see her again.

About a month after the start of our relationship I knew in

my heart I couldn't carry on with it in deceit. Coral had been very open and honest in her conversations with me, but I still hadn't told her of my recent imprisonment. Knowing how I felt about her, I knew that the longer the truth was withheld, the harder it would be for me to tell her. I was suffering from inner turmoil—knowing how much I loved Coral, I was frightened of telling her about the killing I had been convicted of. Would she believe me or would she reject me? After considerable thought, I decided to tell Coral the truth, thinking it would be better to end the relationship now, for I would not be able to cope with the emotional upheaval of rejection later.

That night I picked Coral up from work and we drove back to her house. Danielle had gone to bed and Coral went through her usual routine, checking that the children were all right, before we settled in the lounge with our coffee.

True to form, Coral had detected something was troubling me and said, 'You're quiet tonight, Noel. Is there something wrong?'

'There is something I need to talk to you about, Coral,' I replied.

My heart started to beat faster and faster and the familiar feeling of insecurity from the past caught up with me again. Heart trembling and hands shaking, I knew I had reached the point of no return.

'You know I care for you, Coral, don't you?'

'Yes, I do.'

'The truth is, I have fallen in love with you and there is something in my past I haven't told you about. Because I love you I think it's only fair to tell you about it now, because neither one of us can afford to be hurt emotionally again.'

'Well, tell me about it,' she said.

I related the whole story from my arrest up to my release, honestly and in every detail. It took me the best part of an hour to finish. All the time I was talking I kept looking at Coral, trying to gain a glimpse of her reaction from her eyes or her facial expression. She just sat there with her feet up on the sofa sipping her coffee and showing no hint of surprise or emotion.

Having laid my cards on the table, I said, 'Well, that's the lot. Now you have the story of my life, what do you think of it?'

It felt like an age had gone by before Coral spoke. She just looked at me for a while. Her face again was expressionless.

'All I can say, Noel, is that if you say you didn't do it, then I believe you.'

I couldn't believe my ears! *She actually said she believed me*, I repeated to myself. This is the first person outside my immediate family who believes me. All those years and someone I have known a month actually *believes* me. Now *I* couldn't believe it. All the torment and worry over the last few days had gone. I felt clean again; Coral knew the truth. The adrenalin flowed through my body. The tension of the last hour vanished into thin air.

'How does this affect our relationship, Coral? Believe me, I will understand if you don't want to see me any more. It would be painful for me, but you and the children must take priority over my feelings.'

'It doesn't make the slightest bit of difference to our relationship. You have told me the truth and I honestly believe you. Seeing you have been so open with me, I must tell you something,' she said.

'This is turning into a confession time,' I said.

We both laughed. Then Coral said, 'I just want you to know that I love you.'

The words took me by complete surprise. I knew Coral cared for me, but to hear that she loved me was beyond my wildest dreams. Tears formed in my eyes. My emotions were running high as we embraced.

'This is the happiest day of my life,' I whispered in Coral's ear.

'It's not been a bad day for me, either.'

After sharing my past with Coral, our relationship really took off in a big way. Life was sweeter than I had ever imagined it could be. Now I had someone to share my heart with, someone who knew the truth of my situation. Coral had given me hope and purpose for the future. All I lived for was to please her and the children.

Having worked for a few months, I now felt I could look for a better job in the Bracknell area. I had long since given up the idea of using my educational qualifications outside, as the employers would ask to see them and therefore know where I had obtained them. After a number of interviews and several disappointments, I managed to succeed in finding another job with Expandite, a local sealants company in Bracknell. The company specialized in jointing compounds for the construction industry and my task as a joint-sealer was to travel all over the south of England sealing expansion joints in buildings and bridges. What made the job appeal to me was the incentive they offered—a basic wage with lucrative bonuses and as much overtime as I wanted. This was my golden opportunity—piece-work offered high rewards for anyone who would take up the challenge of work.

I took the job and learnt fast. Within a couple of months I was earning top money. The one disadvantage was that I worked away most of the time, which meant I could only see Coral at weekends. The old saying, 'Absence makes the heart grow fonder' became a reality and it wasn't long before I was phoning Coral up at least four times a day. Just to remind her of my true feelings, I used to send her telegrams regularly as well. If nothing else, being away from Coral during the week proved my love for her.

One Friday night after returning home from work, I changed and rushed straight round to see Coral. Louise answered the door and welcomed me in and I started chatting to her in the hall. Suddenly a voice called down the stairs.

'Is that you, Daddy?'

Taken by complete surprise I replied,

'Yes, it's me.'

Olivia said,

'I knew I had a Daddy.'

Feeling rather awkward, I shrugged my shoulders and

continued to talk with Louise. Coral came down after settling Olivia down for the night and told me the reason for what Olivia had called down the stairs. She had been playing with some of the neighbours' children in their garden, where they had a slide. All the children were standing in a line, waiting to take their turn on the slide, but when Olivia's turn came, things went sadly wrong. One of the older boys had told Olivia that only children with daddies could go on the slide. He said she hadn't got one so she couldn't have a turn. Olivia had come running home upset and had told the story to Coral. The poor child was heartbroken. Children can be so honest and cruel at times. From that day on, Olivia always called me Daddy. When I came home I spent all of my time with Coral and the girls. The extra money enabled me to take the children on trips and spoil them occasionally. We all fitted into each other's lives perfectly, as if we were purpose-built for each other.

After a night wining and dining Coral we returned to her house for the usual coffee and after-dinner chat. In between coffee, cuddles and kisses, I said, 'Coral, will you marry me?'

'Yes, of course I will.'

We decided to announce our engagement to the children over a special dinner party the day before my birthday in September. It was now 1974. It was all I could do to keep the secret until then. Coral had prepared a special meal for the occasion and I bought a bottle of wine to celebrate. Everyone gathered at the table.

'I have a very special announcement to make. Your mother and I are engaged, and with your approval we want to get married next September.'

The children cheered and clapped. They were delighted. It was complete. Coral and I had already decided the children needed to give their approval before we could make our plans.

After the initial excitement had died down, Louise said, 'Does that mean I will be able to call you Dad?'

Her remark really touched me.

'When we're married, Louise, if you want to call me dad you most certainly can.'

'Oh, that will be great.'

The girls spent the rest of the evening making wedding plans. It was wonderful just seeing the happiness on their faces. The next night Coral and I arranged my birthday party, to which we had invited both sets of families. To our delight everyone turned up—both sets of parents and our brothers and sisters. Halfway through the evening I stopped the music and announced our engagement. You could have heard a pin drop.

Rosa, Coral's mother, said, 'You shouldn't joke about things like that, Noel.'

'It's true!' said Coral. 'We're getting married a year from today.'

The place erupted. Everyone was delighted. The children took great pleasure in telling everyone that they had known the day before, which made them feel rather special.

Coral and I, together with the girls, drew up the wedding plans. It was important that the girls felt totally involved in the wedding. Even Olivia used to pitch in with her remarks, which only added to our enjoyment of planning our wedding day. Being in love suited me. Coral had brought real purpose and balance into my life. I just wanted to make her and the girls as happy as I felt. In the time I had known Coral, she had introduced me to her friends, who in turn had welcomed me into their homes and accepted me. There were occasions when they asked questions about my past life in the north of England and Coral would step in and cover for me admirably.

In those early months of trying to re-establish myself, it was easy to chart the continued career development of the man who had put me behind bars, Joe Mounsey. In September 1974, he was called out to the scene of a killing at a post office in Accrington, East Lancashire. Derek Astin, a former Royal Marine, had bravely attacked a masked intruder, despite having been shot in the left shoulder. But a second bullet through his vital organs allowed the gunman to escape.

Detective Chief Superintendent Mounsey immediately linked the crime with a similar raid in Harrogate, Yorkshire—and it was soon clear this was the work of the notorious Black Panther.

With his usual thoroughness, Mounsey ordered checks on two thousand shotguns in Accrington and made plans for his men to interview nearly every man in the town. Harry Hawkes, the author of *The Capture of the Black Panther*, describes how Mounsey felt the solution to the crime was a 'personal challenge' when he stated that: 'Open war has been declared on a cornerstone of British life—the sub post office.' Mounsey later hosted a conference of senior detectives from other forces involved in the Panther hunt—the forerunner of many others throughout the country. Mounsey was one of few officers in the case not selected for criticism when the Black Panther, Donald Neilson, was eventually cornered in December 1975.

Neilson was then a 29-year-old former soldier who planned every crime—including the kidnap and murder of heiress Lesley Whittle—with military precision. When he was arrested in Nottinghamshire, local detectives quickly realized other forces would be eager to question him too. But their chief constable issued an edict barring all other forces from the initial interviews at that stage. He wanted time for his men to work on Neilson before the stampede. Every constabulary agreed, bar one. Joe Mounsey, 'keen as mustard, set out from Lancashire and was soon at Mansfield'. He failed to meet Neilson on that occasion but was not out of the limelight for long. His investigation had unearthed more than enough evidence to put Neilson away behind bars for life—one of five he received at Oxford Crown Court in July 1976.

After a while, a vacancy arose at work for a contract supervisor's job and my immediate manager informed me the Managing Director wanted to interview me for the post. I went to the interview smartly turned out and met Bill Dolan, a Welshman who had worked his way up from being a rep.

He told me he had been watching my performance since I joined the company and I had performed well.

'You're not the average sort of person who takes on this kind of work and you don't speak the same sort of language,' he said. 'Have you any qualifications?'

Not wanting to spoil my chances, I said, 'Just a few 'O' levels and an OND Business Studies certificate.'

'I thought you had been educated,' he said.

I felt rather uncomfortable in his presence. The man was definitely perceptive.

'Well, Noel, I think you're the man I am looking for.'

I couldn't believe my luck. Surely he wasn't going to offer me the job?

'I am offering you the position of Contract Supervisor at a starting salary of £3,700, together with a company car and expenses. If you prove yourself in this position after twelve months, then I will consider promoting you to be a contract surveyor.'

'How long do I have to consider your offer, Mr Dolan?' I asked.

'Give me your answer by Monday morning.'

I left his office in jubilation. I couldn't wait to tell Coral the news. She would be delighted. When I told her the news she was overjoyed. It was the opportunity I had been waiting for. We discussed the finer points of the offer together, as initially it meant a drop in my income. We both decided it was an opportunity to start climbing the management ladder and, as one could only start at the bottom, it was right. Coral gave me all the encouragement she could, by telling me I had the knowledge and potential to succeed in whatever I chose to do. That was good enough for me. If she believed it, then I could do it. I rose to the challenge and gladly accepted the post. Within a few months I had the workforce working at full speed getting good monthly results.

Since taking the supervisor's job I found myself at home more often. Both Coral and I preferred my new status. It meant we could see more of each other in the week. Having completed our wedding plans and drawn up the budget, it was obvious that my salary and Coral's family allowance would not meet the weekly outgoings once we were married. Because Coral was supposed to receive maintenance from her ex-husband, I would be classed as a married man with no children, so I would pay tax at a higher level. It made no difference to the authorities that Coral wasn't receiving any maintenance at all. I couldn't claim the tax relief; it was her ex-husband's entitlement. The problem of finances troubled me more than it did Coral.

'We have each other, love, and together we can manage anything,' she told me.

As usual, Coral had an answer for everything. She was positive and always displayed confidence in me. I only hoped I could live up to her expectations. I wanted Coral to have the wedding she desired so I decided to supplement my income by taking on building work in the evenings and at weekends. As I only charged people one pound an hour it wasn't long before I had a full order book. Every hour I worked was a labour of love. Much to my pleasure and relief, a couple of weeks before the wedding I had reached my financial goal.

But having worked fourteen hours a day through the week and as many as twelve hours a day through the weekend, I was understandably physically drained. It was my own fault. Pride had been my downfall. Many people had offered financial support for the forthcoming wedding, but I had refused their offers as I wanted to meet the costs myself. Receiving presents or gifts from people had always been a problem area for me. I found it easy to give but impossible to receive.

I had been best man at Paul's wedding a year earlier when he married Linda, so I returned the compliment by asking Paul to do the honours for me. He willingly accepted the invitation, and my younger brothers, John and Roger, agreed to be ushers. Now all was ready.

On 27 September 1975 Coral and I were married at the Methodist church in Bracknell. All our hopes, dreams and plans came together in a single moment as we looked each other in the eyes and said, 'I will'. Louise and Olivia stood next to us in their colourful bridesmaid's outfits, tears of joy streaming down their faces. Love had found a way for them as well. There were no yesterdays or tomorrows; I wanted this precious day to last for ever unspoilt, untouched by the passage of time. I loved Coral and the children so much it hurt.

The early months of our marriage were spent learning to live with each other. I was learning to live with four females in the house and they were making constant adjustments to my being a husband and father. Coral and the girls had been used to making decisions themselves; now I was being asked to make the family decisions. It was a whole new ball game to me. I didn't even know the rules of family life, let alone the answers. But it wasn't long before I felt secure in my new-found responsibilities. Coral again was supportive, constantly encouraging me to take the lead in family matters.

In the early part of 1976 there was a sense of purpose and balance flowing through the family. Financially we were just keeping our heads above water. After paying the rent, rates and food bills, there was little extra left to spend. I found the financial pressure a burden. I saw it as my responsibility to provide an adequate income to support the family. Not that Coral complained—she cut her cloth accordingly.

The pressure eased as I was informed at work that I had come up to expectations and was to be promoted to a contract surveyor. It meant more money and an annual bonus scheme measured on performance and profitability. The promotion had come at just the right time. Now I could see light in my darkness. All I had needed was the opportunity to prove myself. My primary objective was to achieve better results than my contemporaries and earn the maximum bonus available. After all, I had already learned that in line management it was dog eat dog. *You were only as good as your last month's figures*, they said. A number of people had tried to stab me in the back, metaphorically speaking, while I was a contract supervisor. Unfortunately for them, I had served my apprenticeship in Wakefield Prison and recognized their knives before they had even drawn them. Consequently their plots against me backfired and came to nothing.

My burning inner desire to succeed became an obsession. After my promotion I cracked the whip to all who were under my direct control. I was going to reach my goal at any price. I had earned respect from the workforce as a supervisor, always paying them their worth with added bonuses for effort. In my new office, that hadn't changed, but I had earmarked the trouble-makers and within a couple of months they sought different employment after I had cracked down on their timekeeping. Now I had the team that would produce the results I needed to climb the ladder of success.

Although work was going according to my plans, I was still walking a tightrope, always fearful that someone would learn the truth about my past and I would be out on my ear. Promotion had both fed my ego and made me even more defensive. To survive, liars have to have good memories and I wasn't too confident in those stakes. I viewed every question directed at my past with suspicion, seeing them as an attack. Up would go the defence barriers and I would purposefully retaliate with rhetoric; this would normally end any reference to the past.

The tightrope was stretched even tauter as night-time brought recurring nightmares of my years in prison. These nightmares were always violent and horrifying. They disturbed me so much that I used to wake from them perspiring and shaking. Coral would ask what was wrong and I would tell her it was just another nightmare. She would ask me to tell her what the nightmares were about, but I always refused as I didn't want to worry her. In the early months of my release, I had hoped the memory recall of prison would fade into obscurity. Now I realized that my dreams were getting worse and not better. The intensity of worrying whether people would discover my true identity, linked with the nightmares, resulted in deeper insecurity, a bout of black moods and depressions.

After a particularly bad nightmare I would wake in the morning physically and mentally exhausted. Coral knew the signs well by this time and would try to reach me with words of comfort and understanding. I used to try and fight my depressed state off, but it had to run its course. When I returned to normality I would then feel guilty about having been depressed, as Coral and the girls were always the ones who suffered through them. Not that I became aggressive or violent; on the contrary, all I did was remain silent, not talking to anyone at all. It was worse for the children as they had no idea what I was going through. To them I was just in a mood. Coral always protected me by saying I wasn't feeling well and would recover soon. It was heartbreaking for me as I saw the four people I loved most of all in my life suffer as a result of the injustice I had suffered in the past. In turn that led to more hatred and bitterness against the people and the system that had damaged me so badly.

I had tried for years to block from my mind the names and faces of some of those who persecuted me during the trial. In 1977, a photograph appeared in the newspaper of a studious-looking man with bushy grey hair and black-rimmed glasses. He was Dr Alan Clift, the expert Home Office forensic scientist who had spent so long in the witness-box under the spotlight of both prosecutor and defence barrister. He had been suspended from his job on full salary—he was now at the Birmingham forensic science laboratory—while police probed his work.

In the September of that year, assault charges against three men were dropped on the orders of the Director of Public Prosecutions, following careful scrutiny of Clift's work. It was the warning sign of an avalanche of criticism which was later directed at Dr Clift.

In another case in June 1981 a lorry driver from Stoke-on-Trent appeared before Appeal judges after serving eight years of a life sentence for the murder of Mrs Helen Will, in Aberdeen. The panel ruled that Clift had been discredited 'not only as a scientist but as a witness'. John Preece was freed to start re-building his life at the age of 49. He later received what was then record compensation of £77,000. At the end of that summer, Clift was told to take early retirement on the grounds of 'limited efficiency'. But that was not the last to be heard of him.

By the end of the year, a 50-year-old man was freed by the Appeal Court. He had been held in a mental hospital for six years following the court testimony of Clift. By this stage the Home Office Criminal Department was working overtime to see whether there were any more miscarriages of justice in over fifteen hundred cases handled by Dr Clift.

They found what they were looking for in the case of Geoffrey Mycock, jailed in 1968 for raping and killing 84-year-old spinster, Miss Adelaine Bracegirdle. Fibres taken from the scene of the murder and those found on Mr Mycock's clothing had played an important part in the case. But Clift's evidence was later found to be 'not up to the standard required for a criminal trial'. No contemporary notes were left and it had been impossible independently to verify all his work. Mr Mycock was cleared.

Findings of a Home Office report on Clift were published in *The Observer*. The department's investigator wrote: 'Dr Clift's work fell short of the requirements in many respects. There was evidence of bias, carelessness, inaccuracy and a failure to have kept abreast of modern scientific work. In many ways, Dr Clift's attitudes reflect those of the very early forensic scientists who saw their function as one of "helping the police" and not, as I would believe a modern forensic scientist would see it, to assist police in their investigation and to assist in the cause of justice in the courts.

'He does not seem to have turned his mind to the possibilities of his evidence incriminating people, trusting that the police were always right in their initial suspicions.'

After leaving the service, Dr Clift was reported to have gone into publishing and book-selling. In a House of Commons answer, it was revealed that he had received nearly £50,000 in salary and allowances during his term of suspension.

Success at work brought me both a new job and greater financial reward but I found it meant sacrificing family life for the prize of recognition and success. In my new job I often had to be away from home. There is a very fine line that divides working for a living and living for work. In those months I was governed by work, knowing that successful results would only add to my prospects of promotion in the future. I tried to explain this to Coral but in her view my attitude to my work was shutting the door on our relationship and our life together as a family. However much I tried it seemed I couldn't strike a balance. When the chips were down I knew that my love for Coral and the children was far greater than anything else. So we agreed on a policy that I would work whatever hours were necessary during the week, which would enable me to devote the weekend to the children. I felt hemmed in by pressure from all sides—work, family responsibilities, and the worst pressure of all: sleepless nights or nightmares related to my past.

By the end of 1977 anyone viewing my life from the outside would see a reasonably successful manager, happily married, living quite comfortably on a secure income. It was all a mask. Work was all right. I had again achieved more than was required of me, but at a cost. Having worked flat out for months on end, I was exhausted. To counter the increasing nightmares I was now staying up until the early hours, tiring myself to the point of physical collapse, so that when I went to bed I would sleep soundly until the morning. My theory was that the less I slept, the less likelihood there was of nightmares. I used to wrestle with the reality of my existence during the hours I was alone downstairs.

I loved Coral, loved the girls, enjoyed a comfortable home, had a respectable and secure career. In fact, I had everything any man could ever ask for, yet I wasn't fulfilled or genuinely happy. I concluded that the reason lay in the dungeon of my mind, wrapped up in a single package labelled 'Injustice'. Whatever I might achieve in the future would never compensate me for what had happened in the past. It seemed that the more time that passed, the worse I felt. Coral had tried everything humanly possible to break through my defences over the nightmares and melancholy moods, but I just couldn't bring myself to share the horror of it all.

As always Coral would just smile and say, 'Don't worry, I still love you.'

If she had said it once over the years, she had said it a hundred times. I doubted that anyone other than Coral could have put up with me and my constant swings of mood. She was everything to me. All I had to do was be everything to her. Perhaps one day I would be. Surely love could find a way.

13

Encounter with God

The year 1978 arrived to the sound of much singing, dancing and cheering on my part. I was in a drunken stupor following hours of heavy drinking. The alcohol had taken effect and now I could feel nothing. My head and body refused to respond to the simplest of commands and I finished up in a heap on the floor. I had really let myself go this New Year's Eve. All the frustration of 1977 had been drowned in beer and whisky. The year was gone for ever, along with its nightmares, horrors, problems and memories—or at least I hoped so.

'It will all be better this year, Coral, I promise you,' I said.

'You've had too much to drink, Noel,' she replied.

'Wait and see. It will be our year.'

'I wish you'd stop drinking now, Noel. You have had enough. Besides, you will pay for it tomorrow with a lousy hangover.'

Coral was right, of course. Whenever I had one over the top I paid for it the next day. Worse still, so did the family. Drinking had become another means of escape from reality. If I could only consume enough alcohol to blur the brain and memory, it gave me some respite. The only problem was that it cost money to drink—and the more one drank, the more one needed to drink the next time to achieve the required result. Just like other escape routes I had tried, drinking led nowhere. Once the effect had worn off I was left to face up to the cold, hard facts of continued mental stress, anguish, remembered pain. Added to that was the sense of guilt at having acted so selfishly and irresponsibly towards Coral and the family. I was so locked up in myself that I didn't have time to consider anyone else's problems or frustrations. I had come to the conclusion that a magic cure for the battles in my mind and resulting depressions could never be found. This was my destiny—a life filled to overflowing with inner hatred, bitterness, anger, frustration and fear.

The one element in my life that still seemed to be prospering was my career. Since starting the new job at Evode I had attained all I had set out to achieve. The reward was promotion, coupled with a fat bonus for target achievement. The extra money enabled Coral and me to buy our house. It was an exciting time as we waited for the final agreement and purchase price to be settled. Neither of us had ever dreamt that we would be able to own our own house so quickly after the financial struggles following our marriage. But when the price was finally agreed, we found our savings were too small to secure the deposit and legal fees for the purchase. Rosa and Brian, Coral's parents, came to the rescue, offering to lend us the balance until my next bonus was due. I really struggled with myself—I couldn't cope with lending or borrowing anything from anyone. At first I refused, but I finally agreed, promising to pay the money back within the year.

Coral was delighted at the prospect of our owning a house but I had reservations about having to find a mortgage payment every month as well as settling the loan from my father-in-law. I knew I had subjected myself to yet another pressure on my life. But we finally signed the contracts and became home owners. The following months revealed a major drop in our standard of living—after the mortgage and the food bill, there wasn't anything left in the kitty at all.

It wasn't long before I was spending sleepless nights worrying about finances and my ability to cope. Together with dreams from my past, this anxiety resulted in even worse nightmares. Now I dreamt I was dead. I died at least twice a week in my dreams, which led to deeper bouts of depression and longer periods of locking myself away in isolation.

My brother John had been visiting us more frequently than I thought necessary. I loved John as my brother, but he was heavily into religion and Christianity. Unlike Roger, who was also a Christian, John couldn't stop talking about

217

Jesus, God and his beliefs. Having totally convinced myself that God did not exist following my prayer in the sweat-box at Lancaster Assizes back in 1970, the mere mention of Jesus or God threw me into fits of rage and resulted in aggression towards anyone who dared mention the words in my company. While I respected both John's and Roger's beliefs, and I saw that their lives reflected what they believed in, I didn't want any of it filtering into my life or my family.

One Sunday morning Coral informed me that she was going to church with my brother John. I knew that Coral had been under tremendous strain and pressure because of my moods and nightmares, so my only response was, 'If that's what you want, you go.'

So off she went to church. Underneath my indifferent response, I was seething with rage. If they thought Coral was going to be another Jesus freak, they had another think coming. I challenged Coral after she had gone to church for the second Sunday in a row.

'Why are you going to church all of a sudden?'

'I don't know really. I suppose it gives me time to think over things on my own.'

'What things?'

'Just things personal to me.'

'There's no way I want you to become one of those Jesus freaks.'

'I don't think I would.'

I made doubly sure Coral didn't get involved any further with the church. Every Sunday following I made arrangements to visit relatives or go to the seaside for the day.

Everything seemed back to normal until Coral and I spent an evening with my brother Paul and his wife, Linda. We had enjoyed our evening having a meal together at Linda's parents' restaurant and I was a little merry to say the least. We all returned to Paul and Linda's home for a nightcap. My parents had been babysitting for Paul and Linda and they asked how the evening had gone.

'Fine. A really good night out on the town,' I replied. 'Plenty of food, plenty of booze and plenty of jokes, so all in all a great night.'

Coral and I decided to stay for the nightcap and catch up on family news from my parents. After the usual exchange of family information my mother turned to me and asked, 'How are you then, son?'

'I've already told you, mother. I'm really fine.'

'I know you said you're fine, but I was asking how you really feel,' she persisted.

'Well, he's still having trouble sleeping,' said Coral.

'Yes, the nightmares have become worse and now I keep dreaming I'm dead. It's becoming quite tiresome,' I quipped.

She looked at me carefully and said, 'Well, I think God is telling you that you're spiritually dead, Noel. I believe the Lord is speaking to you in your dreams.'

I sighed. 'Oh dear, don't give me all the heavy religious stuff, mother. I can't cope with that at all.'

'I really believe it's true, Noel.'

'I can't handle all this Jesus stuff. Besides, they're just bad dreams recalling past hurts.'

But my mother continued along the same line of reasoning. She believed that her God was definitely speaking into my life. I knew my mother was a devout Christian woman; she had lived out her beliefs as far back as I could remember. I tried all ways to trip her up about her faith and beliefs, but she just answered every question I threw at her. She seemed peaceful and secure. It was the first time I had listened to her real beliefs. Coral and I were so engrossed in what she was saying that we forgot about time completely.

'It's four o'clock,' Paul declared to everyone.

'It can't be,' I said.

'It is,' answered my father.

I couldn't believe it. We had sat there talking for the best part of four hours about God and my dreams. Not that I had any revelation about this God, but at least I could appreciate a little more what my mother and two of my younger brothers really believed in.

I spent the next few days thinking over all we had talked

about, and finally came to the conclusion that it was fine for my mother but that there was definitely nothing in religion for me. It was all talk anyway. There was no real proof that God existed at all.

A couple of weeks later on a Saturday afternoon the doorbell rang. I got up from the settee to answer it. My brother John was standing outside the front door, looking rather pale and nervous.

'Hi, John. Come in,' I said. 'What can I do for you, then?'

'I've just been on what should have been a long journey, but was a short journey,' he said.

My heart seemed to skip a beat as I wondered if something untoward had happened to his wife, Gillian, or Mark and Simon, his sons.

'Stop talking in all those parables, John, and tell me what's wrong.'

'Well, it's rather difficult, Noel.'

'For goodness sake, John, spit it out. I can't stand the tension any longer.'

His arm reached inside his coat and produced a book. He looked at me rather sheepishly and said, 'I just felt I had to give you this.'

He held out a Bible.

'Well, put it on the table, then.'

I was just relieved to hear that there was nothing wrong with his family.

'You really mean I can leave it here?'

'It's only a book, John. If it gives you that much pleasure you leave it.'

I found it difficult to understand why he was so excited at bringing a Bible to me.

'What's the big deal?' I asked.

'Nothing. It's just that when God tells you to do something and you obey him, you experience a sense of purpose and joy,' he returned.

By this time all the colour had returned to his face and he was really beaming.

'Why are you so happy, John?'

He half smiled and said, 'Well, normally you would have been aggressive towards me at the mere mention of the word God, but this time you haven't reacted.'

I thought for a few moments and then, 'Have you been speaking to our mother lately?' I asked.

'No, I haven't seen or spoken to Mum for two or three weeks.'

'You haven't heard anything about my dreams or stuff like that then?'

'No. Honestly Noel, all I know is that God told me to bring that Bible round and I was scared stiff at bringing it to you.'

I really knew that John was telling the truth—for all my disquiet about his religious beliefs, I knew he always told me the truth.

'OK. I believe you John, and thanks for the book.'

He left with a smile on his face and a spring in his step. I just sighed and thought how easy it is to please some people. John had no material wealth in his life. In fact both he and Gillian had struggled financially since their marriage. But the one thing that had always struck me whenever I met them was the peace they seemed to have in their lives. Whatever their circumstances, there was a sense of security and love.

Coral and I talked over John's sudden visit and the reason for bringing the Bible to me. I decided it was to try to get us to church, or even to get Coral to church again. Coral felt it was deeper than that and said that perhaps if there was a God he was trying to speak to me.

'Rubbish,' I retorted. 'You're starting to sound like one of them already.'

'Well, like it or not, Noel, that's what I think.'

I gave Coral the benefit of the doubt and took the Bible upstairs and set it on my bedside table. Over the next few days, the Bible seemed to stare me in the face every time I entered the bedroom. The more I tried not to look, the more I actually saw it. A week or so later I returned home from work and went upstairs to wash and change before my evening meal. On entering our bedroom I noticed immediately that the Bible was missing.

'Coral,' I shouted down the stairs.

'Yes, love.'

'What's happened to my Bible?'

'You're never going to read that, so I decided to put it in the wardrobe on the shelf.'

'Yeah, OK.'

I went directly to the wardrobe and rescued it. I opened the Bible for the first time and it fell open at Isaiah, chapter 53. I read the whole of the chapter and immediately felt a small stirring inside to read it again, so I did. After reading, I closed the Bible and thought about all I had read. It really didn't make any sense to me at all. But I knew I had felt something telling me to read more. Over the next week I read a little of the Bible secretly each day, hoping to find what the answer to my problems really was. I didn't see or hear God but I felt there was definitely something happening in my life. There was a new awakening or a desire to seek the truth—something.

Towards the end of September my youngest brother Roger called in to see us.

'Have you spoken to John lately?' I asked.

'Yes, I saw John and Gill last week. Why?'

'I thought John might have mentioned something to you about his message from God.'

'You mean about his bringing you a Bible?'

'So you know about all that, do you?'

'Yes. John told me all about it,' replied Roger.

I began to tell Roger about everything that had happened to me over the last few months—the talk with my mother, John bringing the Bible and the dreams I was still having.

'What do you make of all that, Roger?'

He remained in thought for a time, then said, 'For what it's worth, I really believe God is speaking to you in a big way.'

'Really? Well, how come all of you are hearing him and I'm not?'

'If you're really serious about meeting God, Noel, believe me, he will meet you.'

'I'm serious all right. I really would like to meet him as I have quite a few questions to ask him,' I said angrily.

'He will meet you, Noel, if you really desire to meet him—I assure you.'

'Where is he, then?'

'God is alive and well in a church in Bracknell.'

'Which church?' I asked.

'I'm not telling you. If you really mean what you say, then go out and find him and meet with him.'

'Oh, I see. It's a game of hide-and-seek, is it?'

'It's not a game—it's reality.'

Very shrewd, my younger brother, I thought to myself. He knew I would rise to the challenge of trying to disprove God.

'I might give it a go sometime,' I said.

'It's your choice, Noel.'

The next Sunday Coral and I took Olivia with us to our local church, hoping to meet God. It was terrible. I couldn't cope with the service at all. We came home laughing at ourselves for having gone there in the first place. Unperturbed, we decided to keep up the challenge and visit other churches in the town over the next few weeks. Even if we didn't find God, it would be good for a laugh anyway.

After visiting three or four of the local churches, I was totally convinced God was a figment of all Christians' imagination. There was more life in a graveyard than in some of the churches we visited. I knew I had been conned and I told Coral that the next time I saw Roger I was going to tear him off a strip or two. A couple of weeks later Roger popped in to see us.

'You conned me, you liar. You said God would meet me if I wanted to meet him and we have been all round Bracknell looking. He isn't there and doesn't exist.'

'He's alive and well. I'm sorry but that's the truth.'

'I don't want to hear any more of that crap, Roger. Forget it, will you? Anyway, where do you go to church?' I asked.

'Bracknell Baptist Church,' he replied.

'Where's that?'

'Next to the bowling club near the town centre.'

'You better watch out. I might turn up there one day and tell people what you are,' I joked.

'You're more than welcome any time.'

I talked the whole God thing over with Coral and she suggested there was no harm in going to Roger's church. After all, what did we have to lose? I agreed. It was the very last church I was going to, anyway. On the last Sunday in October, off we went to Bracknell Baptist Church, Olivia in tow again.

We arrived to the sound of people talking excitedly, greeting each other with hugs and kisses. It was quite different from anything I had ever seen in church before. The incredible thing was that everyone seemed so pleased to be there. The whole place was buzzing with life.

I turned to Coral and said, 'These are definitely weirdos. Keep your eyes open.'

Coral just smiled and said, 'Let's wait and see what happens.'

We took our seats in the centre row of the church and a few minutes later the music started. A quietness crept over the congregation and the minister, Ben Davies, stood at the front with some other men. As he prayed simply over the meeting, I detected a Welsh accent which was pure. He boldly spoke out about God and asked us all to stand. As the congregation started to sing a chorus, I couldn't believe my ears! Everyone was singing and people were clapping and playing tambourines. The whole place shook to the sound of people rejoicing. I felt very awkward. It seemed as if everybody was on a high. Perhaps it was pumped-up emotion, I thought to myself. Whatever it was, it was certainly different from anything I had ever seen before.

In the beginning of the next chorus they sang, I found myself suddenly gripped in muscular spasm. I couldn't move. Fear gripped me. I could see, I could hear, but every muscle in my body was totally locked. I tried to move my head to attract Coral's attention, but I couldn't. I tried to speak out her name, but I couldn't. There I stood, full of fear and completely immobilized. Then what can only be described as a heat fell upon me. It came in through the top of my head, spread through my entire body and went out through my toes. Over and over and over again it continued to flow through me.

After what seemed an eternity, but which was probably only a minute or so, I felt the hurt I had carried for so many years coming up out of the pit of my stomach and I broke down. I stood there, tears streaming down my face—unable to control them. As the hurt came out a sense of peace took its place and started to fill my whole body. As the heat continued to flow through me, I knew that I had met God in a very special way. I kept saying in my head, 'Thank you Lord, thank you Lord.' I knew with absolute certainty that I had met the living God.

The heat left just as suddenly as it had come and my body was able once more to respond to my requests. I collapsed on the chair saying, 'Oh Lord, oh Lord.' I could hardly believe what had happened to me. Then I turned to look at Coral. She was still standing and singing. There were tears on her cheeks. Eventually the singing stopped and Coral sat down. I was shaking like a leaf.

I leaned over and said to Coral, 'I have just met God.'

'I know you have.'

I didn't really hear or see the rest of the service. I just kept thinking and reliving what had happened to me. I felt absolutely wonderful.

On the way out after the service Ben Davies stopped me and said, 'You're Roger's brother, aren't you?'

'Yes, I am.'

'You've just become a Christian, I hear.'

Cold shivers travelled down my spine. I thought, *this is unbelievable—the man knows what has just happened to me.*

'No, not me. Definitely not me.'

'Really. Is that true?' he asked.

'Yes, it is, but there was something that happened I need to talk to you about. I met with God here today.'

'Incredible,' said Ben. 'How about coming and meeting with me on Wednesday evening?'

'It would be my pleasure,' I said.

Coral and I arrived home full of everything that had happened to us. I felt completely different. There was a sense of peace and security in my life which God had planted deep within me. My life had completely changed—from the exact moment when I actually met God. Even more precious was the fact that Coral had met God as well, at the same time and in the same place.

I could hardly wait for Wednesday so I could tell Ben what had happened. The day came and Coral and I poured out everything that had happened on Sunday and then, to my amazement, I poured out the whole of my story—the case, arrest, prison, new life—the lot. Ben sat there absolutely transfixed.

After I had finished I asked, 'What do you think of that lot, Ben? Is there any chance for me?'

'Jesus can and will sort everything out for you and as far as I'm concerned, if you say you didn't do it, mate, then I believe you.'

'Really?'

'Honestly, Noel. I believe you and that's it.'

Now I had two people who knew about the case and believed in my innocence. Something had been released inside me to enable the hurt and locked-up frustration to come out and here I was having told my whole life story to a man whom I had only just met. Ben talked about a new life to be found in Jesus, explaining how we could be reconciled to God through Jesus Christ, by being reborn spiritually. The only way was to repent—to turn away from living our own selfish lives—and to put our trust in Jesus, and serve him with our lives. I had heard of the 'born-again' label from time to time, but I had thought it was a new cult, never realizing it was to do with Christianity.

After meeting God in such a tremendous way on Sunday, we didn't need to be persuaded. I was totally convinced, so was Coral. Ben prayed with both of us as we talked to God, turning away from our past lives and sin and asking Jesus to take over our lives.

It was all over in a matter of minutes, but once more a heat poured through me for a few seconds as I spoke out the words of prayer. I felt totally clean and a new security welled up inside my stomach. There was peace, joy, reality, purpose, love—all flowing through my life. Everything seemed so wonderful and perfect. I really felt like a new creation. Coral and I shed a few tears. We felt so privileged to be enjoying God's love together. Since Sunday our whole lives had changed. My face beamed with life and happiness. Coral's was just the same. In fact, she had been wearing the same smile for so long I thought it would become a permanent feature.

Later that evening, I phoned the whole family to tell them of the good news, how God had moved so generously in our lives. My mother, John and Roger and Carole, one of my sisters, all Christians, were overjoyed for us. It was then they told us they had been praying, asking God for several months to touch Coral and me.

Carole said, 'Prayer changes things, Noel. Isn't God good?'

'He's great.'

The following week everybody I met asked what had happened to me as I looked so unusually happy. I told everyone that I had met God in a dramatic way and now I was a Christian.

'Jesus lives in me,' I told them.

Needless to say they were surprised. Before I had been so anti-Christ, so totally opposed to religion. Now there was no stopping me. Everyone who spoke to me—whether at work or in the street—they got the lot. I just wanted everybody to know that Jesus Christ is Lord. Every night Coral and I read the Bible together, 'feeding' on God's word. We couldn't get enough of it. One night, we decided to pray together so we each kneeled down on one side of the bed. We both put our hands together in prayer-like fashion and then stared at each other.

'What do we say? How do we say it?' I asked.

'I don't know.'

'Let's just talk to God then.'

'That sounds all right to me.'

We did just that—talked to God about everything that was on our minds. I asked God to show the whole world I was innocent. I knew that he knew I had nothing to do with the crime and I wanted him to prove to the world I wasn't guilty. At the time I wasn't sure if one was allowed to ask God for things, but I knew he loved me, so I reckoned it must be all right to ask. There seemed so much we didn't know.

Before long, Coral and I joined a 'foundation course' at the church, geared towards new Christians. It turned out to be everything we had hoped for. Within a couple of months we had learned much more about how to pray and the Bible came alive to us. We were thrilled as we began to understand how much we were loved and cared for by God. Louise and Olivia became Christians and so did Coral's mother, my father, my brother Paul and many other people. So many of our prayers were being answered that Coral and I were becoming apprehensive about praying any more in case we were cut off—we felt we had our portion answered already! But we experienced the love of Jesus as he poured out blessings upon us, day after day, week after week, month after month. It seemed his supply was endless. And in early 1979, a couple of months after our conversion, Coral and I were baptized at the church and became members.

How different our lives had become since putting our trust in God. But there was still more. The week following our baptisms I was driving to London on a business engagement and, as usual, I was listening to cassettes on the car cassette player. I was listening to a tape of worship songs, joining in and thanking God for all he was doing in my life. Suddenly my voice changed as a heat came upon me and I started speaking a strange language. I felt frightened—I thought the old devil must have got me! It went on for a couple of minutes, and then I started talking normally again.

I turned the car around immediately and went home. I needed to tell Coral what had happened to me. She was surprised to see me home so early. I quickly told her what had happened and so we prayed about it, asking God to reveal the truth about the experience. The same evening I was in the bath and it came upon me again. I started speaking in that strange language. This time I decided to get help, so I phoned one of our ministers, Alan Marshall, and explained what had happened. He told me not to worry and said he would be straight round.

When he arrived, he asked to hear the whole story again and I told him every detail.

'You have been baptized with the Holy Spirit, Noel,' he said.

'Wow! I knew it was something different.'

He explained to us the work of the Holy Spirit in the life of a Christian. This new experience was a gift called 'speaking in tongues'—a special language given to an individual by the Holy Spirit to use for prayer and worship, when the human part of a person finds that human words are not enough, so to speak!

Alan and I then prayed with Coral and she received the Holy Spirit and spoke in tongues as well. This experience of being filled with the Holy Spirit brought a new dimension to our spiritual lives and we became even more aware of God's presence in our daily lives.

Although my life had changed dramatically since I had become a Christian, many of the old problems still manifested themselves from time to time. The dreams had subsided to a large degree but I still suffered them periodically. However, my real struggle was with forgiveness. As a Christian the Lord had called me to forgive my enemies, but I just couldn't. It was easy to forgive with my lips, but my heart still held bitterness and resentment. I asked God to take away the effects of my past life and show me how to walk in the truth without harbouring unforgiveness. I knew that he could do everything for me, yet I did not experience the outworking of it in my life. I desperately wanted to do his will, yet I failed in so many ways. Sometimes it seemed that the more I tried to overcome sin in my life, the more I seemed to fail. I came to the conclusion it was impossible to be perfect!

A meeting with one of the church elders, Dr Maurice Robinson, who was also our family GP helped me tremendously. Maurice was a man who could take care of all our needs, spiritual and physical. He was a warm, gentle, mature Christian who listened intently to all my problems and the frustrations which I felt were inhibiting my spiritual growth. He gave me very wise counsel.

'Let the Lord wash through your life, Noel, instead of trying to do all the work yourself,' he said. 'Let the Holy Spirit reveal the areas of your life that need to be changed. It is the Lord who is building you into the person he wants you to be. Relax. God's in charge.'

We prayed together and I felt much better. Maurice was right, of course. I had striven to do everything myself and kept falling short of my standards. My standards and the Lord's standards were completely different—after all, he knew I could and would fail from time to time. I hadn't grasped the degree of forgiveness God had given me. The time I spent with Maurice was the first of many times over the following years, each meeting resulting in more change in my life.

I put into practice Maurice's advice and slowly things started working out. My anger started to subside, as did swearing, cursing and a memory for distasteful jokes. It seemed small stuff to me but at least there was movement in the right direction.

In mid-November 1979 I answered the door to two gentlemen with northern accents.

'Noel Fellowes?' asked one.

'Yes, that's me.'

'We are police officers investigating a murder in Shap, Cumbria, and we would like to ask you some questions.'

A man had been found badly beaten and bound up; he had died from the injuries. It was very similar to the killing I had been convicted of in 1970.

'Shap is 300 miles away from here. Why are you asking me about it?'

'We're just eliminating suspects.'

I started to shake with fear. Everything the police had done to me back in 1970 came flooding back. Coral was able to find out exactly what we had been doing on the night in question from the daily diary we kept, and it was a huge relief when they finally left, satisfied with my alibi. It took me a number of hours to settle back into a normal state, however. I wrestled in prayer over the following months about it. It was all very well having assurance that God was with me, but I wanted action. I wanted my name cleared. After all, God knew the truth. All he had to do was reveal it to the world. I just couldn't understand why it hadn't happened.

In 1980 I learned of a man who had received a ministry of healing from God. His name was Ian Andrews and he lived in Chard, Somerset. I managed to get hold of his telephone number and rang him up. I told him of my past life and said that I felt he might be able to help me. He listened to me and then said he would pray about the issues for a few days and if he felt the Lord had given him any answers he would ring me back. I felt rather despondent. How on earth was I ever going to untangle the past if no one would help me to understand how supernatural healing really worked? Since the visit from the police my relationship with God had really see-sawed— up one week, down the next. It seemed I couldn't find a balance.

About a week after my initial phone call to Chard, Ian Andrews phoned back and invited both Coral and me down to his house for the day the following week. I was really excited at the prospect of meeting the great man of God. I hoped to find all the answers and to come home totally free from my hang-ups and free from remembered pain. We arrived at Ian and Rosemary's at half past eight and after coffee together, Coral and Rosemary left Ian and me to get on with the business.

Ian asked me to tell him everything about my past, right up to the present day—hurts, fears, anxieties, relationships, injustice, the lot. I poured my heart out all day. We stopped for an hour at lunch-time and continued into the afternoon. At about five o'clock I had finished. There was nothing left inside me. I had given him the whole shooting match. After long deliberation Ian spoke.

'It's really quite simple, Noel. You need to be healed from anger, resentment, bitterness, rejection and an orphan spirit.'

'How do I achieve all that?' I asked.

'All we need to do is ask the Father and he will do it.'

As Ian prayed over me, I felt the Lord touch me. There was a release from inner turmoil and tension. A new peace welled up inside me, different from the one I had experienced in the church. I felt clean all over. It was as if I was bathing at the seaside, the tide lapping over my body continually. This whole process had taken only a couple of minutes, yet I had spent all day getting it out of my system. Now I had been healed of all these things, there was a new area of freedom to experience.

Now my emotions had been totally unlocked and in the following months I found a new ability to be absolutely open with Coral. For years I had kept my anxieties, fears and thoughts locked away. Now I spoke about them openly and freely—for the first time in our marriage we had genuine open communication. Our marriage took off in a deeper way. Gone was the heaviness that had hung over our relationship for years. Love flowed in both directions—sharing, caring and encouraging one another in everything we did.

Since our encounter with Ian and Rosemary, there was a hunger to seek out the deeper truths about supernatural healing and other gifts that God gives to his people. After considerable prayer, Coral and I felt we were being called out of the church and into a local Christian fellowship, which was partly under the spiritual leadership of Ian Andrews. Ian felt it was right and since he had played an important part in my life, I thought his counsel wise. Ben Davies was really sorry to see us go, but he genuinely wished us well. I felt rather sad at leaving the place where Coral and I had been shown tremendous hospitality, understanding, support and encouragement. The one consolation was that we left on a clean footing and that all the relationships we had established in the church would remain with us in the future.

I had resigned from my job some time previously in favour of a business proposition from a friend who was in the building industry. He wanted me to join him in partnership in order to expand the business on the sales and management side. It was an opportunity I had been waiting for and against the advice of Coral and fellow Christians, I joined the business as a full partner. I threw myself into the challenge and, contrary to everybody's expectations, the business started to take off. It was thrilling to be in charge of something I had part ownership in, as it gave me even more incentive to make it work. The extra profit meant a better wage, which meant a better standard of living. Life seemed so wonderful—business was good, and although the new fellowship had its teething troubles we were learning and growing as Christians.

In the summer of 1981 we had planned to visit Christian friends of ours in America who had invited us to stay in their home in Orlando, Florida for three weeks. We decided to take them up on the offer and sent off for the necessary visa forms. Much to our dismay, the form asked about convictions for crime in the UK and stated that anyone convicted of manslaughter or the like was prohibited from visiting the USA. Coral and I really wanted to go to America, so we filled in the relevant forms honestly and accurately. We prayed over my form, asking God to honour our trip by shielding the form through the necessary channels. Three weeks later we all received our visas to go to America. The Lord had answered our prayers. We were all jubilant, praising God for the small miracle he had performed. The trip of a lifetime was on. Louise and Olivia were really excited at the prospect of going to Disney World. It became their sole topic of conversation.

A fortnight before we were due to fly to America I arrived home from work just in time to see Coral helping Olivia out of the car. Olivia was holding a pair of crutches.

'Guess what I've done, Dad?'

'Don't tell me, Olivia. I doubt if I would be able to take it right now,' I replied.

All I could think about was the trip to the States. It turned out that Olivia had fallen in her gym lesson and torn her cartilage and all the ligaments affecting her knee. The hospital X-rays had confirmed the worst—she was totally strapped up and would be for a further six weeks. Worse still, she wouldn't be able to walk for at least a month. I could just imagine myself having to carry Olivia around on holiday. It would be a nightmare. There was only one answer. We would have to call in the heavy mob—Ian Andrews.

Coral phoned Ian the next day and explained about Olivia's leg. Ian told Coral that it was my responsibility as head of the household to ask God for healing for Olivia. Coral told me the exciting news when I arrived home.

'Great—that's just great,' I said. 'He's the one with the healing ministry, not me. OK, I've prayed with people with headaches, colds, flu and other minor ailments, but nothing like this.'

'If Ian says you have the word for Olivia's healing, I believe it,' said Coral.

'That's all very well for you, love, but I need to know it for myself,' I replied.

A couple of days later after spending time praying and talking to God about it, I felt in a better place and told Olivia I was willing to pray for her if she was ready to accept the Lord's healing now. Olivia agreed and I started to pray. I had barely touched Olivia's leg when I heard a shriek of painful anguish come from her, followed by tears and sobbing.

'It hurts, Daddy, it hurts,' she cried.

'I know, sweetheart, but Jesus is going to heal it right now.' I felt that God had healed Olivia's leg and I declared it.

234

'You're healed, Olivia. The Lord has healed you. Now you must walk in your healing. Get up and walk.'

Tears still flowing down her cheeks, Olivia tried to stand. I held her hands as she stood.

'There. You're standing in your healing by yourself,' I said. 'Now take one step of faith, darling, and walk.'

'I'll try, Daddy,' she said, and took one step forward. A broad smile came over her face as she walked across the room.

'I'm healed, I'm healed,' she kept on saying. Coral and I just gazed at each other. We knew we had just seen a miracle. God had healed Olivia completely. We took all the dressings off and there was no sign of bruising anywhere, neither was there any pain. The next day we took the dressings and crutches back to the hospital and told them of the healing Olivia had received. They couldn't believe it, but the proof was there for all to see—Olivia was dancing around the reception area. From that day I never had difficulty in praying for anyone for healing. Many have been healed, many haven't, but as it is God who heals and not me, I just keep on praying. We all had a tremendous holiday in the States and returned to the UK ready to take up the next challenge.

In the early months of 1982 there was clear indication that my business was in danger of financial crisis. The order book was low, owing to the general decline in the building industry and our profit margin was barely meeting our overhead requirements. We had taken on new business premises a few months earlier, but now the cost of the lease and rent was crippling us. The fellow directors and I tried everything we could to pull the business out of the doldrums, but by May we were forced to make the decision to go into voluntary liquidation.

I was devastated. Everything I owned had been poured into the company. The same was true for the other directors. Two-and-a-half years of hard work and painful sweat had vanished into nothing. It was little consolation when the official receiver told us it happened to hundreds of small companies every year. The one area of my life I hadn't had dealt with stared me in the face—failure. I felt hopelessly lost. Not only had I failed, but I had let down Coral, my family and fellow Christians and, most of all, I felt I had let the Lord down. I was riddled with guilt as I knew that I had compromised my beliefs in some of my business dealings in the past. How could I have failed to heed the warning bells? Now it was too late. I had lost the lot, and, worse still, I owed a substantial amount of money.

Sid Stevens, the leader of the fellowship, was a tremendous source of help and support. He told me to put the whole thing down to experience, and encouraged me to ask God to guide me as to where I should work and who with. Sid continued in this positive approach every time he saw me. Maurice Robinson was another source of encouragement. He played a dual role, treating me as a patient and also as a pastor. My best mate, Keith Jobber, and his wife Betty, swung into action, taking over the responsibilities of all the legal implications of the liquidation and generally underpinning both Coral and me while we recovered from the blow and the shock of it all.

As the trauma of the whole personal disaster began to die down, I realized I had come to the end of myself. Strangely, I had lost everything and couldn't do anything to rescue the situation at all. The only truth in my life that remained was Jesus Christ. I knew in my heart that whatever happened I couldn't lose him. He was there for ever. Coral and I chatted over the whole thing and we prayed together. I told the Lord I was sorry for the mess I had got myself into and asked him to show us the way out again. I also told him I wasn't going to do anything until I knew it was right. We waited for a few weeks and then both Coral and I felt that God was telling me to start my own business.

We shared our revelation with a number of close friends, who confirmed the idea. Knowing that I was being guided by God gave me the confidence to do the spadework on working out the company name, logo and general formation procedures. Although both Coral and I were extremely excited about the new venture, we were desperately short of finance. All we had was two hundred pounds and our outgoings that month were five hundred. I had returned home one evening after praying with and helping a young married couple and told Coral, 'I believe the Lord wants us to give one hundred pounds to that couple. They are in desperate need of it.'

I could see by the expression on Coral's face that she was thinking the same as I was. We needed the hundred pounds just as much as they did.

'If you believe that is what he is saying to us, then give it to them,' she said. 'We both know you can't outgive God.'

So I put the money in a plain envelope and at midnight I travelled to the young couple's home and popped it through the letter-box. Coral and I felt genuinely pleased that we had obeyed the Lord and we both knew he would meet our needs.

We had arranged an appointment with the bank manager and, having spent much time praying about the meeting, we arrived to see him on a Monday morning.

'What can I do to help you, Mr Fellowes?' he asked.

'The truth is I have recently had the misfortune of seeing a small company I was a director of go into voluntary liquidation. After a short rest to assess my future, I feel the Lord is telling me to start a new company.'

'That's an angle I haven't heard used before,' he said.

'That's probably because it's the truth.'

'Why do you think this bank should lend you the money?'

'Because the Lord wants to bless you for helping us get the new company off the ground.'

The manager looked slightly amazed at my reply and seemed somewhat bemused by the whole event.

'How much do you think you will need to borrow?' he asked.

Here it comes, I thought.

'About two thousand pounds,' I half muttered in his general direction.

'How much?'

'Two thousand pounds.'

We discussed the vision for the new business venture and I

produced my portfolio for him. After about fifteen minutes of a question and answer session, he said, 'Well, Mr Fellowes. Thank you for being so forthright in your approach to your new venture. I think we will be able to help you.'

I looked at Coral to check if I had heard right; she nodded. It was true—I had heard right.

'I don't think two thousand pounds is a realistic figure to start your business off with,' he continued.

'I'll be happy with whatever you think is right,' I replied.

'I was thinking more in terms of six thousand pounds,' he said.

I nearly fell off my chair. Six grand . . . unbelievable! He wanted us to have six grand. Once my feet had touched the ground again, I said, 'Thank you very much. I am sure you won't regret it.'

'I know I won't, Mr Fellowes. I have every confidence you will make it work.'

Coral and I left the bank knowing we had a six thousand pound overdraft facility which we could use to launch the business. Everyone we told about our meeting at the bank couldn't or wouldn't believe such a thing happened. God had moved in a massive way, turning the bank manager round to our way of thinking, and we had the proof in our overdraft facility.

By the spring of 1983 Building Crafts, my new company, was running profitably and smoothly. The order book was relatively full and many of my previous debts had been cleared. Coral and I had come full circle. We were happy, peaceful and still head-over-heels in love with each other. There was so much freedom, honesty and purpose flowing through our relationship. It was as though we were courting again. The final chapter of my old lifestyle had gone with my business collapse. Now I was totally free from the effects of my past. Gone was resentment, anger, frustration, rejection, bitterness, fear of failure and, most importantly, unforgiveness. God had taken me apart piece by piece and completely rebuilt me. Now I was walking his path rather than my own.

However, I still prayed periodically that he would reveal the truth about the case and that I would be completely vindicated before man.

One night in July 1983 I experienced a strange dream. Dreams had become few and far between since the Lord had removed the past from my life, but I dreamt I was watching television in the lounge when the doorbell went. It was quite late in the evening and I thought it unusual for anyone to call at such an hour. I answered the door and found two men on the doorstep.

One asked, 'Mr Noel Fellowes?'

'Yes, that's me.'

I recognized his accent as being from Lancashire.

The other one pushed a paper towards me and said, 'I think we have something here that will interest you. New revelations on a killing in 1970.'

That was it. Then I woke up.

I told Coral about the dream the next morning and we both felt that God was telling me something but exactly what we couldn't fathom out. I knew that if the Lord wanted to reveal more to us then he would, so I wasn't anxious. I just left it at that.

One evening in February 1984 I was working in my office at home when Coral opened the door and announced there were two men who would like to see me. I asked them into the office, whereupon they identified themselves as detectives and showed their warrant cards.

'What do you want to speak to me for?' I enquired.

'We have been asked to come and see you by the Lancashire Police about a murder investigation concerning a young man who has been found dead in South Lancashire.'

'Why on earth have you come to see me?'

'It seems the victim was killed in a similar way to the one you were convicted of in 1970.'

I felt the blood drain from my face and my nerves set on edge. Blood pumped furiously to my brain and the adrenalin started to flow.

'For your information I was innocent of the crime in 1970 and here we are in 1984 and you're still trying to destroy me,' I said in an angry voice.

Coral popped her head in the door and asked if everything was all right.

'No, it isn't,' I said. 'These two are investigating a murder which they say is similar to the one I was convicted of in 1970 and they want to know about my movements again. They obviously think I have nothing better to do than go up and down the length of Britain killing people.'

'Don't react to them. They're only doing their job,' said Coral. 'I'll go and get the diary.'

I cooled down and apologized for my outburst. The detectives told me that it was a part of their job they hated doing, but unfortunately it had to be done if another force requested it. Again I gave them details of my alibi and they left, apologizing for any inconvenience they had caused.

I sat in the office for a couple of hours after they had left, completely stunned by the whole episode. I was upset at the way I had reacted to them, but felt justified. I saw it as an attack not only on myself but the whole family. Coral came in and chatted with me for a while, offering her own thoughts on the subject and encouraging me to keep hold of the peace I was now living in. After Coral had left I prayed for a while and then said to the Lord:

'Father, I don't know that I am able or even willing to take any more reminders of the past. You have healed me of all the hurts and injustice; I acknowledge that. Father, please put an end to it once and for all. Amen.'

That was it. I just left it there, believing that the prayer would be answered in God's time.

14

The Supergrass Connection

Lenny Pilot and Fred Scott had two of the best-paid jobs in Manchester. They were experts in their line of business—both in the way they meticulously planned every 'transaction' and in the precision of carrying it out. Armed robbery was not just a tax-free career for Pilot and Scott—it was a way of life.

Pilot's businesslike approach also included a mental index of all cronies he and his accomplices had been involved with. Little was I to know, but the Overton case was just one memory tucked away in his mind.

They had previously dabbled in more legitimate streams of commerce, but willingly discarded them for the high life of professional criminals. Pilot had once been a smooth-talking salesman and Scott had run a string of shops in the city, mainly dealing in pornography.

Pilot and Scott admired and complemented each other's differing styles and criminal talents. While Scott demanded to be *au fait* with every detail of a crime at blueprint stage, Pilot, eighteen years younger, was known throughout the Manchester underworld for his 'bottle'. He would stop at nothing to loot cash from post offices, security vans and company accounts departments. Both of them carried shotguns as easily as most people carry umbrellas.

By 1982 the tie-up robbery committed by Pilot and friends on a Town Hall cashier in Warsop back in September 1970 was small beer. Pilot and Scott were now in the big league. None of their robberies were planned to take more than 90 seconds before fleeing to their hideaways with alibis already in hand. Their stock-in-trade was to wear hideously wrinkled 'old men' masks which would not only shield their identities but also bring a new dimension of terror to their victims. Just for good measure, Pilot would fire a shotgun into the ceiling of the factory wages office if the cashier was being a little sluggish in handing over the money.

On ambushes of security vans, Pilot would leap from the boot of the car in front, surprising the driver with both barrels of his shotgun. Once, a brave security guard threatened to defy the raiders, so an accomplice blasted his weapon directly at the van. Pilot simply explained: 'I was an armed blagger. Firing shotguns was just part of the game. I suppose somebody would have got killed eventually.'

The ferocity of the armed robberies persuaded Greater Manchester Police Chief Constable Jim Anderton to act swiftly and dramatically. He decided that a 74 per cent rise in firearm offences merited armed police units on a 24-hour-a-day mobile duty. This later caused a furore with his left-wing police committee and the plan had to be shelved amid a blaze of publicity. But Pilot and Scott laughed at the feeble attempts to trap them. While Pilot spent around £500 a week on drinking, gambling, fast cars, holidays and designer clothes, Scott's business empire boomed and he looked forward to early retirement and a life of leisure with his wife and two children. Though the police harboured suspicions against the pair, proving anything concrete was extremely difficult.

For the criminals, it had reached the stage where thieving had become nothing more than lucrative fun. Pilot recalls: 'I would pick an area with a few jewellery wholesalers and sit around for an hour or two and study who was driving which car. When I'd decided who was most likely to be a representative for the firm, I would follow him, often for many miles out of town. The rep. would park outside a customer's house, lock up, and take a brochure inside. I would nip out, force his boot open, steal his case with £40,000 worth of gems and take off. Easy as that.'

The Post Office robbery at Moston in June 1982 seemed to be just another job. Pilot parked a friend's Mercedes car several miles away from the scene of the crime while his armed team went into action. But a curious neighbour jotted down the registration number and later passed on the information to the police. After Pilot ditched another get-away car locally and escaped in the Mercedes, he and his associates were arrested and charged with armed robbery. Apart from the Mercedes, the evidence was thin. The court allowed them bail while the case was prepared and Pilot's solicitor advised him there was little chance of conviction on the quality of prosecution evidence so far.

During the twelve months between the robbery and the Crown Court trial, five more similar attacks took place. In April 1983, Pilot was arrested again and questioned over another robbery. Still on bail, he forcefully denied any involvement, which, for once, was the truth.

By then, the police had their own new techniques to try out. Detective Sergeant Henri Exton of the No. 1 Regional Crime Squad asked Pilot for 'a quiet word'. He tried to persuade Pilot to turn informer, prior to his trial, but Pilot would have nothing to do with it. The suggestion went against every criminal code of ethic he had held dear for as long as he could remember.

But Scott had other ideas. He felt that the police had a stronger case against him on the Moston robbery than Pilot would admit. (In the event he was proved right and the pair were jailed for ten years.) Scott was in his early fifties and realized his only hope of gaining a lengthy period of parole would be to turn 'supergrass'—a term which has only become accepted within the last decade, but which has now become a regular feature of news bulletins on criminal affairs in England, and Northern Ireland particularly.

The first 'supergrass', a man called Bertie Smalls, was an informer to Scotland Yard's robbery squad. The information he gave on a series of bank robberies between 1968 and 1972 eventually led to court appearances for twenty-six people, of which sixteen were convicted. Smalls himself was housed, paid expenses and granted immunity from prosecution. Not everybody in the legal field was happy with the changing face of detection. While Lord Justice Lawton said the teaming up of the Director of Public Prosecutions and a professional robber was an 'undignified sight', the Metropolitan Police Commander, Sir David McNee, defended the system. More supergrasses were forthcoming—although total immunity was never granted again.

The urge to turn supergrass gradually overpowered Scott. Under a false name, he left Walton prison—where I had served the first few months of my sentence—and travelled to Wigan police station where he started 'singing like a canary', as one policeman put it. Scott was frank about his and Pilot's exploits, and the identity of their accomplices. He admitted armed raids at a mill in Oldham, a security van at a rail station in Manchester, a wages stick-up in Wythenshaw and others, topping £100,000 in cash. He was later jailed for seven years for these crimes—but the judge ordered them to be concurrent so they would not lengthen his ten-year sentence.

News of Scott's 'defection' took some time to get about. While Scott was still supposed to be at Walton, Pilot was starting his sentence at Strangeways. One of his first visitors was Detective Sergeant Exton.

'He told me the police had a mass of evidence against me on several security van robberies and were preparing a case against me. He then told me some facts and I could not believe my ears. It was obvious someone was talking and giving Exton information. He said he had permission from the top to offer me supergrass status,' recalls Pilot. Exton's offer was attractive, but Pilot turned it down.

The full truth was revealed early in the New Year of 1984. Press and radio reports buzzed with details of *Operation Belgium*, as more than 200 officers had been involved in dawn swoops on thirty homes, all acting on information from Scott. The 6.30 a.m. timing was intended to catch their prey at a psychological low ebb. It worked. They were taken to twenty-four different police stations where they were allowed a tantalizing glimpse of a list of names of their friends also under arrest. Many of them knew their criminal careers were over. And the regional crime squad detectives were rejoicing.

At that point Pilot knew he had to act fast, both to protect himself against Scott's incriminating accusations and to accept supergrass status while it was still available. Pilot claims he also wanted to turn his back on his former profession: 'I was completely disillusioned and sick to the back teeth with it all. I realized it wasn't worth it. I had enough of crime and criminals and decided I would co-operate fully and not only corroborate Scott but help police clear up other serious crimes.'

It was a coincidence that Pilot was moved to Lancaster Castle—scene of my trial—until the Home Office confirmed his status as supergrass. Then his name was changed temporarily to Robert Downes to avoid security leaks and after a fortnight he was released from prison custody into the hands of police guardians. There is little doubt that his new-found allies were determined to keep him happy during their time together, and it is difficult to tell whether the luxury treatment Pilot claims he enjoyed was simply a civilized way of extracting information or a more devious police plan.

Pilot's information and his uncanny knack of remembering names and places produced a flood of details on crimes both petty and serious. In return, he says, he suddenly found himself the next best thing to free: 'I was able to go to the pub for a drink and meet my girlfriend, parents and solicitor. One day I wore a flat cap to disguise myself and went to watch Wigan play St Helens in a rugby cup final, with two cops on either side. I had a colour TV and a video and would sometimes go and choose a film from the local video store. I would go out for a meal or have one brought in from the Spinning Wheel restaurant. The police even left me and my girlfriend alone in my cell for a couple of hours. She brought in cans of booze. It led me to believe in the supergrass status, but it was a false sense of security as I was to find out later.'

Pilot's information gave rise to *Operation Holland*, the successor to *Operation Belgium*, and the arrest of around twenty men. Most names were linked with crimes of a similar pattern, but two immediately stood apart from the rest—Billy Clark, who had joined him on the Warsop raid, and another local lad called Robert Berry, Joey to his friends.

On 13 February 1984—fourteen years to the month since the killing of Harold Parkinson—startling new information came to light. At Littleborough police station, two detectives listened breathlessly as Pilot—or Downes as he was named—began dictating a statement.

In it, he first owned up to the Moston robbery he had denied so vehemently during his trial. Then he confirmed a sheet of twenty-one previous convictions, dating back twenty years. One was the Morecambe optician assault and theft in 1972. But then he began talking in earnest on the Overton crime.

'Around 1970, Joey Berry came into The Church public house on Ashton New Road, Manchester, where we used to drink quite often. Joey said he wanted to see me, and we both went and sat down. Joey said he had to talk to someone as he was very worried and he wanted to get something off his chest. He said he and our mate Billy Clark had been to do a tie-up and Billy had hit this bloke and the bloke had died. Joe was frightened that he could get done for murder. I told him to calm down and not to be so stupid. I asked him what had happened. He said a businessman dealing in one-armed bandits had told him and Billy about a retired coin-dealer who lived Morecambe way, had a safe with plenty of money in it and some valuable coins, and it would be an easy tie-up. Joe said the man had let them in. Billy had given him a crack and the bloke had jossed it [died].'

Pilot then alleged how he and Berry drove to Billy Clark's local pub and met him.

'Billy told Joe not to be so silly and said, "What's done is done. It's best to forget it" or words to that effect. Joe seemed to calm down and I never heard a mention of it again. Some time later I was in Risley remand centre. There was a lot of talk at the time among staff and the cons about an ex-copper who had been done for a murder in Morecambe. I heard it was a coin-dealer but I cannot be positive if the ex-copper was actually in the nick at the same time as me or if he had left and people were still talking about him. I do remember one of the staff telling me that the ex-copper was a nuisance, always going on about his innocence. At the time I heard this, I thought, the man is innocent, there can't possibly be two murders of coin-dealers in Morecambe.'

Pilot recalled just one other detail. 'I remember Joey saying on that night something about the tide having to be out so they could get to the house.'

The four-page statement took seventy-seven minutes to jot down. But it was studied for many hours afterwards by a variety of officers representing different police forces. The first job for the police was to find records and files kept by the neighbouring Lancashire force to confirm a killing had taken place in the Morecambe area at that time. Excitement grew as the first enquiry gave broad details of the death of Harold Parkinson.

The management of the police operation following up Pilot's statement fell to the Regional Crime Squad Co-ordinator Detective Chief Superintendent Bill Lumsden. It was to be his last major case before retiring. He handed the Clark assignment to Det. Chief Inspector Allan Potts, who was well qualified for the sensitive type of work that lay ahead. His initial brief was to make discreet background enquiries, including surveillance of Clark at his home in Staton Street, Openshaw, Manchester. His men also blended anonymously in pubs and other places where Clark called in, meeting friends and associates. Soon they built up a limited picture of Billy Clark, an unemployed cabinet-maker with a list of previous convictions. A similar operation was mounted to observe Joe Berry.

By 13 March, the crime squad had enough definite information to know where to strike in another series of dawn raids. Armed officers were on stand-by as doors were kicked in and suspects were hauled bleary-eyed from their beds. Clark and Berry struggled to make sense of the reasons for their arrests. Berry recalls: 'It didn't register with me when they said it was for a Morecambe job. I told my wife I would be home for dinner, I was that certain they wouldn't keep me.'

Billy Clark was taken to Rochdale police station and Joey

Berry to Whitefield. They were both documented and placed in cells for a short time. Detective Chief Inspector Potts and Detective Sergeant Phil McEvitt began questioning Clark at 9 a.m. in a CID office. When Potts told Clark he was enquiring into a death at Overton, Clark responded: 'Not me, I don't know what you're on about. I've done no job in Morecambe.' The first fifty minutes dragged by in deadlock.

Despite Potts' quietly persistent manner Clark was not about to give ground after such a short period. He was returned to his cell at 10.25 a.m. where he stayed for an hour. Potts pondered on whether all the conditions were favourable. Certainly he had done his best to try to encourage Clark to talk without the sort of oppression I had endured fourteen years earlier. The room was clean and airy, the table and chairs illuminated by natural light from a large window at one end. Potts knew it was a question of reaching a rapport with this man—of 'striking the right chord' as he put it.

When Potts deliberately let slip that the information leading to the swoop had come from Pilot, his one-time buddy, Clark swore vehemently. The interrogators noticed Clark's outward bravado slip slightly as he became agitated and began repeatedly scratching the back of his hands. Just after mid-day, Potts changed tack, mentioning the Warsop tie-up robbery. Potts said his informant had claimed Clark and his friend Berry were with him during the raid. Clark's defences started crumbling. 'All right, you know I was on that one,' he confessed. But he refused to be budged on the Overton killing.

After an hour's lunch break, Potts said: 'We have been looking at the details of the jobs at Warsop and Morecambe and find the tie-ups were very similar. What about that?'

Clark replied: 'We used sellotape at Warsop, and some bandage. I don't know nothing about what was used at Morecambe.'

Potts persisted: 'The man at Warsop was tied up with sellotape and bandages while the man at Morecambe was tied up with webbing and electric cord, all wrapped in similar positions on the body of each man.' Clark realized that he was walking on quicksand and made no reply.

Potts asked: 'Does the name Fellowes mean anything to you?'

'Never heard of him,' came the answer.

Several miles away at Whitefield, Detective Sergeant Derek Gardner was going through the same question-and-answer routine with Joey Berry.

'We have reason to believe that you and some other person in 1970 went to an address in Morecambe, the home of a coin-dealer and, as a result, the man who was tied up died later from his injuries,' said Gardner.

'You're joking, don't know what you're talking about, haven't got the foggiest. All this is through this —— Pilot. We're just small time, I'm a sneak thief and nothing else,' complained Berry, who had heard of Pilot's supergrass activities from his cousin Kenny Connors, awaiting trial following arrest during *Operation Belgium*.

Gardner then accused Berry of being involved in the Warsop crime but this was hotly denied. The detective then produced a number of coins belonging to Berry, some of which were collector's items. Berry said they had been given to him legitimately.

While the interview at Whitefield made little real progress, it was a different story at Rochdale. Potts was winning the battle of wills. He had a gut feeling that Clark was hiding something and his patient build-up of carefully selected questions and off-the-cuff remarks was beginning to make headway.

Potts said, 'We believe that the two of you got in the house using the coin. That, once in, you both tied him up, is that right?'

Clark held his head in his hands for several minutes. Eventually—after what must have seemed an eternity—came six simple words: 'I did it on my own.'

After that admission, Clark recalled how he, Joey Berry and a 'cockney' called Peter had travelled to Overton. The other two had stayed in a nearby pub as Clark went to Mr Parkinson's house. After showing the old man some half-crowns and two-shilling pieces, Clark was allowed in. Mr Parkinson even made tea for him.

'He went upstairs and I was rooting around to see what I could find. I got £55 and shoved it in my pocket,' Clark admitted.

Potts glanced at his sergeant to make sure he was noting every remark. There seemed no stopping Clark now as he described how the old man surprised him in the act of pilfering: 'He jumped on my back and started hitting me with karate chops . . . I had to fight him off. We were fighting for a while, then he just went on the floor and was gasping for breath.'

'I had to tie him up so he couldn't follow me. I got some flex, a tie and a belt. Then I run out the front door and went back to the pub. We got a taxi to the station and a train back to Manchester.'

Clark then elaborated further. He described how, after arriving in the coastal area, he had telephoned Mr Parkinson 'as an excuse to get in the house. I told him I wanted to show him some coins.'

Clark also wanted to make clear he had only hit the old man with his fists. 'I just kept lashing out at him to get him off. I don't know, it was just a fight that went all wrong. I didn't mean to do that. I didn't mean to hurt him, I just wanted to get away. If he had not have gone upstairs I'd have tried to unlock the back door and come back later. I never meant to harm him. I suppose I'll get twenty years for this.'

Despite the rising panic in Clark's voice, his memory of that dreadful day fourteen years ago was crystal clear. He remembered both knocking over a kettle in the fireplace during the struggle and leaving the front door ajar on his way out. When he and the other two had successfully returned to Manchester, Clark had continued to worry about the old man left tied up in the lonely cottage. It was he who phoned Lancashire police and reported an accident at 19, Main Street.

Potts was astonished. 'How do you come to remember the address?' he asked.

'I've lived with it for fourteen years!' came the reply.

He was not the only one!

Potts and McEvitt tempered their delight at Clark's confession with the knowledge that, despite the unabated outpouring, it could still stand for little at the trial. A record of conversation can be doctored—as I found out to my cost back in 1970. A statement was needed to verify the remarks in print. But Clark even obliged on the same day by repeating how he had tricked his way into the cottage, fought with the old man and tied him up. He added: 'I have been told that a man called Fellowes was convicted of this job but he did not have any part in it and I do not know any person of that name. I'm very sorry it happened this way but I never dreamed it would. I'm glad it's all over this time. If only he [Parkinson] had not sneaked up on me like that it would never have happened that way. I can't express how sorry I feel for his family.'

Clark added finally his confession to the Warsop crime, which brought a very satisfactory day's work to an end. Detective Chief Superintendent Lumsden felt proud of his team and exhilarated by what was becoming one of the most bizarre cases he had ever handled.

Meanwhile Berry was proving stubborn. Potts decided to visit him the following day and broke the news that Clark had admitted involvement in the Morecambe case and had also been charged with the robbery of £660 in Warsop. Berry's replies to all points had a familiar ring to them: 'It's nothing to do with me . . . I'm saying nothing . . . It's not down to me . . .' The interview was terminated inconclusively.

Berry had given nothing away a couple of hours earlier when Detective Sergeant Gardner had tried to use the psychology of confronting the suspect with his accuser—Lenny Pilot. The meeting in the Whitefield cells began with Pilot saying: 'I'm wiping the slate clean, Joe, I've told them everything, about the job at Warsop when you, me and Billy tied that kid up . . .' But Berry shut his ears and repeatedly interrupted Pilot with the words, 'Goodnight Lenny'. He later told police: 'I don't want to hear his name again, he's dead as far as I'm concerned.'

The confrontation idea was pursued the following day when Berry had another caller—Billy Clark. For twenty minutes Clark told his friend what he had admitted to police. But he was anxious also to impress on him that he had neither betrayed nor implicated him. 'I've told them, Joey, you had nought to do with it . . . I tied that fella up and you and cockney Pete stayed in the pub.' Berry—under the glare of his friend and three policemen—refused to be budged. When police charged him with the Warsop robbery five hours later he remained silent.

Berry was under intense pressure as he sat alone in his cell for the next few days. Eventually he realized that Clark would end up in the dock and said, 'I don't want to end up as a prosecution witness against Billy and be called a grass like that —— Pilot'. On 29 March, in the central detention centre at Manchester, Berry suddenly found his memory flooding back.

He related how he travelled to Overton with the others and stayed for 'one or two pints' in the pub while Clark disappeared to commit the crime. Berry had originally planned to join in a 'sneak theft' of the coin collection but his courage had deserted him. He added that years later he had heard 'about a kid getting time for murder' in Morecambe. He did not know me and had never heard of the name Fellowes, he stressed. Berry too agreed to make a statement.

The path was now clear for Lumsden to launch another side of the operation—to validate Clark's and Berry's admissions and compare them with the Lancashire constabulary version of the death of Harold Parkinson.

Three teams of officers travelled to Overton, first alerting Lancashire police as a matter of inter-force politeness. Detective Chief Inspector Potts remembers those early enquiries: 'First I wanted to check whether the telephonist existed, whom Clark said he rang before being put through to Mr Parkinson, prior to the crime. She did. Then we found the policeman who had answered his call reporting the accident in Main Street. Around 800 statements were taken at the time of the incident, but many of them had been destroyed. But we recovered more than thirty from Lancaster station. We were less successful trying to trace fingerprints taken at the house because they had long since been destroyed by the criminal records office.'

'A description of a village with two pubs cut off by the tide turned out to be correct, and we knew we were getting somewhere. The adrenalin was running but this had to be a calm, clinical examination.'

Joe Mounsey, by now the longest-serving assistant chief constable at Lancashire, handed over photographs of the body and Det. Chief Supt. Ray Rimmer, head of the county CID, was appointed liaison officer between the two forces.

It wasn't long before news leaked to the newspapers. On 4 April 1984, the *Lancashire Evening Post* front page headline read: 'Police Turn Up Death Links.' The crime reporter, Bob Westerdale, said: 'Detectives are studying startling new evidence about the killing of a Lancashire coin-collector fourteen years ago.' The story rightly merited front-page treatment—but there was one central element missing—the whereabouts of the man who was convicted in the first place. Enquiries by Bob Westerdale and his colleague Nic Fogg in the Morecambe and Heysham area drew a blank. But one former neighbour remembered I had originally come from Windsor and, as a last chance, Bob Westerdale telephoned directory enquiries. Luckily for him, my initials and the distinctive spelling of my surname threw up just a handful of possibilities. Eventually—after sweet-talking the operator— Westerdale managed to get a home address despite my ex-directory status. Before long, he and Terry Bromley, a photographer, set off down the motorway.

Following a fellowship meeting at our home, I turned on the television to watch the highlights of the football international between England and Northern Ireland. The doorbell rang. I glanced at the clock. It was quarter past eleven. Slightly annoyed at having to answer the door because Coral had gone to bed, and I might miss a vital goal, I raced to the door, opened it and said, 'Yes, what is it?'

In my innocence I had thought perhaps someone had forgotten their Bible and had called back for it. Standing on the doorstep were two strangers.

'Noel Fellowes?' asked one.

'Yes, that's me.'

'I've got some very important news about the Overton killing.' Then I saw him produce a newspaper and offer it to me.

'Two men are being questioned about it.'

They stood there, half expecting me to slam the door in their faces, even though they had made a four-hour journey from Preston to Bracknell to tell me the good news. They didn't know at the time that the few words they had spoken triggered my memory about the dream I had had in 1983. It was a complete re-run, only this time it was happening for real.

'I've waited fourteen years for someone like you to come along. Come in. You're messengers from God.'

They looked a little puzzled at my last remark.

'Don't worry, I'll explain it all later. Come and make yourselves comfortable in the lounge.'

I couldn't contain my excitement. I shouted upstairs to Coral.

'Come down. I've some really exciting news to tell you.' I half said it and stuttered the rest. Coral was down in a flash.

'What's all the excitement?' she asked.

'Let me introduce you to Bob Westerdale and Terry Bromley, a crime reporter and a photographer with the *Lancashire Evening Post*. They're here to break the news about new developments in the Overton killing.'

Coral and I just hugged each other. We could hardly believe what was happening. My head was still in the clouds as together we read the front page story over and over again. I was shaking with excitement. 'At last. At last. It's finally going to be sorted out,' I kept saying to myself. 'All these years and now I can see the beginning to the end of the whole nightmare.' Bob and Terry just sat there, trying to assess the situation. In between reading I kept leaping up and down, praising God for answering my prayers. I just couldn't contain myself.

Eventually I calmed down and Bob started to press me for a response. He wanted to run a headline story the next day with my reaction. As Coral and I talked it over, we decided it would be better to have a third opinion, so I rang up Sid Stevens and explained what had happened. He and his wife Ann came round in a matter of minutes.

Bob felt he had lost the moment and asked,

'Why can't you make the decision yourself? Surely you don't need anybody else to make the decision for you?'

'We need wisdom in this situation,' I replied. 'Besides, the press haven't got the best record in the honesty stakes,' I said. 'I need to protect Coral and the children at this time. Also our home address and my business. Before I give you a story I want to make sure all the angles are covered and that I have witnesses to verify what I have actually said.'

Bob felt a little happier after I had got that off my chest. We talked over all the issues, and decided that I should give Bob a story. I set out the rules before I gave the interview. He wasn't to print Coral's name or the children's. He wasn't to print my address or whereabouts. He would quote me completely accurately. If he abided by the simple rules that I had laid down, then I would remain exclusive to him as far as the media was concerned. Bob promised to abide by my wishes and even accepted that I wasn't going to let his colleague, Terry, take any photographs so his journey was somewhat wasted.

I related the dream I had had in 1983 to Bob. He just sat there open-mouthed as he realized the impact of it.

'I told you I thought you were God's messengers and I firmly believe he has selected you to report everything I have to say now and in the future.'

'I'll buy that, Noel. That'll do me,' said Bob. 'I give you my word that I won't let you down.'

I had warmed to Bob. He was naturally relaxed, blunt and to the point. Besides, he was a fellow Manchester United supporter, which was even better. It was about two-thirty in the morning when we finished the interview. Both Bob and Terry were delighted with the quality of material they had gathered. They left to find their hotel and compile the notes into a story, which had to be telephoned through by breakfast-time to catch the early issues of the paper.

Coral and I talked for a while longer with Sid and Ann before retiring at about three-thirty. We were both still too excited to sleep. We both knew these were early days, but thanked God for making the all-important breakthrough on my behalf.

15

'I am Innocent!'

The reporter and photographer had come a long way for a story, but the trip had been worthwhile. Bob Westerdale explained to me the angle he would be pursuing—that of a wronged man proclaiming, 'I am innocent'. And those three words were the headline on the front page of the *Lancashire Evening Post* as it went to press. My trust in Bob had been repaid; it was the start of a firm friendship.

The story quoted me as saying: 'I am absolutely innocent. Now I want my name cleared.' That summed it up—I had kept my story secret for long enough. Now was the time for everyone to know I was not a killer. Bob's article also added that Detective Chief Superintendent Lumsden and his men had 'uncovered some elements of confirmation'—this referred to the statements made by Clark and Berry, neither of whom had yet been publicly named. And Mr Lumsden disclosed the existence of a 'third man' wanted for questioning over the Overton death during a confidential briefing with Bob. He said, however, there was little chance of capturing 'cockney Pete' unless one of the two men being questioned gave a more easily identifiable name.

Within a few days of Bob's news I travelled to Salford with Ian Andrews to meet Detective Chief Superintendent Lumsden, who was spearheading the enquiry into the Overton case. The reason I had invited Ian to come along with me was two-fold—firstly, I wasn't too happy meeting police officers by myself after my last encounter with them in 1970 and secondly, I valued Ian's discernment of people. As it turned out, Mr Lumsden was a delightful man whose only interest was to establish the truth in Pilot's allegations. Both Ian and I were satisfied that my side of things was safe in the hands of Bill Lumsden. Ian observed afterwards that whilst I and Mr Lumsden were engaged in conversation, we looked at each other eyeball to eyeball, neither one looking to the left or right. It seems we were both engaged in the same operation—trying to get the measure of the man. I found Mr Lumsden to be open and affable, just as Bob Westerdale had promised. Following our brief but fruitful interview, Mr Lumsden advised me to get hold of a good solicitor as he felt I would need one to act on my behalf even at this early stage of the proceedings.

I told him that I had already engaged a solicitor, Mr Graham Hughes of Robinson, Jarvis and Rolf on the Isle of Wight.

He looked a little perturbed and said, 'But you live in Bracknell, Berkshire.'

'Yes, that's right, but it's a long story. I'll explain it to you some time.'

In fact, Ian had advised me that a friend of his, Clive Rolf, a Christian solicitor practising on the Isle of Wight, was the man to speak to about the new revelations in the case. I phoned Clive on Ian's recommendation and explained my situation. He in turn passed me on to one of his partners in the firm, Graham Hughes, who specialized in criminal law.

After our meeting, Mr Lumsden told the press: 'He has no animosity towards the police and wished us every success in our enquiry. I have a very open mind on his guilt or innocence and we are working hard to establish the truth.'

That was the official line. Off the record he told Bob, 'You will do well to stick with this story; it's going to get more and more interesting.'

Coral and I travelled to the Isle of Wight to meet Graham Hughes. When we got to his office I asked Graham what he thought about the case on the strength of the documentation he had been able to examine to date.

'I believe you're innocent, Noel, and there seems little evidence against you in 1970. If the same thing happened today you would never be charged.'

'How do you feel about handling the case totally on my behalf?' I asked.

'It would be my privilege, Noel, and I can assure you I will endeavour to make certain nothing goes wrong this time.'

On the outward seventy-mile journey we had been asking ourselves why we were going to see a solicitor so far away. As we talked, it was obvious to both Coral and me that Graham was the right man. He was both 'a brother in Christ' and professionally second to none. The one element in Graham's approach which struck me was that he paid great attention to detail—I knew I needed a man who would dot every 'i' and cross every 't'. I had complete trust in him. Before we left his office, all three of us prayed together, asking God to assist Graham in every step he took regarding the defence procedures for my vindication. Coral and I returned home feeling secure in the knowledge that now we had two people—Bob Westerdale and Graham Hughes—fighting all the way for us.

Meanwhile, Detective Chief Superintendent Lumsden's travelling team of men were consistently reporting back with snippets of information which he pored over long into the evenings. The first information he latched on to was the reported three sightings of Harold Parkinson on Wednesday 25 February 1970—the day after the time the Crown had claimed I had killed him.

Men got to work on this line, with mixed results. Retired fisherman Jimmy Braid, who had described talking to Harold Parkinson over the back garden stood by his earlier statement. But the barman Charles Ramsey who had told Joe Mounsey's officers he had 'easily recognized' Mr Parkinson now had other ideas: 'At that time and even now I was not positively sure that it was Parkinson . . . I had had a few drinks that day.'

The bus-driver, Richard Luke, was much more positive, though. Fourteen years earlier he had described seeing the old man on the morning of the 25th, 'he lifted his hand to me in acknowledgement when he saw me'. Mr Luke didn't reveal at the time that he had stopped his bus and given Mr Parkinson a lift to Heysham village. To have admitted it then could have invited trouble because his official trip wasn't scheduled to start for another half hour.

Lumsden's men continued to bring in other results during April, including interviews with one-time GPO telephonist Sylvia Kinnaird, retired PC Alan Knowles and serving constable Joe Howarth, all later to play a part in the case against Clark.

While all this activity was going on, Lenny Pilot was preparing to face another moment of truth in front of a judge forty miles away at Preston Crown Court. Every national newspaper was represented for his half-hour appearance in Number Two court before Judge Mr Justice McNeill, QC. They were intrigued by Pilot's supergrass activities and the 'spin-off' statement he had made concerning Overton. Pilot later admitted it 'took some bottle' to stand flanked between prison officers in the dock and plead guilty to no fewer than twenty-three charges involving robbery, arson, conspiracy and theft. Several times he nervously peered to his left at the locked doorway leading into the court as if expecting retributions from the Manchester gangland he had turned his back on.

Pilot sat uneasily in the court as the Crown he had reluctantly made a pact with laid bare his years of wrong-doing. The counts included the occasions when shotguns were blasted in an office at an Oldham mill, a Manchester dairy and the side of a security van. Pilot also admitted ramming a company director's car, shooting at a tyre and stealing £7,300 from a businessman in Failsworth. Another incident was described when Pilot ran over a pub landlord as he was taking £800 takings to the bank. In all, he had netted £121,000 in these raids, and a further £42,000 in thirty other offences he asked the court to take into consideration.

The first glimmer of something more positive in his life came as Detective Superintendent Bernard McGourlay from the Regional Crime Squad took to the witness-box. He complimented Pilot on the 'spot-on' quality of his information, which had resulted in a confession rate of around 70 per cent. He had been 'no respecter of persons' in the names he had forwarded to the police but there had already been repercussions after two incidents 'believed to be reprisals'. Pilot's defence counsel continued on this theme, saying the professional villain would 'always be looking over his shoulder' when he left the isolation unit he was caged in. He commented that: 'The people arrested were among the hardest and most violent criminals in Manchester. So many criminals have been forced to confess that in future organized crime should be much reduced in the Manchester area.'

The barrister also drew attention to the Overton killing and to Clark, adding, 'If any question arises of a man having been wrongly convicted in the past, Pilot's information may well serve to right that wrong.'

Jailing Pilot for six-and-a-half years—concurrent with the ten he was already serving for the Moston post office robbery—Mr Justice McNeill remarked: 'There have been threats to your life which have been taken seriously by the police. Your career in crime is finished and your life in Manchester is finished. No criminal will ever trust you again.'

Pilot nodded respectfully before being ushered down the steps to the cells. He had won a concurrent sentence and the only charge he had pleaded not guilty to—conspiracy to murder—had been allowed to lie on the file. In other words, no action taken. It was a victory of sorts.

Within five days of the Pilot case, Lancashire Chief Constable Brian Johnson decided to send Mr Lumsden's report on the Overton crime to the Director of Public Prosecutions for his advice.

So far, I had no reason to feel anything but elated over the way everything was going in my fight to get justice. Nor had I anything but respect for the way the *Lancashire Evening Post* had handled the story. Bob Westerdale had pledged to protect Coral and the children by not printing my address but he also repeatedly warned me it was only a 'matter of time' before it would be leaked to a rival media man.

At the end of May, some seven weeks after the *Evening*

Post had traced me, the national press heard of it and I was confronted by a *Daily Mail* reporter and photographer. Eventually, I showed them some of the quotes used by the *Evening Post* and invited them to use the same words. The pair agreed not to take my picture and we parted amicably enough.

But some hours later as I walked from my home to the car, out of the corner of my eye I spotted a camera lens zooming on me from a car parked down the road. Within an instant I knew I had been betrayed. With a screech of tyres, the vehicle disappeared, leaving me feeling my trust had been misplaced and my home had been invaded. Bob had warned me specifically about the 'snatch-photo' technique but now I had been caught like a fish on a line. A telephone call to the London offices of the paper had little effect and the story was used two days later with an unflattering picture of me and quotes I could scarcely recognize.

The encounter did not spoil my relationship with Bob, who immediately invited Coral and me to go up to Lancashire. He booked us in at a hotel in Morecambe. Bob's idea was to upstage the *Mail*'s trickery by taking legitimate photographs and a cover story. We discussed the idea in the hotel lounge quite late into the evening and finally agreed the pictures would have most impact if they were shot in Main Street, Overton, outside Harold Parkinson's home.

The next morning Bob, myself and Terry Bromley, the photographer, travelled to Overton. I was a little nervous as it was the first time I had set foot there since my arrest in 1970 when the police took me to their Murder HQ in the Memorial Hall. It was a bright day and Terry asked me to stand outside the house so he could take a few shots. After that he had me walking up and down Main Street for more active shots. While doing this, I noticed an elderly man with white hair enter the gate of Harold Parkinson's old home. Before I even thought about my actions I found myself walking hastily towards him.

'Excuse me, is this your house?' I asked.

'It certainly is. Are you from the press?'

'No, actually my name is Noel Fellowes. I am the man who was convicted of killing Harold Parkinson in this house in 1970. Now new evidence has come to light, I am fighting to have my name cleared.'

'So you're the unfortunate man who has suffered all these years, are you? My name is Ernest Staples. I'm pleased to meet you,' he said, offering me his hand.

'Likewise,' I replied.

By this time Bob and Terry had caught up with me and I introduced them both to Mr Staples. I told him the reason for my being in Overton and the need to take photographs to counter the *Daily Mail*'s snapshots.

'Would you like to come inside the house?' asked Mr Staples.

I could hardly contain myself.

'It would be nice to see the room where I was supposed to have killed the poor man,' I said.

'Hang on a minute and I'll ask the wife if it's all right.'

A few seconds later he was waving me forward to join him at his front door. He introduced me to his wife and then invited Bob and me into the front room. I felt a chill run up my spine as I stood there. I recognized it as the room where the killing had taken place as I recalled the photographs that Mounsey had kept thrusting in my face in 1970. Now here I was, standing in the room where it actually happened, for the first time in my life.

'So this is where it all took place?'

'Yes, I'm afraid so,' said Mr Staples.

'I do wish it was all finished and they could leave the poor man to rest in peace,' said Mrs Staples, fighting back emotional tears. Now I understood why I had felt chilled on entering the house. Poor Harold Parkinson wasn't at rest at all. In fact, as I closed my eyes it seemed as though Harold Parkinson's blood was screaming from the ground just as Abel's in Genesis.

'Do you still feel a presence in your house, Mrs Staples?' I enquired.

'Yes, we do. I wish he would rest.'

Without a moment's hesitation I said, 'You have probably read in the papers that I am now a Christian. With your permission I'd like to pray over everything that happened in this room all those years ago.'

'We would be very grateful if you would,' replied Mr Staples.

I just closed my eyes and started to pray, asking the Lord to bring his peace back into the house and to rid the place of unwanted spirits. I prayed over every room, and within minutes I felt the assurance that it was done. Peace had returned to the house and the occupants. Both Mr and Mrs Staples thanked me and confirmed they felt much better after my prayers.

'It has been my privilege to meet you and share these moments with you,' I said as we left.

I felt really honoured to have been used in that way. I turned to Bob and said, 'It's incredible. As God is my judge, I have never stepped foot through that door before today, yet the Lord has brought me two hundred and fifty miles to visit the house and indeed the room where the crime was committed. Then, on top of all that, he commissioned me to pray over all that had taken place here.'

'Nothing surprises me any more where you're concerned, Noel. It's just amazing to see it all,' replied Bob with a smile.

So we left Overton with the photographs and an incredible story for Bob. That evening the newspaper headline read 'Convicted ex-PC prays at house of death'. There was satisfaction knowing the *Daily Mail* had truly been upstaged.

A month later, the Director of Public Prosecution's office returned an interim report on the case. The Chief Constable of Lancashire police knew a full-scale enquiry had to be commissioned and picked 50-year-old Eric Evans to head it.

The Deputy Chief Constable of North Wales was kindly, yet needle-sharp. My first reaction was relief. I knew there would be no whitewash now.

Mr Evans needed a fortnight to relinquish his normal duties and select his squad from regional crime offices across the North West. He was lucky to have at his immediate disposal two Detective Chief Inspectors—Allan Potts, who had already proved himself in Overton, and Tom Eyres. Together they would run the incident room, set up on the first floor of Morecambe police station. Their task was to re-investigate the killing. It would be done the same way as it was in 1970—but with the most precious of gifts, hindsight. The dozen men who began sifting through mountains of details on 10 July were to spend weeks away from their families, but they knew they were working on a unique assignment with prestige status. The workload would include interviewing 300 people from as far apart as Sussex and Cumbria.

Mr Evans recalls: 'The major obstacle right from the start was the lack of written information readily to hand. We could not find a transcript of the trial in 1970 and most of the police papers had been disposed of. The time gap was insurmountable for some witnesses; we were unable to get much detailed information for instance from either Mr Mounsey or Mr Sanderson Temple. But that, of course, is understandable.'

The squad started with the first man to find Harold Parkinson's body—Bernard Darby. He inadvertently cast doubt on the belief that the purple material gagging the victim's mouth was associated with me. 'When I discovered the body I saw that he was tied up with various articles including a purple scarf and paisley patterned cravat and to the best of my knowledge I believe that both articles were his own property,' he said.

There was a similar revelation along this line from the cleaning lady, Mrs Josephine Hockenhull, still living in the village in a local farm property: 'I know for a fact that Parkinson did not have a lot of clothes but he was a maniac for buying and collecting ties and cravats for himself. These were in various colours. His favourite items were without doubt his cravats. The cloth covering his chin [showed to her in a police photograph] is a purplish-coloured loose-cover from off the back of the settee. I can identify this by the stitching round the edges. I know this stitching was made by Harold Parkinson himself.'

Mrs Hockenhull's statement was a glaring indictment of the 1970 police investigation on its own. How could this crucial evidence about the purple cloth have been overlooked all those years ago? At my trial Mrs Hockenhull had not been asked about any of the bindings or clothing. She also gave a broad hint of the way the officers had made her feel. The last time she had seen Parkinson alive he had been carrying a brown leather night-safe purse. She recalled: 'After Harold had been found dead, I made a statement to the police but forgot to tell them about the purse. When I remembered I went back to the police and asked them if they had found it. They didn't seem interested in what I had to tell them about the purse and I can't remember what they said to me, only that I felt a bit foolish that I'd mentioned it.'

Mr Evans was pleased with these revelations so early in the re-investigation, so he decided to approach two other witnesses who could have a lot to say—my ex-wife and former mother-in-law.

The Deputy Chief Constable decided to talk to Michele personally. She told him: 'It seems the police believed that I or my family may have hired a private detective to get evidence for my divorce. I told them that was utter nonsense and told them to check with my solicitors. I did not need any further evidence to obtain a divorce as my solicitor already had ample grounds. I was very concerned about the evidence the police seemed to have against my husband. I have always felt strongly that he was not guilty and had been wrongly convicted.

'The other thing that puzzled me about the trial was that the property missing from the house was never mentioned. It was never suggested that robbery might have been the motive. It seems unbelievable that someone would go to the lengths of tying a man up just because he was being followed.'

At the same time Detective Chief Inspector Potts was being given the precise reason why my mother-in-law's name had been in Mr Parkinson's book. Mrs Iris Castagnini explained how coal deliveries had come monthly from a Lancaster firm and how her husband had always dealt with the bills personally: 'During late February 1970, two detectives called at my house and showed me a photograph of an old man standing near a china cabinet. They asked me if I knew this man and I told them I didn't. They then said, "How does your name and address come to be in a book at this man's house?" I told them I didn't know. When they told me it was a coal receipt that had been paid to a man who represented the coal firm, I realized that he was the person whom my husband paid when he called at the house. I had never met him.

'Initially I jokingly said to the detectives: "Have you come to arrest me?" I thought that Noel, my son-in-law, was playing some joke on me. I then spoke to them about Noel being in the police some time ago and that he was a "villain"—something of a jack-the-lad. I did not mean this in any malicious way.

'Neither my daughter nor myself have ever contemplated having any person or private detective to follow Noel. She was going through with her separation and had enough grounds.'

To Allan Potts it was obvious—there had been no real motive to implicate me in the first place.

Following their early successes, Evans, Potts and Eyres pressed on relentlessly. The team had to know more about the quality of the evidence given at the trial by the nightclub pair, John Bamborough and Carey Thornton. The former had changed his name to Omega and was eventually traced to Cowling, near Keighley in Yorkshire. He was asked what credence he had given to some of my jocular remarks and he replied: 'I thought it was all bravado,' but added: 'I cannot remember if in fact I said it at court.'

It took longer to find Thornton, who was also living the other side of the Pennines. Now a computer salesman in Leeds he had this to say about the standard of his evidence: 'I was what you would say prompted. I had never heard the name Parkinson before. I can recall being shown a plastic bag

267

with what appeared to be a purple scarf. It was never taken out of the bag and shown to me properly. I was led to believe during the course of the interview that my evidence was being used to assist Noel Fellowes and it left me very confused. I would just point out that it came as a big shock to me when Noel was convicted.'

Mr Evans' squad effectively broke the back of the case against me during the middle weeks of July 1984. Their speed and expertise at prising long-forgotten knowledge from so many parties was an example of British policing at its finest. Hard work seems easier when you get results, of course, and there seemed to be surprises around every corner.

Some information came their way without them even having to exert themselves. Such was the case in the testimony of Mr Parkinson's next-door neighbour, Mr Ronald Carey. Back in 1970 he had given Mounsey's men a blurred description of two men he had seen standing on Main Street. But in later years—too late to help me unfortunately—Mr Carey had had a surprise memory flashback.

'I was leaving my home to go to the Globe Public House [when] I saw two men coming from the front door of the [Mr Parkinson's] house. One of them shouted, "We will see you then, Harold" after looking in my direction and seeming hesitant.' Both men were in their twenties.

As the squad worked on, they were relieved that, although they were in effect scrutinizing the local constabulary, there was little or no ill feeling directed towards them. Most officers involved in the 1970 case, both retired and still serving, were as frank as their memories would allow.

One former Chief Superintendent, Mr Alf Collins, even gave a crime squad interviewer a startling piece of information which revealed how much John Bamborough had it in for me: 'While Noel Fellowes was in custody I was on duty at Lancaster police station when I received a telephone call at 3 a.m. from John Bamborough (I recognized his voice). He said, "You've got the right man" or words to that effect. I questioned him about it and he just said that we had got the right man for the Parkinson murder. Mr Mounsey was made aware of this call.'

If that was one example of co-operation, there was the odd exception to the rule. PC Alan Knowles had been the officer on duty at Lancaster on the night when the telephone message about an accident on Main Street came through. Detective Constable Colin Russell visited him at his Lancaster home and showed him a copy of the statement he had made at the time. He admitted a CID colleague had typed it out but he could not vouch the date recorded was correct—even though he had put his signature at the end. Mr Knowles declined to make a new statement when DC Russell returned on 26 July and made a curt response: 'I don't wish to get involved, I'm out of the police now, I'm a civvy. If you want me to give evidence you'll have to subpoena me.'

My solicitor, Graham Hughes, had been feverishly busy since our meeting on the Isle of Wight. He had chased Mr Lumsden, the Director of Public Prosecutions and the Home Office on my behalf. Then I received a call from Graham confirming that Mr Evans wanted to interview me in connection with his enquiry into the 1970 case. Much to my surprise, Mr Evans travelled from Wales to the Police HQ at Reading, where Graham Hughes and I met him on 23 August 1984.

Mr Evans was a tall, lean, middle-aged man with silver-grey hair and a voice that was both gentle and authoritative. It was obvious that he had been carefully selected for the enquiry as his record in the police force was of the highest standard. He was, as many probably called him, a wise old fox beneath the warm smile and relaxed manner. He opened the meeting by outlining his brief and his responsibility in the enquiry, assuring me that his only objective was to establish the truth. Whoever it affected was not his problem.

Mr Evans advised us that there were three basic options available to him by way of recommendation to the DPP— that there were no grounds whatsoever to doubt my conviction; that there were insufficient grounds to suggest that

269

any further action should be taken; or alternatively, that the enquiry cast great doubt on my conviction and that I should be allowed to continue with an appeal against conviction in the higher court on which the prosecution should raise no objection. Mr Evans in fact indicated that on the basis of his enquiry to date he considered the third option to be that which he was most likely to recommend—although he could not of course make any comment as to what the Director of Public Prosecutions would advise following any recommendation he might make. He stressed that the information he had just voiced was given off the record and requested that neither Graham nor I compromise either his, or indeed our, position by any comments made at the present time. Both Graham and I confirmed that we would not abuse his confidence in this respect.

I was thrilled to have heard it coming from his own lips in front of my solicitor. At last things seemed to be moving in a positive manner and favourably in my direction. Mr Evans informed me that I was the last person to be interviewed in his enquiry and proceeded to ask numerous questions regarding my arrest, detainment in police custody and the 1970 trial. I answered all his questions honestly and openly, as I could remember events back in 1970. Unlike the last interview I had had with a senior police officer in 1970, this one was both pleasant and fulfilling.

We spent a long time establishing the fact that I was finally convicted of killing Mr Parkinson on the Tuesday night or the early hours of Wednesday morning. Mr Evans informed me that he was now almost certain that Mr Parkinson met his death on the Wednesday evening. The longer the interview continued, the more I learned. All the questions I had asked myself over the years regarding witnesses and evidence were beginning to be answered.

One of the greatest surprises was when Mr Evans produced duplicated copies of the taxi-drivers' record sheets covering the time of the killing back in 1970. I was stunned for a moment as I read through the sheets. I thought they were supposed to be missing from the taxi office in Euston Road, and I had carried the can for it. It finally sunk in that these sheets may have been lying amongst the sheaves of prosecution and defence documents actually in court during my trial. If only they had been produced at the trial, things could have worked out so differently. I told Mr Evans that to the best of my knowledge these sheets were the only record sheets I ever saw used in the taxi office. Mr Evans admitted that it seemed the administration of the taxi office left a lot to be desired.

At the end of our meeting I said to Mr Evans, 'Do you believe that I had nothing at all to do with the killing of Mr Parkinson, or indeed anything at all to do with this case? I must stress that it is very important to me and I can understand if you want to answer off the record.'

Mr Evans looked me straight in the eye and said, 'Absolutely not. I believe you're innocent.'

'Thank you, Mr Evans. I really appreciate your honesty and I pray continually that everything you need to establish the truth will be forthcoming.'

'It's been a pleasure to meet you, Mr Fellowes.'

Both Graham and I left Reading Police HQ quite ecstatic. We could hardly believe what Mr Evans had shared with us off the record. It only reinforced our determination to pursue my vindication whatever the cost.

By the end of July, officers Evans and Potts knew they had enough to justify what had been on the cards from the moment Lenny Pilot became a supergrass—a charge of manslaughter against Billy Clark.

At lunch-time on Thursday 2 August, the pair faced Clark in an interview room in Manchester's central detention centre. Mr Evans attempted to clarify a few points Clark had touched on during the initial interrogation, but Clark was classically non-committal. He repeated the phrase, 'nothing to say' thirteen times. Three hours later, Detective Chief Inspector Potts spoke out the words that Clark had been dreading for fourteen years: 'You between Monday 23 February 1970 and Thursday 26 February 1970, at Overton in the County of Lancaster, unlawfully killed Harold Parkinson, against the peace of our Sovereign Lady the Queen, her Crown and dignity contrary to Common Law.' Clark winced but made no reply.

The following day Clark appeared at the magistrates' court in Crown Square, Manchester, just a flight of steps away from the Crown Court where he would eventually face trial. He looked agitated and passed frequent messages to his common-law wife, sitting at the back of the courtroom, as the manslaughter charge and the Warsop robbery allegation were put to him. His unprofessional attempts to persuade a somewhat short-tempered stipendiary magistrate into allowing him release on bail fell on deaf ears. He was remanded in custody at Strangeways prison for one week.

About a dozen newspaper, radio and freelance journalists, including an ITN film crew, had been present to witness the brief hearing. Media interest in the case was growing every day. But as their attention was focused on Clark, the other man slipped away. On 16 August, the Director of Public Prosecutions ruled that Joe Berry would not have to face any charges connected with the Overton crime, in spite of his admission that he had conspired with Clark and the mysterious 'cockney Pete' to carry out the 'sneak' theft. The London ruling surprised officers working on the case in the north. The charge of robbery at Warsop, which Berry had always denied, was also dropped and Berry was free to return to his wife and children.

Berry, never particularly anxious to talk about crime to policemen, certainly had no inhibitions when questioned by Bob Westerdale. The *Evening Post* reporter was impressed by the terraced house Berry and his family lived in. Despite a poor employment record, Berry's front room boasted expensive furnishings of the most elegant style—not at all bad for a man who could not read or write. Berry spoke willingly of how he and the others had hoped to find £25,000 worth of gold coins in Parkinson's house—and also of his amazement at being arrested and detained over offences he thought had long ago been forgotten. He told Westerdale he would never

272

come to terms with the betrayal of Lenny Pilot: 'He is worse than most of the people that he turned evidence on. We were all born and brought up in the same part of Manchester and he was a regular guest at people's homes. I even took his wife Eileen to see him in Blackpool police station once. I don't even like thinking of him now.'

In October, Pilot was released from prison into the custody of armed Manchester policemen, in readiness for the *Operation Holland* and *Belgium* trials, to be held at Lancaster Castle. He enjoyed his limited taste of freedom. He claims his guardians dropped him off at a 'safe house' where his girlfriend was being kept and he was able to make use of local pubs and the sauna. He tried his best to give the police their money's worth and almost competed with Fred Scott as to how much information he could recall against one-time criminal colleagues.

Judge Morris Jones, QC, ordered a press blackout from the beginning of the trial for several weeks. But it was eventually lifted as the sentences of the guilty men began to be determined. The most spectacular jail terms came during the *Belgium* part of the trial, thanks mainly to Scott. But Pilot did his best to share the credit by corroborating whenever he could get in the witness-box.

The top sentence of fourteen years went to scrap-dealer David Thompson for three armed robberies on security vans and a bank robbery conspiracy. Defence counsel said the 34-year-old villain had only been a 'petty crook' before he met Scott, the man who eventually shopped him. John Ward, already serving eight years for the Moston post office raid which netted the supergrass pair, received another eleven years for two other similar 'jobs'. Kenny Connor—the cousin Joe Berry had been so worried about—went down for ten years. John Shirley was jailed for nine years for robbery and there were three terms of five years, and numerous other lighter penalties handed out. These included a suspended sentence for Pilot's girlfriend Margaret Goodwin, who operated as a messenger girl for the gangs. She was reminded by the judge that she would 'continue to walk in the shade for many years to come and live in fear' as a result of her relationship. Even Pilot's next-door neighbour, a Dutchman, Gerrard Pronk, got six years for firearms offences and perjury.

Pilot had given fourteen witness statements against defendants in the *Belgium* trial, providing evidence on oath three times. There were twenty-one more statements ready when the *Operation Holland* trial began, although Pilot was restricted to taking to the witness-box on only one occasion in the Crown case against prison officer Tom Field, whom Pilot had accused of joining him in crimes. The prosecuting QC, Mrs Helen Grindrod, had a curt introduction for her star witness: 'For a lenient sentence he told the police all and became a grass, a most unpleasant thing. Nobody likes sneaks but it has become an accepted public policy that people should be encouraged to reveal what they know about the crimes of others because silence in the criminal world is usually impenetrable.'

Pilot's story that he and Mr Field had become friendly while he was serving four years in Strangeways prison for burglary and wounding was not believed by the jury, who found him not guilty. In fact, prior to Clark's trial, the standard of Pilot's information leading to *Operation Holland* arrests alone had been anything but sensational. Seven men, including Joe Berry and the slot-machine man Pilot claimed had masterminded the Overton robbery plot, had been questioned but not charged. Two were not arrested, three shared jail terms of just six-and-a-half years between them, two received suspended sentences and there were fines or community service awards against five others. Evidence was left on file against another pair and there was none offered against three.

One man in this category was Billy Dalton, a cafe owner who lived in Strood, Kent. He too was seized in a dawn swoop and charged with conspiracy to commit armed robbery. He was remanded in a prison cell for two weeks before being released on bail. Nine months later he was told at Lancaster Castle that there was no evidence against him. Understandably incensed about the treatment dished out to him by the police, he alerted *Daily Mirror* journalist, Paul Foot, to the real story.

Both Pilot and Scott had eaten at Billy Dalton's transport cafe. When Pilot was captured, he had asked Dalton to provide a false alibi. Dalton had refused so Pilot had named him as an accomplice. 'The police were prepared to believe the flimsy statements of two hardened criminals, one of whom had been convicted of perjury. Why believe them and not me?' complained Dalton.

This was a slight embarrassment to some of the policemen who had spent so much time feather-bedding Pilot. But the supergrass had done an important job. At the end of the trials, Scott disappeared south to one prison with a supergrass unit and Pilot to another, never to meet again.

Meanwhile, Mr Evans had completed his enquiries in the Morecambe area and sent his squad of officers back to their separate bases in Manchester, Cumbria and Cheshire. He completed his report and delivered it to the Lancashire Chief Constable, the Director of Public Prosecutions and the Home Office. Back in his small, functional office in Colwyn Bay, Mr Evans had chance to reflect on his mission. He was pleased that at the end of it there was to be no mud-slinging at the discredited forensic scientist, Dr Alan Clift, who, in Mr Evans' eyes, had been unfairly pilloried.

In an interview with Bob Westerdale, Mr Evans told him: 'The case against Noel Fellowes was not strong to begin with and our enquiries make it a lot weaker still. This has been a unique job and there have been so many problems to overcome which I have never come across before—particularly the gap in years. It has been complicated—but always interesting.

'But my satisfaction will have been to assist an innocent man to prove his innocence . . .'

16

Truth on Trial

After all the frustrating years of waiting for a major development, the months preceding the trial of William Christopher Clark were probably among the worst. Any hopes I had about a quick listing were dashed time and time again. There were rumours that the case would go to Lancaster Castle, which would have been in line with the way other alleged crimes uncovered by *Operation Holland* had been tried, and near enough to Overton for the jury members to have a good knowledge of the locality. Eventually though, the trial was scheduled to take place at Manchester Crown Court. And after yet another postponement which tested my patience to the full, it was pencilled in for Wednesday 17 April—some thirteen months after the arrest and remand in custody of the defendant.

The prosecution run-up to the case stumbled over an unforeseen obstacle. The star witness, Lenny Pilot, clashed with the police over the 'terms' of his trip from the supergrass unit in the south to the courthouse. Versions of exactly what did go wrong differ. Detective Chief Inspector Allan Potts refused to negotiate with Pilot over his demands. 'He wanted to be put in a police station cell for a few days so his relatives could visit him in Manchester whenever he wanted them to. He wanted a video recorder, films, TV and all sorts of other perks, including restaurant-standard food. I just was not prepared to give in on the issue. Instead I had planned to put him on the hospital wing at Preston prison where he could have travelled every day. His refusal caused me a lot of problems because I obviously wanted to present the best case I could. I left it with Pilot that if he refused to leave his cell to go to the vehicle supplied for a certain time I would have to do without his evidence.'

There is some evidence to suggest Pilot genuinely did want to give evidence in court—if only to give more strength to his own appeal against sentence which was expected to be heard within the next few months. He fired off a salvo of letters on the subject to his solicitor in Blackburn, the prosecuting counsel at the Clark trial, Mrs Helen Grindrod, QC, Greater Manchester Police Chief Constable, Mr James Anderton, and his MP, Mr Tom Pendry.

Pilot wrote: 'They told me I was to be treated as normal prison production for Clark's trial, taken from Preston prison to the court every day. I could not believe my ears. What about all the promises that I would have protection and never have to go inside a northern prison again? It was completely out of the question. Not six months ago I had been under armed escort all the time to and from court and kept at Wigan and Littleborough out of the way. But there was absolutely no way I would ever voluntarily set foot in an ordinary prison—a supergrass in contact with ordinary prisoners—the consequences are too frightening to ever contemplate.'

Pilot says he wrote to DCI Potts telling him he would appear as a witness if he had the same protection as he had been afforded during the Lancaster trials. But within two days of the hearing, Pilot was terrified to hear that the only transport laid on was a taxi trip accompanied by unarmed prison officers. 'This was completely unacceptable and unfair, it was my life that was in danger.' Pilot's stand on the issue caused him considerable heartache and soul-searching. With the Court of Appeal hearing only a short time away, he needed to be making friends in the law-and-order community rather than enemies.

Pilot described in one letter how he could hardly eat or sleep as the trial date neared and he eventually collapsed on the eve of it. But, like DCI Potts, he remained resolute. Pilot knew there were many people still on the outside with a score to settle—only a few weeks earlier a threatening note and a wreath had been delivered to a relative's home. In fact, Manchester police had arranged an armed presence at the law courts in the city centre, and it was with reluctance that DCI Potts ordered them to stand down.

On the morning of the trial, the corridors of the courts were buzzing with rumours that Pilot had 'gone moody' and had refused to appear. There was also some pretty wild guesswork on the media's behalf about whether I would attend as an interested observer in the public gallery. The BBC had a camera team waiting outside and one reporter told a group of fellow journalists that he had just been chatting with me in the gents. Bob Westerdale smiled at this. He had just phoned me at my home in Berkshire!

I had considered whether to attend part of the hearing, if only to see what the man whom police said had committed the crime actually looked like. But I didn't want to distract the jury members who might start comparing us as we sat in different parts of the same court room.

The judge was Sir Joseph Cantley, OBE. He was 65 years old but as quick-witted as the day he became a barrister in 1933. His phenomenal attention to detail and concentrated thoroughness were legendary. After the jury of six women and four men had been enrolled, the Crown prosecutor, Mrs Helen Grindrod, QC, opened the case.

The stage was similar, the actors wore the same wigs and gowns of office and the script closely followed the opening lines of my trial fifteen years earlier. The only difference was that the lead performance was being played by Billy Clark, not Noel Fellowes.

The QC immediately made it plain that 'one unusual feature' of the case about to be put before the jury was that the events had taken place back in 1970. She outlined how Harold Parkinson had met his death in such a bizarre manner in the small village of Overton. She said the time of the killing had been put at between 11 p.m. on 24 February and 7.30 a.m. on the 26th, before adding pointedly: 'The prosecution say that he died on the evening of the 25th and whoever tied him up was responsible for his death.'

From his seat in the dock behind her, Clark could not have

278

had a good view of the prosecuting speaker, but he listened intently. Occasionally he allowed himself an anxious glimpse over the high glass-walled dock behind him to acknowledge his wife.

'The death was caused by strangulation. It seems that such were the methods used in the tying, that the efforts made by Mr Parkinson to release himself tightened the bonds around his neck and caused his death,' continued Mrs Grindrod. 'That is manslaughter.'

Mrs Grindrod had only been on her feet for minutes when she uttered the words I had been longing to hear for the last third of my life: 'On the 8th of March 1970 a man named Keith Noel Fellowes was arrested for the murder of Harold Parkinson. He was tried and convicted of manslaughter on the 29th of June 1970. The Crown now say that was a tragic mistake. William Christopher Clark, say the Crown, was the man who went into Mr Parkinson's home, motive theft, tied him up and caused his death.'

The reporters sitting in three rows adjacent to the well of the court couldn't write it down fast enough. Bob Westerdale was so anxious to tell me the sensational opening remarks that he jammed a coin in the press-room telephone box and eventually had to ask the operator to make a transfer charge call. I was overjoyed by the content of the Crown's admission at such an early stage.

Meanwhile, Mrs Grindrod was eloquently describing how Clark had admitted entering the home, how he panicked when he was discovered rooting through the old man's belongings and assaulted him before tying him up. 'There were marks on the face consistent with having some sort of struggle or fight before he was tied up.' She also introduced the importance of two telephone calls—one which Clark had made to his victim—overheard by a GPO telephonist; and the other later made by Clark to Lancaster police, informing them of an 'accident' on Main Street, Overton. Later she went on to mention the police interview with Clark, which had begun with denials and ended with a full account of the clash in the cottage. She echoed Clark's words: 'It was a fight that went wrong. I didn't mean to do that.'

The first witness called by Mrs Grindrod was the former Lancaster policeman who had told officers re-investigating the case the previous year: 'I don't wish to get involved—if you want me to give evidence you'll have to subpoena me.' Alan Knowles could never have guessed when he resigned from the service that he would be back giving evidence from the witness-box at the age of 63. It was clearly something he was not relishing either. The court had in fact just re-assembled after the lunch-break but all movement ceased as Knowles held the testament in the air and repeated the words of the oath.

Knowles recalled being on night duty at Lancaster police station when the early morning phone call came in: 'It was a man's voice saying there had been an accident in Main Street, Overton. That was all that was said. I couldn't guess at age or anything else. I would have written it on a scrap of paper and then on to an official message pad and passed it on to the Morecambe sub-division to check.'

There was a slight pause and the defence QC, Michael Maguire, made his case début. He reminded Knowles that his original statement had clearly pointed to the caller being a young, well-spoken man. The jury must have been wondering if there was to be any profound significance to Mr Knowles' evidence. But the Crown was slowly building a picture of what happened from sources other than the defendant's statement.

Then PC Joseph Howarth came to the witness-box to relate how he was called out to Overton to investigate the telephone message. Both witnesses confirmed they had not given this information at my court hearing in 1970. But then police had discreetly overlooked its significance at the time.

As there was no possible conflict over the next witness, his testimony was read to the court from his statement. The description of Bernard Darby's discovery of his friend's body that winter morning held the jurors' undivided attention. For the first time they had a full, graphic account of how the body was bound. 'I saw a bundle lying on the floor. I went to

280

it and realized it was a body. It had a gag around the face,' said Darby.

Mrs Grindrod chose to break the routine of reading statements by then introducing a witness in person—Mrs Josephine Hockenhull, possibly the most important person police had discovered who could help clear me. She was not in any position to point the finger at Billy Clark, for she had never seen him before in her life. But the fact that she put doubt on my conviction meant that the blame lay elsewhere. Mrs Hockenhull's big moment had been carefully planned by the prosecution. A projector and screen were erected in court and some slides of the state of the body were shown. Far from being upset by these disturbing photographs, Mrs Hockenhull soon lost her initial nervousness and began pointing out from the witness-box which bindings on the body she could identify. A buckled strap round his knees came from a big trunk upstairs; another piece of material had once been used to strain wine with.

Eric Evans was sitting in the court patiently waiting for Mrs Hockenhull to mention the all-important purple material, masking the lower half of the battered victim's face. This was the cloth that was supposed to have been my cravat. Mrs Hockenhull had now identified it as a runner from the back of Mr Parkinson's settee. All that was needed was for the witness to say it in court . . . Somehow the evidence slipped her mind and she left the witness-box without mentioning it. Even the best-laid plans go up in smoke under the unnerving atmosphere of a Crown Court.

The situation was not irreversible and on the following day the cheerful figure of Mrs Hockenhull made a surprise reappearance in court to tell the judge her thoughts on the purple antimacassar. It was certainly an unusual twist for any trial—calling back a witness after she had finished giving evidence. But the Overton woman seemed to enjoy her fleeting time in the limelight. And her homely, Lancashire expressions were a pleasant departure from the judicial jargon. A cream-coloured ligature was 'mucky white' to Mrs

Hockenhull; and Harold Parkinson's eccentric behaviour was simply him 'acting the fool'.

On that second morning of the trial, people outside court and in the public gallery were avidly reading the account of the trial in national newspapers. The 'King Midas' killing—a journalistic reference to Mr Parkinson's love of gold coins—was big news in the northern editions of most of the dailies. It merited just a few paragraphs in the Fleet Street printed editions, probably because my exact address had never been made public at that time. I was grateful for the limited coverage in the south as it afforded a shield of protection over Coral and the girls.

The headlines were on much the same theme: 'Ex-cop did not kill Mr Midas'; 'Innocent man was jailed for killing' and 'Man convicted for killing in "tragic mistake" '. The stories were factual accounts of the case, mainly I suspect because of the strict reporting guidelines enforced by law. Although the *Daily Star* did describe me as currently running a taxi firm in Berkshire.

The harrowing pictures of the tied and gagged body of the coin-collector were to stay on the screen for most of the morning. The Crown relied on the man who took them, retired Detective Sergeant George Brogden, to explain the nature of the bonds. It was obvious that time and care had been employed to ensure the old man would not be able to struggle free, Brogden told the court. He added that it had later taken many hours to remove the ligatures in the morgue. George Brogden was the third Lancashire policeman to give evidence at the Clark trial; none of them had been anywhere near the court for my hearing.

Bob Westerdale hardly recognized another witness who was escorted to the box by a prison officer. He was Robert 'Joey' Berry, the petty villain Westerdale had interviewed at his home some months earlier. Then he had been in the full bloom of health, having been told that he would not face prosecution over the Overton crime. Now he seemed to have aged fifteen years, his features were gaunt and his complexion decidedly yellow. He was obviously being held by the police on an unconnected charge. But it probably wasn't just the stale air of prison life which had altered his appearance so drastically. More likely it was something to do with the 'honour among thieves' code so besmirched by his one-time friend Pilot. Berry had already told one officer: 'I don't want to end up as a prosecution witness and be called a grass.'

Berry's escort officer sat inches away from him as he gave incoherent answers to questions. Expressions like, 'Billy, me and cockney Pete had gone to do a creep' had to be explained to the judge. 'Billy was going to talk to him [Parkinson] and open the back door for me. I was going to look for the coins. We went to a pub in the evening but my arse-end went about doing the job.' Mrs Grindrod explained this charming colloquialism with another piece of slang: 'you mean you lost your bottle'. Eventually all the people in the courtroom understood—Berry's nerves had let him down, and he had stayed in the pub with the cockney while Clark disappeared. 'We didn't ask him where he had been,' claimed Berry. Throughout this fifteen-minute ordeal in the box, Berry had been conscious of the unbroken stare from his friend in the dock. There seemed no hostility in the gaze, for Clark realized more than most how awkward the situation had been for Berry.

Berry's exit left observers wondering how Clark could possibly defend himself after such a damning start against him. It seemed even more like a cast-iron case as Detective Chief Inspector Potts read out his interview with Clark to the jury. The nub of the police case was here, in Clark's confession: 'I did it on my own. I got fifty-five pound and shoved it in my pocket. He jumped on my back and started hitting me with karate chops. I had to tie him up so he couldn't follow me.'

Clark lowered his face to avoid glances from the jury as each sentence seemed to become more incriminating than the last. 'I never meant to harm him, I suppose I'll get twenty years for this.'

Mr Michael Maguire's cross-examination of the Detective Chief Inspector Allan Potts subtly brought my name back into reckoning. The next few minutes were critical. The QC had to raise a doubt against the case which had gone against his client so badly thus far.

Maguire: 'In 1970 were all the exhibits considered relevant put before the jury?'

Potts: 'Probably, yes.'

Maguire: 'Fellowes was a taxi driver. Was there some connection between Fellowes and the deceased?'

Potts: 'In the deceased's house there was a notebook with Fellowes' mother-in-law's address. He was a debt-collector . . .'

Maguire: 'It was also believed in the village that Mr Parkinson was not only a debt-collector but a private investigator. Was that fact known to Fellowes?'

Potts: 'I think it probably was.'

Maguire: 'The enquiry was conducted by senior police officers under Joe Mounsey. The case was put before magistrates. There were committal proceedings and Noel Fellowes was charged with murder. A jury convicted him of manslaughter. Was the 1984 enquiry deprived of seeing most of those exhibits?'

Potts: 'Yes.'

The QC used the opportunity to add that no fingerprint evidence used during the 1970 case was available now either. Mr Maguire was suddenly gaining the upper hand, at just the right time. For the defence case was just about to begin. And William Christopher Clark grabbed the opportunity I had lost—to give evidence on his own behalf.

The pure drama of watching a defendant on a serious crime walk from the dock to the witness-box is never lost, no matter how many times you have seen it. It is like a boxer coming out of his corner for the all-important last round. Clark had prepared well for a battle to final bell.

The court filled up for the event, most on-lookers curious to know what line of defence Clark and his QC would pursue to justify the plea of not guilty. It came as a surprise when the first words uttered by him were that 'apart from a few slight differences' he agreed with Detective Chief Inspector Potts' account of the interview after his arrest.

In a broad Manchester accent, Clark told how he had read in the papers that Mr Parkinson had died through strangulation—and took this to mean someone had manually throttled him with their hands around his throat. He only learned the real truth about strangulation from the bindings five months after his own arrest, while browsing through post-mortem reports in jail. Clark admitted he had tied the old man up after a clash. But referring to the description given of bindings and injuries he claimed: 'Things were done to him that were completely wrong to what I'd done to him. I compared how I tied him up and how the papers said he had been tied up.'

Clark, with the help of Mr Maguire, then carefully went through the full catalogue of bindings on the body. He said he did not apply webbing, the purple material gagging the mouth, and white bandage across his chest. However, he did use a tie across his wrists and the hoover flex around the shoulders. A black cable binding the thighs might have been his work, he admitted. 'I left him near the centre of the living-room, no mistake about that. His legs were straight and he was all right. Just a bit out of breath.'

Clark then offered two versions of what he surmised could have happened after leaving the old man on the living-room floor. First, he suggested 'cockney Pete' could have nipped in to the cottage to steal the coins and finished him off. Or it could have been me. 'I would clear Mr Fellowes if I could. I would say I did it. But there are too many things wrong,' he said.

Judge Mr Justice Cantley interrupted at this point, seeking clarification. It was explained that Clark felt somebody must have followed him into the cottage and killed the old man. The judge observed drily: 'That was tremendous bad luck for Mr Parkinson.'

Clark then gave a detailed account of his activities in the Main Street house: 'The idea was to open a window catch and go back in the middle of the night. Joe Berry got it wrong when he gave evidence. We were both to go back. Cockney Pete said the coins were somewhere downstairs. Instead of sticking to the idea I decided to have a quick look while I was in and stuck £55 in my pocket. Suddenly he set about me side-on. I clouted him, not very hard, on the head. I was lashing out to stop him hitting me. I punched him in the stomach to wind him. There was no more need to hit him as he was out of breath so I sat him down on the floor. That's when I tied him up, in the middle of the living-room.'

The judge—remembering that Clark had agreed to all but a 'few slight differences' in the Potts interview—interjected, saying this was not what he had said to the detective.

Clark continued saying he could never understand why the man had died: 'There was no blood at all on his face. He even had his glasses on. I have been living with it all the time. The man is never far away from my mind. I have always felt really bad about it. I thought I was responsible for him dying because I wasn't aware of the full facts. It is time to tell the truth. Joe Berry had nothing to do with it. As far as I knew then, Noel Fellowes had nothing to do with it. If I could clear him, I would do. If I had done these things, I would plead guilty to them,' he repeated.

Clark was becoming agitated now as he again tried to find a solution to the puzzle behind the killing. At one point he even told the judge he thought I was an 'out-and-out murderer'. Clark managed to compose himself as his QC sat down and Mrs Grindrod stood to cross-examine him. She immediately wanted to know how Clark could feel responsible for the death for so long and yet on the other hand believe that the old man had been manually strangled. Clark then said: 'I stopped thinking I was responsible when I saw in the paper that Noel Fellowes was being remanded every week.' But then he added: 'After so long there had been nothing in the paper and I took it for granted that Noel Fellowes had been released with no charges whatsoever. I'd have gone to my grave always believing I was responsible for Mr Parkinson's death. I blamed myself all the time. I thought for fourteen years it was the flex that killed the man. The feelings of guilt were not lifted until I read the pathologist's report.'

Clark said that a gesture of how much he had worried about the trussed-up old man was reflected by the phone call he had made to Lancaster police, alerting them to the scene. Having got that off his chest, Clark returned to the dock to await final speeches by counsel, which started on day three of the trial.

All the newspaper representatives were still in the court precinct, from the *News of the World* down to the local freelance reporter. The *Daily Mail* used one single-column story headlined, 'Clear me, pleads jailed PC' quoting me in full. They must have spoken to another Noel Fellowes because they had not spoken to me. I had vowed not to co-operate with them after they first let me down at my Bracknell home.

On day three of the trial, Mrs Grindrod concluded: 'It is very rare for the Crown to say to a jury that another jury has been mistaken. You know for a fact that another man was convicted in 1970 but we know very little about what was said on that occasion and very little is relevant for you to know. Clark seems to be saying I tied him up but "only a little bit". Use your common sense, apply it in the way you do for normal walks of life.'

She then suggested that Clark hit the old man, tied him up, gagged him to prevent him calling for help—'surely he would want to have prevented him from shouting?' Then, echoing the judge's words, she said that Mr Parkinson had been in for another piece of 'very bad luck'. After Clark had left, 'by an awful mischance, somebody else arrives at the house.' She suggested that the second intruder decided to 'improve on the process' of tying the stricken pensioner up, putting a table-runner underneath the existing flex, a paisley cravat round the wrists among other bindings. Then the QC stressed it wasn't all bad luck—there was good luck for Clark because 'Fellowes had been arrested'. She finally added that Clark had never mentioned to the police the possibility of a second intruder following him in. 'If gloss has been put on the evidence by the defendant you will have to study it carefully.'

Mr Maguire responded for the defence admitting the law was not perfect but, 'when the Crown opens the case with the words that a tragic mistake was made and really the man now in the dock is truly the guilty one, one has to be exceedingly careful.' He continued, 'You may think that fifteen years ago twelve men and women sitting in a different jury box were also conscious they had to be extremely careful.' Mr Maguire said that the nation rightly prided itself on its jury system and the Crown's ability to put every single piece of evidence possible before those jurors, he said. 'But to say a tragic mistake has been made was a mere assertion as far as it relates to Mr Fellowes. Noel Fellowes remains convicted of manslaughter and no Court of Appeal ever changed it. The prosecutor must have told the jury they could not convict Noel Fellowes unless the evidence adduced satisfied them, so that they were sure of guilt.'

After both final speeches, the judge wisely decided that Friday afternoon was not the best time to start his own deliberations, so he adjourned the hearing until Monday morning.

The suspense of waiting was becoming almost overpowering for me and I took up Bob Westerdale's offer to bring my family up to stay at his home until after the verdict. It served two useful purposes—throwing other reporters off the scent and bringing me closer to where the action was. I agreed to take part in one radio interview in Lancashire, to be embargoed until after the Clark case was over. They wanted to record two reactions from me—one to Clark's conviction and a substitute for his acquittal. This seemed strange to me, as I had not given much thought to the idea of Clark walking free after the balance of evidence.

We all managed to relax during the rest of the weekend, Bob's three-year-old daughter, Emma, keeping us amused with her antics. But the pressure was back on again when Bob left home to cover the last stages of the trial on Monday morning. The others all left the house soon after—leaving me alone to pace up and down and wait for the telephone to ring. Bob is no DIY genius and I passed the hours by re-wiring some of his plugs. It had been a miracle he had not electrocuted himself long before then!

Meanwhile, in his summing-up Mr Justice Cantley was agreeing with earlier remarks that the legal system was far from flawless: 'A perfect system would ensure that in every case a guilty man was found guilty and an innocent man was acquitted. This burden is put on the prosecution—weighted to guard against something which they say happened in this case, the conviction of the innocent.

'We do not know what evidence there was against Mr Fellowes but there must have been some which pointed to him as the guilty man, or he would not have been convicted. On the other hand, it would seem that there was absent from that trial any information at all pointing to, or even mentioning, this defendant. The prosecution say that conviction was a tragic mistake and Mr Fellowes was innocent of the charge. If that is right and this defendant before you is the real guilty man, it certainly was a tragic mistake and it is disturbing to any lawyer to think it could happen. But there we are.'

The judge said that the case was not a contest between Fellowes and Clark and that the jury must decide solely on what they had heard over the last few days: 'Before you can convict you have to be sure of three things. The first is that the defendant used violence upon Mr Parkinson which was unlawful violence; I do not think that will give you any difficulty. If this defendant, who has admitted theft, hit and winded Mr Parkinson to prevent him from detaining him, that in itself is unlawful violence because there is no possible justification in law for it. The second thing is that the violence he used was the kind likely to cause some bodily harm. Again, it may well be that that will not give you much difficulty. The third thing, and really the most important one, is this: you have to be sure that what this defendant did was the cause of Mr Parkinson's death.'

The judge recalled the evidence of telephonist Sylvia Kinnaird, who had eavesdropped on Clark when he arranged to meet Mr Parkinson over the phone. Mrs Kinnaird said Clark had asked: 'Will you be on your own?' before the conversation ended. Mr Justice Cantley went on: 'The defendant agreed with every bit of the conversation except that last part. It is for you to make up your minds whether the last part was included or not, and one question you might ask yourself is this: if you were coming to steal from the house, would you want to do it if there was somebody else in the house? How were you going to open the window with two men in the house?'

The judge's attention next focused on Joey Berry: 'Remember that character who came up from below to tell us as much as he thought wise? Did you think he was a willing candidate and forthcoming witness?' If Berry had been correct, then it was the mysterious Londoner who knew about the coins at the Overton house. 'Amazing what they know, these cockneys,' said the judge pointedly.

After mulling over the main points of the case, judge and jury retired and Clark was taken away to suffer the same nail-biting tension I had undergone in the same way all those years earlier.

Two hours later, the female-dominated jury filed back in court, their faces not betraying what their verdict was about to be. Clark sat at the edge of his seat, his eyes fixed on the foreman.

NOT GUILTY.

A spontaneous burst of applause and cheering erupted in the public gallery. A wide grin beamed from Clark's face as he sought a glimpse of his wife through the crowd. Mr Justice Cantley angrily ordered silence and expelled all those who were seated in that area of the court. Some of the police officers tried unsuccessfully to hide their disappointment behind granite stares at the jury. One young detective moved his head close to a colleague as if to whisper something, but then changed his mind as a look of helpless acceptance passed across his face.

But the court had not finished with Clark yet. He pleaded

guilty to robbing Warsop Town Hall clerk Neal Hunt of £660, the crime committed with Lenny Pilot back in September 1970. Clark did not seem to be listening as Mrs Grindrod described how he and his friends tied up the cashier with pieces of bandage and sellotaped his mouth; he seemed in a different world now. He was perhaps thinking of being re-united with his wife and child after thirteen months in Strangeways. But the full list of his previous convictions were being read out, starting twenty years earlier with stealing and shop-breaking which led to Borstal training, graduating to burglary, arson, criminal damage, assault occasioning actual bodily harm, offences which led to twenty-three appearances in court. In mitigation, Mr Maguire described his client as a habitual small-time crook who would learn from this experience that however long ago the crime, the Crown never gives up.

Judge Cantley told him, 'You are a persistent criminal and unjustifiably pleased with yourself. Tying somebody up is a serious aggravated burglary.' He added that in other cases— and he made clear he was not referring to the Harold Parkinson affair—victims had suffocated and died after being bound and gagged. Taking into account his pleas of guilty, he sent Clark to jail for four years. The sentence and the verbal rebuke certainly took the edge off Clark's early celebrations which had included a wink and a thumbs-up sign to his wife.

Back at Bob's house, I sensed the outcome the instant he rang to break the news. There wasn't much to say. Our telephone conversation was full of awkward silences. Finally I told Coral and Bob's wife, Gill, of the verdict and tried to disappear inconspicuously by wandering upstairs to a bedroom. I was shell-shocked. I had come all this way and now I felt back at square one again. When Bob arrived home we sat together round the dinner table and feebly tried to cheer ourselves up. In a deep depression I realized that everybody would still think I had done it. How would this affect my chances of vindication? How would I ever pick myself up?

The only one unaffected in the house was Emma, the toddler. But even she could not understand why her uncle Noel was not quite as willing to play games and read her books as before.

Coral was doing her best to find a thread of reason in the whole catastrophe. She was sure we had not come all this way for nothing. She kept repeating that she knew God was in charge. She didn't know the reason for what he was doing, but she said it would eventually become clear. Bob admitted he could not find favour with her argument. He voiced his own strongly-held opinions about the jury system.

At 6 p.m., the others left me alone in the kitchen and went to sit in the lounge. My ears pricked up as I heard the Clark case being discussed on the television news. The final few words on the item were amazing confirmation of Coral's pledge: 'Tonight the Home Office said they would consider as a matter of urgency the plea by former policeman Noel Fellowes for a declaration of innocence.'

Yippee! All was not lost at all. The Clark verdict would have no bearing at all on my quest for vindication. All of a sudden, the atmosphere was transformed. It was party time. Gone were the half-hearted plans for a quiet evening—tonight we were going to an expensive restaurant with Bob and his family! It was quite remarkable how our depression had been banished by those few words. God was on the move.

The following day I took part in a television interview with Granada, and a question-and-answer session was transmitted into millions of homes in the north-west three times during that day. I returned home bursting with enthusiasm for the next event in this dramatic story.

The breakthrough came within days. The Home Secretary, Leon Brittan, sliced through red tape with a rarely-used section of the Criminal Appeal Act to secure me an early listing in the Appeal Court. Now I knew my goal was almost achieved. And this time I would not be denied.

17

Free Indeed!

Even before the Home Secretary had referred my case back to the Court of Appeal under the rarely-used Section (17)1A of the Criminal Appeal Act 1968, my solicitor, Graham Hughes, had engaged the services of a top London barrister to fight my case—a Mr Ian Hughes. Graham, in his usual manner, had left nothing to chance and had already forwarded all the documents regarding the 1970 case and new evidence from the 1984 enquiry to Ian Hughes, asking him for a written opinion. Much to my relief, his opinion formed a seventeen-page document that favoured every aspect of my grounds for appeal. So most of the groundwork had already been undertaken prior to Leon Brittan stepping in and ordering the case back to the Appeal Court. This left us in a more comfortable position, knowing we would be ready for an appeal date whenever it cropped up.

I was totally confident that I now had the best legal counsel around. And I was sure that this was all God's work. The fact that these were top men in their chosen professions made me feel privileged to have them representing me. (It was sheer coincidence that both men were called Hughes.) Having such confidence and assurance in counsel's ability and dedication to my cause left me able to sort out with God other important issues such as my own spiritual life.

Following Clark's trial and its outcome, I really had to examine my reaction to the verdict. Although I had prayed prior to the trial that the Lord's will would be done, and not mine, I still felt cheated and resentful with the result. I felt a little disgusted with myself. After all, I had been convicted for a crime I had never committed, so who was I to judge another man on the premise of new evidence, whether he actually meant to kill or not? This close examination revealed my heart—I still felt that justice hadn't been done on my behalf.

After much praying about it with Coral, I finally realized that God's way wasn't necessarily my way. I was trying to control the timing and result of the whole case myself. Indeed, that had been my folly for the last few months. I had been so mentally, emotionally and physically involved in the case that I had stopped listening to what God was saying. It had become *my* battle, *my* fight, *my* injustice, *my* case, and so on.

Not only that, but my whole life as a Christian had been thrown into utter turmoil. With heavy hearts, Coral and I had decided we would leave our fellowship, following a number of problems which remained unresolved, in spite of all our efforts to reconcile people. Through all the subsequent heartache and spiritual mourning we knew that it wasn't the end, but that God had a future for us. But it felt like a mess. My life seemed to be turning upside down again. Although everything seemed to be going against me, this time I recognized that God was in it and was probably teaching me something for the future. I knew that the whole situation was in his hand. All I needed to do was accept it, then he in turn would reveal everything to me.

One evening we were invited to attend a guest service at Bracknell Baptist Church by our friends, Keith and Betty Jobber. We hadn't been back to the church since our departure years before but we decided to go. We were received like the prodigal son as everyone responded very warmly to us. We could sense an abundance of life and purpose in the church and we both felt we had come home, that God was calling us back into the church where we had first known him.

We continued to attend the church and felt very comfortable in the knowledge that this was to be our spiritual home again. It all seemed to make sense to me, yet I was still nervous about committing myself to the church before the Appeal had been heard.

I sat at home in the evenings thinking about what was

going to happen when I was vindicated. While I knew all the glory would go to God, I wasn't sure I wanted to pay the price. It would mean more pruning in my life, more cutting back and changing to steer clear of hypocrisy. I was probably judging myself too hard, but it all seemed pretty heavy stuff to me. Coral had filled in the commitment form to join the church as a member. She asked me if I had filled mine in.

'No, I haven't done yet,' I said.

'Why's that?'

'I'm sure that's where we are meant to be, but I'd rather wait until the Appeal is finished. Then I'll be able to decide. If it all goes wrong or against me, I really don't know what I will do or how I will react. I just feel unable to make the decision now.'

'That's all right, love. I understand. Let's wait until you're sure.'

Typical Coral, I thought. Still positive in everything, still able to see the brighter side of such decisions. For some unknown reason I felt I was wrestling with God again. It seemed that he was calling me into the church but I was dragging my heels.

About a fortnight before the Appeal, I woke up and sat on the edge of the bed, trying to come to terms with the fact that morning had arrived more quickly than I wanted or expected. Suddenly I had an incredible revelation of Calvary— I was picturing Jesus on the cross, suffering such a painful, undignified, cruel death. He hadn't deserved it. What made it even worse was the inner conviction that he had died for me.

I sat there shaking my head and saying, 'Oh, Lord. Oh, Lord. Forgive me for my attitude.'

Something broke inside me as I realized the full meaning of the cross—that Jesus Christ had paid a price far greater than that of anyone before or since. He had laid down his life for me.

I fell to my knees and said, 'Lord, whatever happens in the Appeal Court, whether I am vindicated or not, I am still going on with you. Whatever the cost. You are the only truth in this darkened world. I want to go on with you. I want to fulfil everything you have called for in my life.'

At last I had come into the fulness of receiving God's love in Jesus Christ. Whatever else happened in my life, nothing could ever match up to the sacrifice he had made for me.

I remained sitting on the bed, drinking it all in, then a soft, still voice whispered in my head, 'I know your heart, Noel. I know your heartbeat is for me.'

'It surely is, Lord, it surely is.'

I hurriedly washed and dressed. Then, trying to contain my excitement, I went into the dining-room and said to Coral, 'The Lord has given me an amazing revelation of Calvary. He has broken through the defences I was building around the Appeal.'

Coral was delighted and we hugged each other. I shared everything that had happened to me in the bedroom with her.

'That's really wonderful. Isn't God good to us?' she said, tears streaming down her face.

We both thanked God for his word in season and then filled in the commitment forms for the church. At last we were home, both with the Lord and the church. What more could we ask for?

We were now in the final days approaching the Appeal date of 12 July 1985. Both Graham and Ian Hughes were busy preparing their final arguments for the case and collating the documents. We were not only going to the London law courts, we were actually going to be heard in the top court before the Lord Chief Justice of England, Lord Lane. You can't get any higher than that, I thought to myself. Since that precious moment when God revealed the extent of his love to me, I had enjoyed a new peace in my life and a deeper assurance about the vindication than I had ever felt before.

I had arranged for Bob Westerdale to stay with us for what we hoped would be the final story and for Keith Jobber, a very close friend, to drive us all to the Appeal Court on the day itself. Danielle, Louise and Olivia were disappointed that they could not come too, but I felt it was better to keep all the children away from the media. Although we were walking in total faith we couldn't predict the outcome of the day.

Bob arrived in the late afternoon of 11 July in bright sunshine. Within minutes of his arrival he was eagerly talking about the big day that lay ahead for us tomorrow. I assured him I felt relaxed and confident in God. After dinner things really started to hot up. Friends and relations kept popping in to see us and wish us well for the Appeal hearing. There was an air of excitement and expectancy flowing through everybody. It made me realize how fortunate I had been to establish such good friendships since I came to Bracknell in 1974. I felt really moved by the commitment, sincerity and love our friends had shown us since the Pilot revelations in 1984 and now, on the eve of the Appeal, they came to assure both Coral and I of their continuing support.

It was well after midnight before we went to bed and I crashed out within minutes of setting my head on the pillow. I woke to the sound of the alarm clock. It was 6.15 a.m. on the twelfth of July 1985. The big day had arrived. Unlike the previous day when I had felt totally relaxed and in control of things, today I had a nervous stomach and a distinct feeling of nausea. In a few hours' time I knew that the final chapter would be written in the case and I would be either ecstatic or devastated. I was locked into a battle of the mind. Positive and negative thoughts kept passing through my head. I knew which I preferred and kept trying to dismiss the negative ones. *Keep walking in faith. Keep feeding on the promises of God*, I kept saying to myself, trying desperately to will my measure of faith to increase.

Keith arrived at about 7.15 a.m. Coral, Bob and I jumped in the car and we headed for the Strand in London. Everyone seemed to be locked into their own individual thoughts. Most of the journey was spent in relative silence, with the exception of a few carefully chosen comments such as, how are you feeling? Or, it's going to be a good day.

We arrived outside the law courts about ten past eight,

parked the car and then proceeded to find the listings for the day, which would tell us what court we were in. As I walked through the court entrances and corridors hand in hand with Coral, I felt a sense of walking through the corridors of legal history. How many people had come to these courts over the centuries hoping to find justice that had escaped them for so long? How many men before me had appeals turned down and were later executed for crimes they hadn't committed? How many times had the paragons of virtue made a mistake and sent men and women to face a cruel existence, strangled by the repercussions of injustice they had suffered? If only the walls could speak.

Having determined which court we were in, Keith ushered us to a small cafe where we had breakfast. We settled for bacon sandwiches and coffee. If the truth were known, all four of us were in a state of nervousness, yet each one kept producing a bright smile and a glance of assurance to the next. I could feel the tension mounting. It was nine o'clock. Only another hour and we would be in the court.

I had arranged to meet Graham Hughes inside the court building between nine-fifteen and nine-thirty to discuss the final points of the proceedings. We arrived back at the courts and Graham arrived a couple of minutes later. He looked in a similar state to the rest of us—excitable and nervous. He told us that he had got out of bed at one o'clock and prayed about the case, again at three, and finally at five, when he had to get up and make his way from the Isle of Wight to London.

'You're in safe company, Graham. Both Coral, Keith and I have been praying since we woke up this morning,' I said.

Graham wanted to show me the brief for the proceedings but I declined. I felt I wanted to stand in the faith I had—that the Lord was going to vindicate me and I didn't want to muddle myself with a lot of information.

The corridors were buzzing with people and court officials. The whole place was a hive of activity. Graham, Keith, Coral and I stood in a small circle and prayed together. We asked God to guide both Graham and Ian Hughes as they presented the case to the court and to move on the three judges to come to the right decision—a complete vindication, leaving no loose ends or doubts in people's minds about what had taken place in the past.

We walked into the court at five to ten, ready for the hearing at ten. I sat in the gallery with Coral and Keith, just behind my counsel. A quick glance around the court revealed the press-box was full to overflowing. I saw Bob among the national newspaper men and he acknowledged me with a wave and a smile. The public gallery was quite full and the counsel representing the Crown were busy putting their papers together and chatting to Eric Evans, the Deputy Chief Constable of North Wales, and Allan Potts, Chief Inspector with the Greater Manchester Police. I thought it strange that they were attending the hearing.

As the clerk of the court asked that everyone be upstanding for the entrance of the judges, a shockwave shot through my body. It reminded me of the same scene in Lancaster fifteen years earlier on the first day of my trial. The judges took their seats, which faced us directly. All the players in the legal theatre of justice were wigged, gowned and ready for the first act. Here I was before the High Court again—judges, barristers, ushers, press and public. I was unable to say anything, do anything or decide anything. My whole life once more rested in their hands, or so it seemed. I was in a state of tense nervousness. My brow was perspiring and my limbs shook as I fought to keep control of myself. Suddenly the words of Jesus came to memory, *Where two or three are gathered in my name, there am I also*. There was Coral, Keith, Graham, myself—and Jesus. Thank you, Lord. Welcome to the proceedings. Please take over.

Ian Hughes opened with the grounds of appeal and his skeleton argument on my behalf.

'Mr Fellowes' conviction for manslaughter on the twenty-ninth of June 1970 is unsafe and unsatisfactory for the reasons I intend to bring before the court this morning,' he said. He went on outlining the relevant points to the case. The purple cravat which supposedly belonged to me had now been identified as belonging to the deceased. Evidence given by Dr Alan Clift, the forensic biologist, suggested possible physical contact between myself and the deceased. It was now indisputable that no reliable scientific evidence was adduced to link myself with the death of the deceased. Mr Hughes went on to relate my twelve-hour ordeal of being interviewed by teams of police officers in an unsuccessful attempt to obtain a clear admission of guilt, and he produced a schedule of police interviews to the court.

I was listening to every word intently and periodically glancing at Lord Lane, Justice Skinner and Justice Macpherson, trying to get a hint of how they were thinking. They just sat there, peering at Ian Hughes and showing no expression at all. It all sounded convincing to me and by this time, some ten minutes into the hearing, my nervousness had gone and I was growing in confidence with every word that was spoken. The courtroom was hushed and I noticed journalists busy writing down every word.

Ian Hughes continued with his submissions. He made reference to the missing taxi records which hadn't been missing at all. Then he went on to my apparent motive, that I was being followed by the deceased and that my mother-in-law had hired the deceased to follow me. He told them it was now known, and indeed had always been known, by the police that her name was in the deceased man's notebook not as a private investigation but as a coal debt, the deceased being the debt-collector. Ian Hughes piled it on and on until his final submission which concerned the alleged time of death.

Mr Hughes established the fact that Mr Parkinson had met his death not on the Tuesday night or early hours of Wednesday morning, but on the Wednesday night, for which I had always had a cast-iron alibi. He concluded that in 1970, had the defence known of a number of statements and the accurate time of the deceased's death, they would have been able to prove conclusively that I couldn't have been the killer; and had Clark's evidence been available in 1970 it was inconceivable that I would ever have been charged with the offence.

Ian Hughes sat down. His submission was finished. I had been impressed by his timing and delivery of the facts on my behalf and was convinced everybody must know by now I was innocent. I felt like giving him a round of thunderous applause for his efforts as they were in complete contrast to my experience with counsel in 1970. Coral and I just sat there, gripping each other's hand in excitable anticipation of the final result.

I whispered in Keith's ear, 'How do you think it's going, mate?'

'No problem. We're on a winner all the way, kid,' he said, with a broad reassuring smile all over his face.

Lord Lane then invited Mr Clegg, counsel for the Crown, to present his case. He informed the Lord Chief Justice that he felt his learned colleague, Mr Hughes, had covered the case quite thoroughly and adequately. Therefore the Crown had nothing to add other than to say it was a disturbing case all round. I could hardly believe my ears. I was hoping for a replay of what I thought I had just heard. There was a definite buzz in the courtroom. Everyone, it seemed, had been taken by surprise. Mr Clegg sat down and then I realized that I had actually heard right. The Crown were not going to raise any objections to my appeal. I felt like dancing up and down the courtroom. A new nervousness had gripped me, one of excitement. The adrenalin was flowing through my body. It took all my inner discipline to refrain from jumping up and thanking Mr Clegg personally for making such a decision.

Lord Lane and the other two presiding judges huddled their heads together to agree the terms of their judgment. As all this was taking place, Ian Hughes turned around to face me and nodded in my direction as if to say, don't worry any longer, Noel, it's done. Although all this only took a few minutes, it seemed more like an eternity waiting for their Lordships to resume with the hearing. The judges returned to their proper places. The courtroom hushed in anticipation as the Lord Chief Justice prepared to pronounce his verdict.

In the last seconds before Lord Lane spoke I felt distinctly nervous again. My stomach started to turn over as I realized the next few minutes would reveal whether or not I was to be vindicated. It was a tense moment. All these people have been discussing me as if I was an object, I thought to myself. It's my whole life they're talking about.

I was actually sitting in the courtroom. It seemed strange sitting a few rows back from all the legal submissions and questions, yet feeling totally isolated from the main stage. *Still, never mind, at least they can't send me to prison for seven years this time*, I joked with myself.

Lord Lane began to speak.

'It would be an understatement to say that this is an extremely disturbing case. If it does nothing else, it demonstrates the fallibility of any system which is operated by human beings. One hopes that many of the disquieting features which emerged from this case would no longer take place.'

A gasp echoed through the courtroom. What a staggering opening from the Lord Chief Justice of England! I was flabbergasted. To hear that in the summing-up was beyond my wildest dreams. Lord Lane went on to outline the background to the case, the way the deceased was found, how he had been bound, gagged and intricately tied up. Then he said,

'The prosecution case, again very much in outline, was as follows. The motive was said to be a grudge which it is alleged the appellant had against Mr Parkinson. The grudge was against Mr Parkinson in his capacity as a part-time private detective. It was said that Fellowes at the time was carrying on with another woman and he suspected that Parkinson was keeping a watch upon his activities. That really arose from a book found in Mr Parkinson's house when it was searched, which contained the name of Mr Fellowes' mother-in-law, a lady who was not very much liked by Mr Fellowes. The conclusion was jumped to that her name was in the book as a client of Mr Parkinson, she having, it was assumed, instructed Parkinson to keep a watch on her son-in-law and his extra-marital activities. In fact it transpired at a later stage that the entry in that book was simply an entry relating to his debt-collecting activities, because the mother-in-law owed some money in respect of delivery of coal, for which she had not paid. This is one of the matters which combined to produce this very serious miscarriage of justice. The opportunity alleged by the Crown was that this man had the time to get from his place of work, he being a taxi-driver, to Mr Parkinson's home to kill him at some time between 23 and 28 February 1970. The third matter was that he had allegedly made admissions to acquaintances and to the police, or, if not admissions, references to the killing which might on one view be construed as admission of guilt. Fourthly, it was alleged that he told lies to the police.'

Fifteen years later and now Lord Lane was saying that I allegedly made admissions or told the police lies. The reverse was true. All I had ever done was make flippant remarks which could have been construed to be in bad taste. I had told the police the truth. It was they who had refused to accept it. It disturbed me to hear Lord Lane saying such things. I began to feel a little uneasy. Surely he wasn't going to do a whitewash job where the police were concerned? He continued.

'It is conceded on all hands that the conduct of the original trial by Mr Justice Caulfield was impeccable. On the way the case went, on the evidence which was actually available to the jury and owing to the lack of evidence which is now available to this court, it is not altogether surprising that things went as they did. Keith Noel Fellowes was advised that there was no prospect of success as far as an appeal against conviction was concerned. It is now clear that despite that apparently strong case against him at the trial, Keith Noel Fellowes could not have committed the crime of which he was convicted. It is not a case of unsafe or unsatisfactory. It has now been proved conclusively to the satisfaction of this court that this man did not commit this crime. As with the case of all disasters, whether they be forensic disasters or any other kind of disaster, it was a combination of events which led to this miscarriage of justice: a combination of misfortunes, one must

303

also say misbehaviour or errors, and of mistaken conclusions which conspired to produce this result.'

At last I knew the answer to the Appeal. It was over. I was going to be vindicated. The last few sentences kept turning over in my head. *You've won, Noel. You've won, you're free, it's over.* And a million other such thoughts passed through my mind. At the same time Coral was hugging me and fighting back her own tears of joy because it was over for her as well, all the heartache and suffering she had endured, coping with me over the years. Ian Hughes turned towards us with Graham Hughes a close second, trying to congratulate us with an expression and a smile. They couldn't say anything as Lord Lane was still speaking. My head was in a spin. I noticed Bob staring at me from the press-box. He gave a victory smile and salute in my direction. I desperately tried to concentrate on the remainder of Lord Lane's summing-up, as there were obviously more revelations to come.

He continued.

'The mistake would never have been discovered had it not been for the activities of a gentleman called Pilot, who chose to act as a large-scale informer, a "supergrass" as the jargon now goes. Among the many other crimes in which he gave information to the police was one in which he himself was not involved, namely this case, the "Morecambe murder" as it came to be known. He told the police that it had been committed by two men, neither of them Keith Fellowes, one of whom was a man called William Clark. Inquiries were made, as a result of which it was established beyond doubt, and is now in fact conceded by the Crown, that the following matters were true:

'First of all, Parkinson met his death between 6 p.m. and midnight on Wednesday 25 February 1970, a very important fact indeed. It was also established and conceded that on that afternoon of Wednesday 25 February Clark travelled from Manchester to Morecambe expressly to steal from Parkinson's house. He had an underworld tip-off that there were valuables available in that house upon which he proceeded to act. It is established beyond doubt that Clark telephoned to Parkinson to make an appointment to see him, on the pretence of selling to him or buying from him, it matters not which, some antique coins. That telephone call was overheard by the operator, the reason being that he had had difficulty in establishing contact and had to make the call through the operator. The journey to Morecambe had been undertaken by Clark in the company of two other people, a man called Berry and a man called Cockney Pete. Those two gentlemen, although originally minded to accompany Clark on his thieving expedition, got cold feet. They opted out and instead of going with Clark to the house in Main Street where Mr Parkinson lived, they stayed behind in the public house.

'Some time shortly after the telephone call Clark called on Mr Parkinson in accordance with the appointment that he had made, and was admitted. Mr Parkinson left the sitting room for some reason or other for a time and Clark took that opportunity to start rummaging round the room to see if he could find the valuables which his tip-off had said were there. Unfortunately for Mr Parkinson, he came back into the room to discover Clark rummaging. A fight took place. Clark punched Mr Parkinson, knocked him to the ground and, according to his own account of events, tied him up with a series of ligatures. He had a necktie round the ankles, electric flex round his knees, dustette cable round his shoulders and a necktie around his wrists. There were other materials binding him.

'After having done that, Clark went back to Manchester. When he got to Manchester he phoned the police to tell them in effect that there had been an accident at a house in Main Street, Overton and he invited them to go along there and see what had happened. That call was timed at 1.22 a.m. on the 25th or 26th February: it is plain from some other evidence that it must have been the early hours of 26th, Clark having travelled back from Overton to Manchester over the night of 25th/26th February.

'In due course Clark was seen and he admitted that he had gone to Morecambe in the way I have described and he admitted that he had been with Berry and Cockney Pete. He

305

described the fight and he described how he had tied Parkinson up and he described how he had gone back to Manchester and made a phone call to the police.

'He was shown the photograph of the trussed-up corpse. Having seen that, he admitted that most of the ligatures had been applied by him, but he denied that he had been responsible for either the calico, which the pathologist thought had been the immediate cause of the strangulation and death, or the cravat which had been used as a gag.

'The strange thing about that, if what Clark was saying was true, was that it means that somebody else must have come into the house, discovered presumably the still alive Mr Parkinson on the floor and that somebody else must have completed the job of tying this man up, and not only applied the calico and the cravat, but must, according to the way that the ligatures were found, have threaded the calico underneath the ligatures which had been applied by Clark. Little more need be said about that, save to say that it is a little hard to believe that that could possibly be the truth.

'So as a result Clark was charged with manslaughter. He was tried at Manchester Crown Court before Mr Justice Cantley and a jury quite recently. The jury were told—obviously they had to be told and very properly were told—of the conviction of this man, Keith Fellowes. That conviction was described by prosecuting counsel at that trial as a tragic mistake. However that may be, the jury, understandably, acquitted Clark: it is not difficult to see, when someone else has been convicted of the crime which they were considering in respect of Clark, that a reasonable doubt was strongly on the cards and that is what they plainly found.

'Those facts alone would have been enough to drive us to the conclusion that the conviction of Fellowes was unsafe and unsatisfactory. But the matter can be taken further than that and we think probably should be.

'First of all, according to the pathologist at the trial of Fellowes, death could have occurred at any time between the night of 24th and midnight of the 25th. If Mr Parkinson had died on the night of the 24th, then it was possible that

Fellowes' movements would have allowed him to be present: in other words, put bluntly, he had not got an alibi for the 24th. But from 6 p.m. on the 25th to 11 p.m. on the 25th Fellowes, without going into details, had a cast-iron alibi supported by a number of impeccable witnesses. It is now known for certain that the death of Mr Parkinson, from the evidence of Clark alone, must have occurred during that time. Consequently it is quite plain that Fellowes could not have been the killer.

'Scientific evidence at the trial came from Dr Clift. It was unchallenged, although it seems from the evidence itself without more, and now particularly so from further evidence from Dr Rothwell, a senior scientific officer, that the evidence was, even taken at its face value, of very little worth, if any at all. It was (as already explained) to the effect that fibres were found in nail scrapings taken from the deceased man's coat and they matched fibres from a Gannex coat which had been borrowed by Fellowes and worn by him on the night of the 24th but not on the night of the 25th. It is now clear that the night of the 25th is the material time. That evidence was, in retrospect, irrelevant.

'What is more disturbing is that at least three people had seen Mr Parkinson alive on 25th February. They were Braid, Ramsey and Luke and that evidence was in fact before the jury. The jury plainly, and mistakenly, again in retrospect, did not accept that evidence—they thought these people must be mistaken. So the effect of that evidence of Braid, Ramsey and Luke was lost.

'The next matter is more worrying. It will be recollected that the purple cravat which was used as a gag was said by some witnesses to have resembled a cravat which was worn by Fellowes. At Clark's trial Mrs Hockenhull, who was the daily help employed by Mr Parkinson, said that she recognized the gag as being the one which Mr Parkinson himself owned: not only that, but Mr Parkinson himself, in his capacity as a needle-man, had in fact stitched. She recognized the stitching. So one of the main points of the prosecution evidence at the original trial was shown to be false.

'There are certain other disturbing features about Mrs Hockenhull's evidence and why it was not more fully explored at the original trial which it is not necessary to go into now.

'There remain two further points. The prosecution had put forward as a motive, as already indicated, for Fellowes killing Mr Parkinson that Fellowes may have had a grudge against him for his private detective activities. As already indicated, that in its turn was supported by the entry in Mr Parkinson's book of the mother-in-law's name. It was known to the police that the reason for that entry was not the private detective activity, but the debt-collecting activity. How it was that that knowledge did not percolate from the police to prosecuting or defending counsel is one of the more disturbing mysteries about this case.

'Likewise the suggestion already mentioned about the disappearing two log sheets: there was evidence available, which once again does not seem to have got as far as counsel, that the log sheets could not have been removed by Fellowes, because his movements in the office were always in the presence of other people, and those other people would have been in a position to say, had they been called as witnesses, that Fellowes could not have removed the log sheets. Hence the suggestion about the removal of the documents was one which should not have been made.'

Lord Lane concluded his summing-up by saying,

'It is only fair to pay tribute, if we may, to Mr Justice Caulfield, not only for the way in which he conducted the trial, which is what one would expect from any judge and particularly from this judge—that has earned him tribute from all sides—but also for the assistance which he has given to this Court by explaining his system of annotating written statements and by the immaculate notes of evidence which he took. The documents of the trial (the shorthand transcript of the trial and of his judgment) are not extant, and without that assistance from the judge it would have been very difficult, if not impossible, for counsel to have presented the case and prepared it in the immaculate way in which they have, and for this Court so readily and easily to come to the conclusion that this trial went sadly wrong.

'Accordingly this Appeal, for that is how the reference from the Home Secretary dated 7 May 1985 must be treated, is allowed and the conviction is quashed.'

Coral and I just sat there, unable to say anything to each other. We were both lost in our own thoughts. Only an increased grip on her hand which I was holding confirmed I was actually here, that it was actually over and I was actually totally and universally vindicated. At that point Ian Hughes applied for costs back-dated to April 1984 when I had engaged Graham Hughes. They were granted. A few tears formed in my eyes. They were tears of relief and joy. I brushed them off with the back of my hand and continued to sit in my moment of triumph. *Thank you, Father. Thank you,* I kept saying to the Lord.

For years I had wondered how I would feel when the whole nightmare was over. Now I knew. I felt as though a heavy weight had been removed from my life. All had been revealed. The Lord had answered my prayers and vindicated me totally before mankind. As I sat there a mental 'video' switched on and gave me instant playback of everything that had happened to me over the past fifteen years. The good times, bad times and the in-between times. The whole show was over in a few seconds and then I said a strange thing.

'What a privilege!'

'Pardon?' said Coral.

'What a privilege to have been used like this,' I replied.

It seemed such a stupid thing to say after all that had happened and especially after the events of the last hour, but I really meant it. Deep down in the pit of my soul I felt that profound statement coming out over and over again—what a privilege. We descended from the Court into a small passageway where Keith, Bob, Ian and Graham, Coral and myself handed out congratulations to each other. Everyone was overjoyed. Justice had been done. It was a triumph for the British legal system. This same judiciary had incarcerated me fifteen years earlier. Today the wrong had been righted.

The press were gathered outside the door, eager to interview both Coral and me.

Ian Hughes said, 'You're a man of deep faith, Noel. Go out there and treat them in keeping with your beliefs. Then come over to Chambers and we'll celebrate with coffee and cakes.'

We walked through the doors and there before us was a whole barrage of reporters, microphones and a host of questions being asked, all at the same time. I had arranged with Bob that he would assemble the press and we would have an orderly interview. He was nowhere to be seen!

'No comment at the moment. I will answer your questions as soon as Bob Westerdale arrives,' I said.

We carried on walking down the corridor, the press hot on our heels and still firing questions. Keith had gone to try to find Bob. He caught up with us and told us that Bob was already on the telephone filing his story. Typical journalist! The very time I need him, he's filing his own copy to beat the rest, I thought to myself. We stopped and Keith and Graham managed between them to bring about a degree of order so I could answer all the journalists' questions one at a time. My mind was working overtime, trying to keep up with them but I felt calm, collected and assumed that they could only print what I had actually said. After all, today was good news day.

About twenty minutes later they were all happy with what I had given them and we departed for our meeting with counsel in his Chambers. Again we were stopped, this time by a representative for ITN television. He wanted to arrange an interview. I agreed to do an interview after we had fulfilled our engagement with counsel. Then Alan Potts and Eric Evans came up to me and offered their own sincere congratulations on the outcome of the Appeal. I thanked them both for all their dedicated work and effort. After all, without them today might never have been. Also I asked Mr Evans to pass on my thanks to the whole team of detectives which had worked so hard on the case. We shook hands in sincerity and they departed to carry on with more normal duties.

We went for coffee as planned. In Chambers we found

both Ian Hughes and the representative for the Crown, Mr Clegg. It was strange celebrating our victory with both sets of counsel. Even more strange was Mr Clegg's remark after congratulating me on the outcome.

'It's good to have a case you really believe in,' he said. I wondered how many cases go before the courts that counsel doesn't believe in.

After a little while we left for the television interview outside the law courts. Having had the opportunity of giving a television interview once before, after the Clark trial, I knew what to expect. The whole interview went like a dream, from the dizzy heights of my euphoria. Then we headed for home. We couldn't wait to see Danielle, Louise and Olivia and to start the celebrations. The journey home was so different from the outward journey. Keith, Bob, Coral and I were jubilant. Each of us was fighting to get a word in edgeways. I kept cheering and shaking my fists in the air. I had to let the emotion out.

'I'm free, I'm free,' I kept shouting.

Nearer home, Keith turned to me and asked, 'What are you going to do with the begging letters?'

I thought for a split second and replied, 'I intend to keep sending them.'

The whole car rocked to the sound of uncontrollable laughter. It all added to the party mood. We felt so carefree. We arrived home to the sound of the telephone ringing. That was the first mistake I had made all day. I answered it. It was the first of hundreds of well-wishers who kept the line busy for the rest of the day and much of the following week. I had already bought champagne in anticipation of the day's result and asked Keith and Bob if they fancied a glass. They declined. What we all really fancied was a cup of tea! Coral put the kettle on and, before it had time to boil, another TV film crew turned up at the house from the BBC.

'Oh no, I don't think I can handle any more of the media right now,' I said.

'Listen, mate,' said Bob. 'It's been a big day. Let the world know what it's like to be vindicated. You might as well get it

311

over with now. Then they will leave you in peace.'

In trooped the TV crew and again Coral and I gave an interview. In truth, the media had been very considerate towards us. It was understandable that everyone wanted an angle on such a 'human interest' story. I hadn't really imagined the impact of this final day in my struggle for justice and all this attention had taken me by surprise. I hadn't expected to be on national television.

I was still eager to see the girls and within the hour the TV crew had left and all three girls had arrived home—Danielle and Louise from work and Olivia from school. The lounge was awash with tears of joy as we all hugged each other and sobbed in unison.

'It's finished. It's finally over. Isn't God good?' I said.

No one really answered. They just hugged me and shed more tears of love and joy on my behalf. It was a very precious moment for me as all that I had given them in the past was returned to me in their reaction to my news. They loved me and weren't frightened of showing it.

In between taking turns answering the phone, I decided that we would have fish and chips from the takeaway to celebrate. But Coral and the girls were having none of it—they wanted the full treatment in a restaurant. I bowed to their request. Besides, we could escape from the phone and any more media men. Before going out, we watched both ITV and BBC news reports, cheering wildly as the two stations ran the full interviews and gave background information about the case. That morning we had been two unknown people; now, on the biggest day of our lives, we were being screened to millions of people. Following the news reports I sat in the easy chair and thought how incredible all the support and media coverage was. I wondered where they all were in 1970 when I really needed them? It was a strange thought to have, but I felt it was significant all the same.

We found a quiet restaurant and celebrated with a fine meal together, but by then the girls had got the TV bug and wanted to get home for the next news broadcast so they could video them. I didn't put up much of a fight—I wanted to see them as well! It was such a special day. We spent the rest of the evening watching news bulletins and cracking open the bottles of champagne Bob and I had bought for the occasion. Shortly after midnight, physical tiredness started to overtake me. I wanted to fight it into submission—I didn't want today to end in case I woke up and it had all been a dream. But I finally submitted and went to bed. What a truly remarkable day it had been! I had been vindicated, the Lord had been glorified and I could look forward to living in that certain truth.

I woke up at six forty-five on the Saturday morning, washed and dressed, dropped Bob off at the station to catch his train home again and then bought every single national newspaper. I quickly returned home and was staggered to find all of them had covered the story comprehensively. So it wasn't a dream, it really was true. I had been totally vindicated and it was tomorrow already. Leaning over the breakfast bar reading about myself, I suddenly put the newspaper down as I remembered the words of a man I had much admired ever since I had read his speeches while in Wakefield Prison.

Martin Luther King had said in his Nobel peace prize speech, 'Free at last. Free at last. Lord God Almighty, I am free at last.'

A few tears welled up in my eyes as I now understood and experienced the full meaning of those words. They echoed the words of Jesus, *If the Son shall set you free, you shall be free indeed*. What more could any man ask for? Now I had it all, because freedom of thought, speech, choice and movement is it all.

18

On Reflection

Since the time when I 'went public' and the case came to Appeal in April 1984, many people, including Christians, have asked about my feelings towards the police and the witnesses who were hostile towards me and who, to a large degree, were responsible for the injustice I suffered. People expect to find hatred and bitterness firmly rooted in my answers to their questions, but now there is no ill feeling in me towards any of those people because God has totally healed me and set me free from all of those negative emotions.

As a little boy, living in a cold council house in Heysham, near Morecambe, Lancashire, I used to dream about what I would do when I grew up. In the innocence of those dreams and childish fantasies I wanted to be loved, liked, secure, successful, have a loving wife and family, nice car, home, be my own boss and, most of all, be happy. What I hadn't allowed for was all the interim years before the fulfilment of those dreams. Whilst writing this book, there have been times when I have felt detached from the person I was writing about. It seemed somewhat strange to describe yesterday's pain, suffering and injustice, knowing deep inside I was the victim.

All I have written is a true account of my personal experiences over the past fifteen years, starting as an ordinary young 22-year-old man who had lost his way somewhat. It was then I found myself neatly packaged on a murder charge and conveniently disposed of, carrying a seven-year prison sentence for a crime I had never committed.

I don't really know why it happened to me, but now I believe God was in it somewhere along the line. 'All things work together for good for those who are in Christ,' as it says in the Bible. However, it is possible that the same thing could happen to anybody at any time, given the right circumstances and timing. I sincerely hope that many lessons have been learned from this case and that steps are already being taken to make sure there are more safeguards against such an event happening again.

It was ironic that the very same system which helped to imprison me also helped me finally to prove my innocence. Eric Evans and his own hand-picked team of police officers dedicated themselves to finding the truth. They went in with no preconceived ideas, and no intention to cover up or white-wash events. Thankfully, they found the truth. Any system operated and controlled by man tends towards errors and mistakes, but those errors only come to the surface when an individual falls victim to such a system, as I did. It would be easy and probably fashionable to judge and criticize the police over what happened to me, but that would be totally unfair upon the thousands of policemen in this country who have always played it by the book. I do, however, have a word of advice for a number of policemen who were hostile towards me back in 1970: 'sorry' is one of the most powerful yet underused words in the English vocabulary.

One morning in March 1986, a letter dropped through my letterbox. In it was a cold cheque from the Paymaster General's Office, and an impersonal, duplicated letter, with my name typed in, informing me of my compensation for the four years I had spent in prison. This was an ex gratia payment, calculated by the system, and non-negotiable. I could either accept the amount, or get nothing. The letter contained no words of regret or apology.

If I were to take a yardstick and measure which element of the past did the most damage to me—the police, remand, trial or the prison sentence—without any doubt I would say it was the years in prison that all but destroyed me as a person. The primary problem for any individual entering prison for the very first time is survival, in a world governed by humiliation, degradation and isolation. For most of the individual's sentence there will be little direction or meaning-ful guidance for the future. In the majority of cases, vocational

315

and educational training is given to the brighter inmate, and the less fortunate semi-literate or illiterate inmate will probably leave prison the way he entered.

The Victorian prison buildings and cells reflect Victorian attitudes towards its inhabitants. The prison system still deprives the inmate of any form of responsibility for himself, which traps him into being totally dependent upon the system. Throughout his sentence he is told what to wear and when to wear it, what to eat, when to eat, how much to eat, when to sleep, when to wake, when to shave, have a haircut, when to slop out, when to work, when to smoke, when to have a bath, change clothing, when and how to speak to prison officers, when he is allowed to see the chaplain, social worker, doctor, dentist, assistant governor, governor, visiting magistrate, and a host of other rules. All a man has to do is try to remain sane and survive it.

In an age when man visits space regularly by space shuttle, east and west super-powers have overkill capability with nuclear weapons, and the world is in the middle of a new electronic technological revolution, the daily procedures of prison life remain very much the same as they were a hundred years ago. Every long-term sentence seems coldly calculated and regulated to achieve the maximum possible humiliation for the individual. It starts the moment he arrives when he is subjected to the dreaded sweat-box treatment to await processing. Then he is stripped of his clothing and personal belongings, given a uniform which is ill-fitting and usually unkempt. As for accommodation—if an inmate is serving a life sentence then he will probably be allocated a single cell, but the less fortunate man could find himself having to share a cell with one or possibly two others.

With little, or, in many cases, no meaningful work, an inmate could spend up to twenty-three hours a day locked away in those conditions. Even the simple things like letters from family and loved ones are censored and visits are strictly supervised, with both the inmate and visitor knowing they are open to body searches at the prison officer's discretion.

The whole system is supervised by prison officers who

spend most of their working lives locking and unlocking doors, counting heads and generally being bored out of their minds. Many of the prison officers I met didn't enjoy their role in the archaic system and would have preferred the inmate to have been given more individual responsibility and freedom in decision-making, allowing the prison officers to develop a more meaningful relationship with the inmates. Unfortunately, the prison department at the Home Office seems to be reluctant to change.

I am not defending prisoners, criminals or the like. If the man is guilty of breaking the law, then let the sentence reflect the crime. On the other hand, just because some people have 'behaved like animals'—or worse than animals in some cases—is it right to treat the whole prison population as animals in cages? I think not. Having spent a number of years living with such people, I know that many of them deserve the chance and opportunity to change and become assets to society again. If, as many socially-minded people take the view, prison is not a punishment but an opportunity towards rehabilitation, then let's provide and implement the changes in rules and procedures to achieve it. In my experience, long-term prisons are run on the goodwill of the inmates, not, as many believe, on the harsh discipline of the prison officers. If changes are not made towards more flexible regimes, then the alternative is frightening—anarchy, riots, untold violence and even more bitter and twisted people being returned to the outside world. As it stands today, the prison system does nothing more than reflect man's inhumanity to man. Neither side wins but one side holds the key to change.

Having served his sentence, an inmate is discharged and goes back into society again, having done his time. He has two choices—one is to pick up the threads of his past life; the other is to start again from scratch. In my case, there was no alternative other than to start again, in the hope that I could rebuild my life out of the ruins of yesterday's measured injustice. New start, new town, new relationships, new job and a new hope for the future. That was the tack I wanted to sail, leaving the past far behind me.

In my new life I never bargained for a visit from the police four years after my release. They were investigating a murder in Cumbria, 260 miles away from where I was living. It seemed there was some similarity with the Parkinson killing. Then there was another visit in 1984 for elimination purposes —a man had been killed in South Lancashire in similar circumstances. One can understand the police having to interview habitual criminals from time to time, but surely not first-time offenders who have kept the slate clean and built a new life? In my own experience, there was no consideration given to my new life, work colleagues, wife, family and need for privacy.

There is supposed to be a time limit for a person's criminal records to remain on file, after which they are erased from the Criminal Records Office computer, but my records were still on file ten years after the offence. I believe it would be in the interests of both the public and the police if an independent person was given the responsibility to make sure records are being erased or destroyed correctly. If the need arises for police officers to interview an ex-con within the context of elimination, I respectfully suggest it should be exercised more discreetly and with extreme consideration towards the individual concerned. Otherwise it could, and indeed has in many cases, destroyed everything that has been built and achieved in a new life.

Having shared some of my experiences and observations on the judiciary and penal institutions, let me say that if the vindication of the terrible injustice I suffered helps to alter and improve the system, by however small an amount, then for me it will all have been worth it.

In telling my story I have opened the way for others to question and assess the merits for judicial and penal reform. For me there is yet another dimension—the hope, forgiveness and justice from a source within the grasp of every man, from God! In my long search for reality, I travelled down many cul-de-sacs. There was no purpose, security, justice, fulfilment or reality to be found in anything or anybody. 'Trust' was a word reserved exclusively for dictionaries.

Having spent a number of years persecuting Christians and trying to disprove the existence of God, I met him in a very supernatural and personal way. I found the reality and truth that had escaped me for so long. Since that day, much has happened to change my emotional, mental, physical and spiritual life. I have received healing in all those areas and I have become a new person in every sense of the word. I'm not a religious freak or someone hiding behind an ideal or finding an escape route from the past; I am just an ordinary, simple, earthly man who met the living God and went on to know him personally.

It would be very nice to be able to say that since becoming a Christian everything in the garden has been rosy. As you have already read, I have had to put my faith on the line many times. There have been many instances when God seemed to be taking me apart bit by bit and rebuilding me; it was then that I felt like throwing in the towel. Through all the peaks and troughs of my Christian experience, God has never forsaken me. Many times he has stretched out his hand to pick me up, to strengthen me in a time of weakness and set me on the right path again.

The thing is, Christians aren't perfect, they are just forgiven. Indeed, there are still areas in my life that God is chipping away to shape me into the person he wants me to be. I sit here writing in the knowledge and confidence that whatever happens in my life from here on God will be with me every second of the way. From the deep and utter depths of despair, suffering and injustice, I found life in abundance. I thank God for the love, peace, joy and absolute freedom he alone can give.

Perfect justice, perfect truth and reality are only to be found in Jesus Christ. The Holy Spirit is moving today through reconciliation, healing and restoring people's broken lives. How can I be certain of these things? I have personally experienced them in my own life and continue to do so every day. It is my desire that everyone who reads this book will enjoy the same freedom and fulfilment that I now have. Through him, all things are possible.

Acknowledgments

I would like to say a special thank you to all my family and friends who have loved and supported me over the years. To name you all individually would require too long a list, but each of you knows who you are. I am sincerely grateful for your friendship, compassion, commitment and encouragement that has sustained me through the testing years. You indeed are all part of this book.

I would also like to extend special thanks to Bob Westerdale and his wife Gill. Bob, who tracked me down and championed the story of my innocence in the *Lancashire Evening Post*, has helped to make this book possible. I am especially grateful to him for his detailed research and contributions in various areas of the book, particularly in the background information on Harold Parkinson, Joe Mounsey, and the trials.

Noel Fellowes

Picture Credits

The publisher wishes to thank the following for permission to reproduce their photographs:
The *Lancashire Evening Post* (2, 3, 4, 6, 7, 11, 14, 15, 17)
The Royal Courts of Justice (16) Crown copyright
Derek G. Widdicombe (9)
Topham (10)
North Wales Constabulary (13)
The Press Association (18)